THOR:

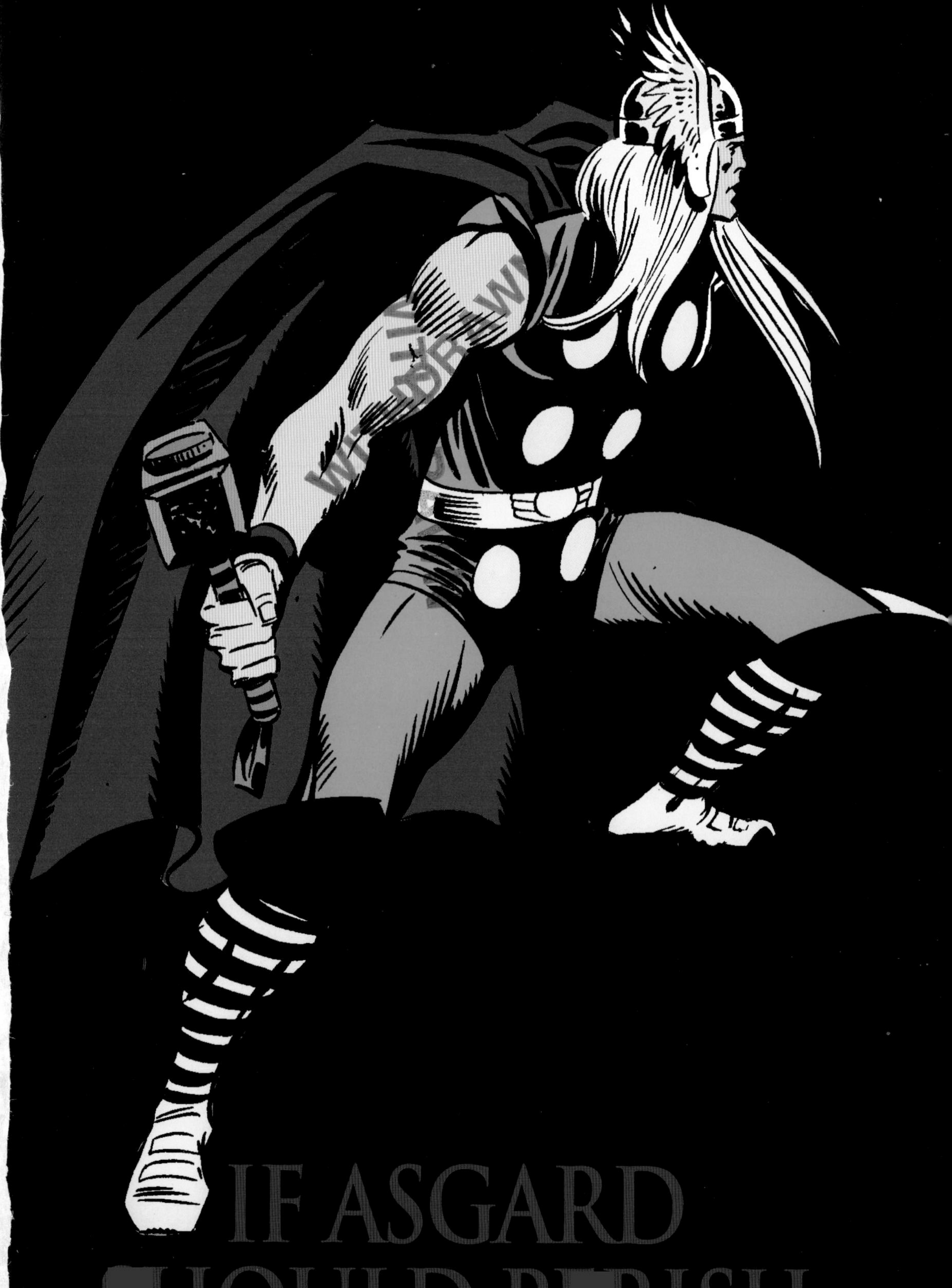

IF ASGARD SHOULD PERISH

THOR: IF ASGARD SHOULD PERISH

WRITERS
LEN WEIN
& DAVID KRAFT

PENCILERS
JOHN BUSCEMA
& PABLO MARCOS

INKERS
JOE SINNOTT,
TONY DEZUNIGA
& PABLO MARCOS

COLORISTS
GLYNIS WEIN
& MARIE SEVERIN

LETTERERS
JOE ROSEN,
JOHN COSTANZA,
CONDOY
& IRVING WATANABE

EDITOR
LEN WEIN

COVER PENCILS
JACK KIRBY

COVER INKS
JOE SINNOTT

COVER COLORS
THOMAS MASON

COLLECTION EDITOR
JOHN BARBER

EDITORIAL ASSISTANTS
JAMES EMMETT
& JOE HOCHSTEIN

ASSISTANT EDITORS
NELSON RIBEIRO
& ALEX STARBUCK

EDITORS, SPECIAL PROJECTS
MARK D. BEAZLEY
& JENNIFER GRÜNWALD

SENIOR EDITOR, SPECIAL PROJECTS
JEFF YOUNGQUIST

RESEARCH
JEPH YORK & DANA PERKINS

SENIOR VICE PRESIDENT OF SALES
DAVID GABRIEL

EDITOR IN CHIEF
JOE QUESADA

PUBLISHER
DAN BUCKLEY

EXECUTIVE PRODUCER
ALAN FINE

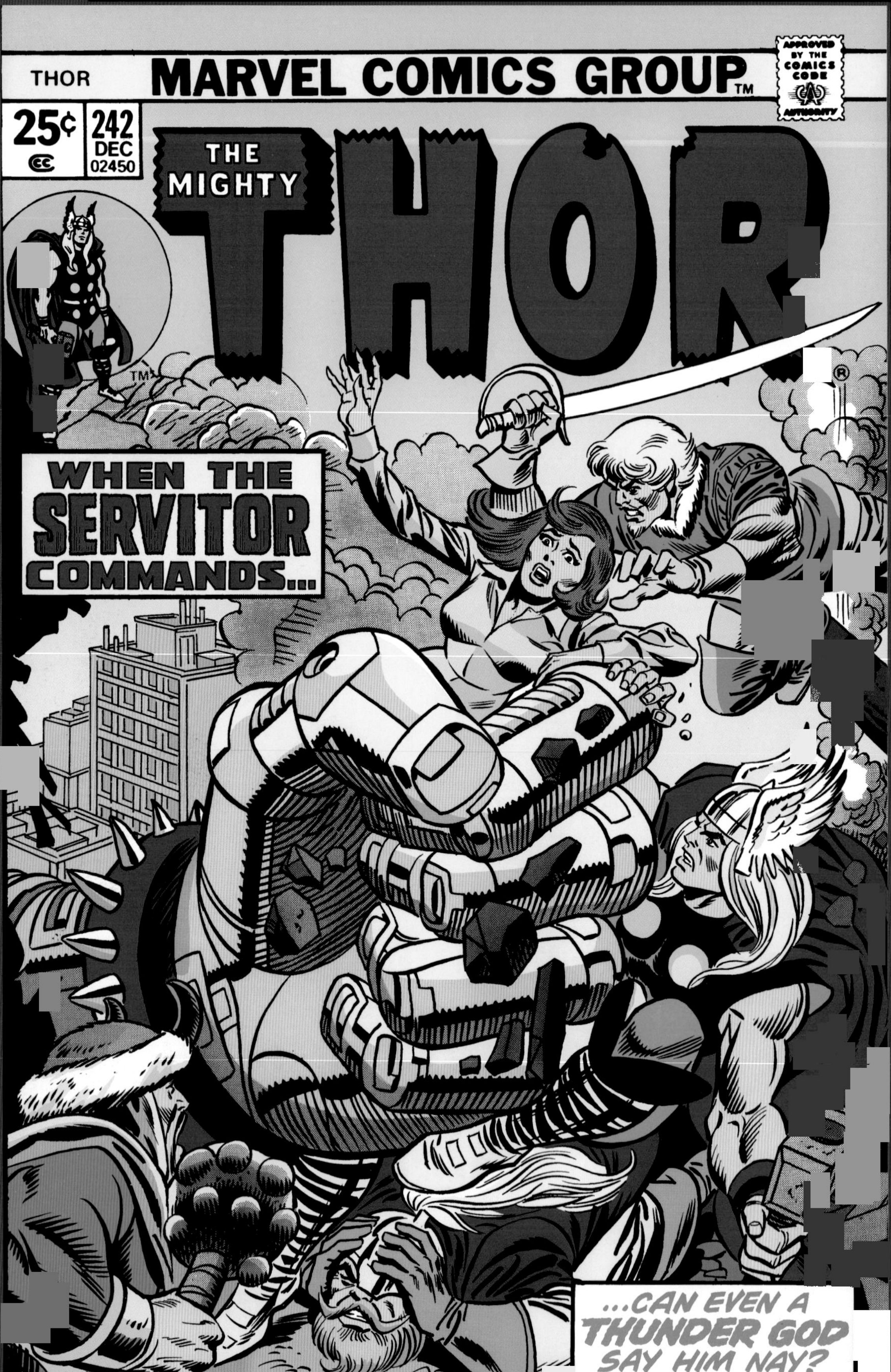
THOR
MARVEL COMICS GROUP™
APPROVED BY THE COMICS CODE AUTHORITY
25¢
242
DEC
02450
THE MIGHTY
THOR
WHEN THE SERVITOR COMMANDS...
...CAN EVEN A THUNDER GOD SAY HIM NAY?

WHEN THE SERVITOR COMMANDS!

LESS THAN A *MINUTE* PAST, THE GOD OF THUNDER *THOR*, HIS LADY *JANE FOSTER*, HIS AMNESIAC FATHER *ODIN*, AND THREE BEINGS WHO CLAIMED TO BE THE EGYPTIAN GODS *HORUS, OSIRIS,* AND *ISIS,* ENTERED THIS DUST-CAKED *PYRAMID* THAT HAD SPROUTED FULL-BLOWN AMID THE ORANGE GROVES OF *SAN DIEGO, CALIFORNIA.*

NOW, THE TWO ASGARDIANS AND THE MORTAL WOMAN SUDDENLY *EMERGE* FROM THE ANCIENT STRUCTURE *ALONE*-- AND THE *EXCITEMENT* THAT RUNS RAMPANT THRU THE CROWD IS AN ALMOST *TANGIBLE* THING...

THANK HEAVEN-- THEY'RE NOT *HURT!*

HEY, HARRY-- C'MERE *QUICK!* THIS YA GOTTA *SEE!*

I SEEN LONGHAIR *FREAKS* BEFORE-- BUT *THESE* DUDES TAKE THE *CAKE!*

POMP AND PAGEANTRY ON A *COSMIC* SCALE WITH:
LEN WEIN
SPANKING-NEW SCRIPTER/EDITOR
JOHN BUSCEMA & JOE SINNOTT
SAME OLD ILLUSTRATORS

GLYNIS WEIN
colorist

JOHN COSTANZA
letterer

HONORARY ASGARDIANS ALL!

THOU MAY SEND THY WARRIORS *HOME*, COLONEL. THOSE THOU DIDST SEEK TO BATTLE SHALL *TROUBLE* THEE NO LONGER!

YEAH? AN' GIMME JUST ONE GOOD REASON I SHOULD TAKE YER *WORD* FOR THAT, GOLDILOCKS!

FOR, 'TIS THE WORD OF THE *SON OF ODIN*, BRASH MORTAL--

--AND THOSE THAT DOTH DARE TO *DOUBT* IT, DO SO ONLY *ONCE!*

OKAY! DON'T GET YER WINGS IN AN *UPROAR!* SO I *BELIEVE* YA!

BUT I STILL GOT ME A *JOB* TO DO!

"THEM EGYPTIAN WEIRDOS MAY BE *GONE*--

"--BUT JUST WHAT'RE WE SUPPOSED TO DO WITH THE LITTLE *SOUVENIR* THEY LEFT BEHIND?"

IF YON *PYRAMID* BE ALL THAT DOTH *PLAGUE* THEE, MORTAL--

--THOU NEED NOT *WORRY!*

GET THY WARRIORS *BACK*, COLONEL--

--AND LET THE *GOD OF THUNDER* DO WHAT *MUST* BE DONE--

--AS ONLY HE WHO WIELDS MYSTIC *MJOLNIR* CAN!

FOR A MOMENT, THE ENCHANTED HAMMER *CIRCLES* THE TIMELESS TOWER--

--UNTIL THE SOMBER PYRAMID IS *LOST* WITHIN A HOWLING *VORTEX*--

--THEN, AS ALWAYS, MIGHTY MJOLNIR **RETURNS** TO ITS MASTER'S **HAND.**

THE DEED IS **DONE,** MORTAL!

SWELL! NEAR AS **I** CAN SEE, ALL YOU DID WAS EXCHANGE **ONE** EYESORE FOR ANOTHER!

GRIMLY, THE THUNDER GOD **STUDIES** THE NATIONAL GUARDSMAN, THEN **GESTURES** IMPATIENTLY--

--AND, FOR AN INSTANT, THE VORTEX TREMBLES, **QUAVERS--**

--THEN CEASES TO **EXIST!**

HUH? THE BLASTED PYRAMID IS-- **GONE!**

AND THE **ORANGE GROVE** IS B-BACK-- GROWING **BETTER** THAN EVER!?!

AT THAT, THE PRINCE OF ASGARD **SMILES.**

I TRUST THAT WILL AT LAST **SATISFY** THY,,, EH?

THOU HAST DONE **WELL,** MY GOOD AND FAITHFUL **SON.**

THAT **VOICE--!** CAN IT **BE--?**

AYE, NOBLE THOR--THY **FATHER** HATH AT LAST **RETURNED** TO HIS **SENSES!**

THY REMOVAL OF THE PYRAMID HATH **FREED** ME FROM THE EGYPTIANS' SPELL -- **AND** FROM THE SPELL OF **FORGETFULNESS** I HAD PLACED UPON MYSELF!

THOU ART ONCE MORE **WHOLE?** THEN MY HEART SOARS, MILORD --AND THE HEARTS OF ALL **ASGARD!**

FOR IF E'ER THE REALM ETERNAL HAD **NEED** OF ITS **LIEGE,** 'TIS **NOW!**

I **BESEECH** THEE, ALL-FATHER-- **RETURN** TO THY THRONE WITH **HASTE!**

IN THY **ABSENCE,** MOST NOBLE ONE--THY FAITHFUL SUBJECTS HATH GROWN **LISTLESS,** WEAK OF **WILL--!**

THEN *COME*, THOR! 'TIS INDEED *TIME* THE LORD OF ASGARD RETURNED *HOME!* AND WHAT A *GLORIOUS* HOMECOMING IT SHALL BE!

NEVER WILL MILADY *JANE* AND I BE *PROUDER* TO STAND AT THY SIDE!

WHAT? AGAIN THOU DOST KEEP COMPANY WITH THAT *MORTAL WENCH* -- DESPITE MY ROYAL *DECREE?** THEN-- *SO BE IT!* ODIN DOTH BE *ALL-FATHER* ONCE MORE-- BUT THOU BE *NOT* HIS *SON!*

NOT TILL THOU HAST *FORSWORN* JANE FOSTER *FOREVER!*

* HANDED DOWN BACK IN THOR #136. --LEN.

MY LIEGE, I *PRAY* THEE--LET ME *EXPLAIN*--!

NO! I WILL NOT *HEAR!* BEGONE FROM MY *SIGHT*, THUNDER GOD --BEGONE!

THEN... THERE IS NOTHING MORE TO BE *SAID.*

DARLING...?

COME, MILADY.

THOR'S *DUTY* HERE IS *DONE.*

NOW LET US *DEPART* THIS DARK PLACE.

LOVE AND *DUTY*: ONCE AGAIN, THE TWO EMOTIONS *CLASH* WITH A RUMBLE LIKE A BREWING *STORM*--

--A SOUND THE GOD OF THUNDER KNOWS ONLY *TOO WELL!*

ORRIN? BUT THEN... YOU'RE NOT *REALLY* CALLED ORRIN, ARE YOU?

I-I GUESS I ALWAYS *KNEW* THAT.

JUDITH! COME *CLOSER*, CHILD. THOU HAST LEAVE TO APPROACH THE *PRESENCE.*

APPROACH YOU *HOW?* YOU'RE SOME SORT OF *GOD*, ORRIN.

I DON'T KNOW WHETHER TO KNEEL OR CURTSY OR...OR *WHAT!*

AH, CHILD--THERE DOTH BE NO NEED FOR *THEE* EVER TO KNEEL BEFORE ME.

NAY, JUDITH...NOT *THEE.*

THOU HAST SHOWN ME *MUCH* OF THE WAYS OF *HUMANITY* DURING MY STAY HERE--

--AND FOR THAT-- AND SO MUCH MORE *UNSPOKEN*--

--*ODIN*, RULER OF THE REALM ETERNAL, IS FOREVER IN THY *DEBT.*

BUT NOW, CHILD-- I FEAR I MUST TAKE MY *LEAVE.*

ONCE MORE, ENCHANTED ASGARD DOTH *SUMMON* ME--AND ITS *MONARCH* AS EVER MUST *ANSWER.*

FOR THY *SAFETY,* JUDITH-- STAND THEE *BACK.*

AND I PRAY THEE, CHILD... *REMEMBER* ME!

FOR IN SUCH MEMORY *ALONE* DOTH A GOD BE TRULY *IMMORTAL...*

A HOWL OF *WIND,* A CLAP OF *THUNDER,* A CRACK OF *LIGHTNING*--AND THE ALL-FATHER IS *GONE--*

CROOM!

--LEAVING *NOTHING* TO SHOW HE HAD EVER *BEEN--* SAVE A GOLDEN *TOKEN* IN A TREMBLING HAND--

--AND A SINGLE *TEAR* IN THE EYE OF THE GIRL CALLED *JUDITH!*

NIGHT HAS CLOAKED GRAY CLOUDS OF POLLUTION WHEN AT LAST THE GOD OF THUNDER AND HIS LADY COME STREAKING THRU THE CRISP MANHATTAN *SKY.*

DARLING, *FORGIVE* ME! IT'S *MY* FAULT YOUR FATHER HAS *FORSAKEN* YOU.

I'VE COME *BETWEEN* YOU BOTH AGAIN...JUST AS I DID IN THE *OLD* DAYS!

NAY, MILADY-- 'TIS NOT *TRUE!*

THESE BE *NOT* THE OLDEN DAYS-- AND THOU ART *NOT* THE JANE FOSTER THAT *ONCE* THOU WERE.

WITHIN THEE NOW BURN THE FIRES OF A *GODDESS BORN**--

* THE SPIRIT OF THE SELF-SACRI- FICING *SIF,* TO BE PRECISE--SINCE *THOR* #236. --LEN.

--AND ERE LONG I SHALL OPEN MINE FATHER'S TOO-WISE *EYES* TO THAT...

EH?

I HEAR... *VOICES!*

METHINKS BASE *INTRUDERS* DOTH AWAIT US WITHIN THY *DWELLING,* BELOVED.

IF THEY DO COME SEEKING *BATTLE*--

KRASH!

--THEY SHALL FIND THE GOD OF THUNDER *READY!*

WELCOME, THOR! A MOST *DRAMATIC* ENTRANCE INDEED!

TOO DRAMATIC, IF THOU DOST ASK *ME*. SOOTH, I DID ALMOST *DROP* MY MEAGER *REPAST.*

DASHING *FANDRAL* --VOLUMINOUS *VOLSTAGG*-- GRIM *HOGUN*--! IT DOTH SEEM I HATH ACTED TOO *RASHLY!*

MORE'S THE *PITY*, VAST ONE. 'TIS *UN-SEEMLY* TO GREET THY BROTHER-AT-ARMS WITH THE STENCH OF *PEANUT BUTTER* 'PON THY BREATH!

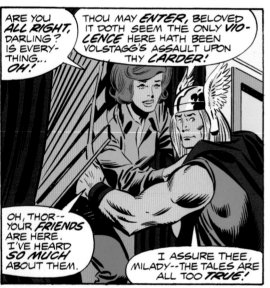

ARE YOU *ALL RIGHT,* DARLING? IS EVERY-THING... *OH!*

THOU MAY *ENTER,* BELOVED IT DOTH SEEM THE ONLY *VIO-LENCE* HERE HATH BEEN VOLSTAGG'S ASSAULT UPON THY *LARDER!*

OH, THOR-- YOUR *FRIENDS* ARE HERE. I'VE HEARD *SO MUCH* ABOUT THEM.

I ASSURE THEE, MILADY--THE TALES ARE ALL TOO *TRUE!*

BUT WHAT *DO* YE HERE, MY COMRADES? I HATH CHARGED YE WITH THE *SAFETY* OF ALL-HALLOWED *ASGARD*--!

--UNTIL THY FATHER DID *RETURN,* MILORD--AS NOW HE *HATH!* AND THE REALM ETERNAL COULD BE IN NO *SAFER* HANDS THAN THOSE OF ITS MOST NOBLE *LIEGE!*

OUR DUTY WAS *DONE*--AND THUS WE CAME IN SEARCH OF *THEE,* FRIEND THOR--FOR WE THREE HUNGER FOR *ADVENTURE*--

--AND THERE BE NO *BETTER* PLACE TO FIND IT THAN AT *THY* SIDE!

AS ALWAYS, GLIB FANDRAL-- THOU DOST *FLATTER* ME.

BUT STILL THOU MAY *STAY*-- AND BE *WELCOME!*

WELL, YOU FELLAS *HEARD* THE MAN! MAKE YOURSELVES *COMFORTABLE.* I'LL GO FETCH SOME *REFRESH-MENTS.*

ZOUNDS-- BUT THESE ROLLS OF JELLY DOTH TASTE *SWEET!*

BUT NOT NEARLY SO SWEET AS THE *CHARMS* OF THE COMELY WENCH REVEALED UPON THESE FOLDING PAGES.

IN TRUTH, THE GRAND VIZIER'S LEARNED *PARCH-MENTS* ARE SORELY *LACKING* BY COMPARISON.

AND ALL JOIN IN THE *LAUGHTER*-- SAVE A *BROODING* GOD OF THUNDER.

I'M AFRAID YOU GENTS WILL HAVE TO SETTLE FOR *LEMON-ADE.* THAT'S ALL THAT'S *LEFT* IN THE REFRIGERATOR.

'TWAS ALMOST--ER-- *EMPTY* WHEN WE *ARRIVED,* MILADY.

THOU ART A MOST *GRACIOUS* HOSTESS, JANE FOSTER.

THY COLD BEVERAGE IS *MORE* THAN ENOUGH.

MORE THAN ENOUGH FOR DOUR *HOGUN,* MAYHAP--

--BUT *NOT* SO FOR FANDRAL THE *CONNOIS-SEUR!*

HAST THOU NOTHING *STRONGER,* LADY JANE?

WELL,...THERE'S A WARM BOTTLE OF *PEPSI* IN THE KITCHEN.

SOMEHOW WE *DOUBT* THAT'S EXACTLY WHAT THE DASHING FANDRAL HAD IN *MIND,* JANE FOSTER--

THRAM!

--BUT NOW WE'LL PROBABLY *NEVER* KNOW FOR *SURE!*

WHAT--!?!

ODD'S BLOOD! A HUGE GAUNT-LETED *HAND* HATH *SUNDERED* YON WALL--!

AND NOW IT HATH *GRASPED* MY *BELOVED JANE!*

QUICKLY, MY FRIENDS-- *TO ARMS!*

'TIS *TOO LATE,* MILORD! THE HAND DOTH *WITHDRAW*--

"--AND IT TAKES THY LADY *WITH* IT!'"

NO! IT ISN'T *POSSIBLE*--!

JANE FOSTER'S SUDDEN *SCREAM* SHATTERS THE STILL NIGHT *AIR*--

--AND GALVANIZES FOUR GAUDILY-GARBED *ASGARDIANS* INTO SWIFT AND VIOLENT *ACTION!*

ATTACK, MY BROTHERS!

WHATE'ER AWAITS US *BEYOND* THIS WALL-- WE SHALL FACE IT AS *WARRIORS BORN!*

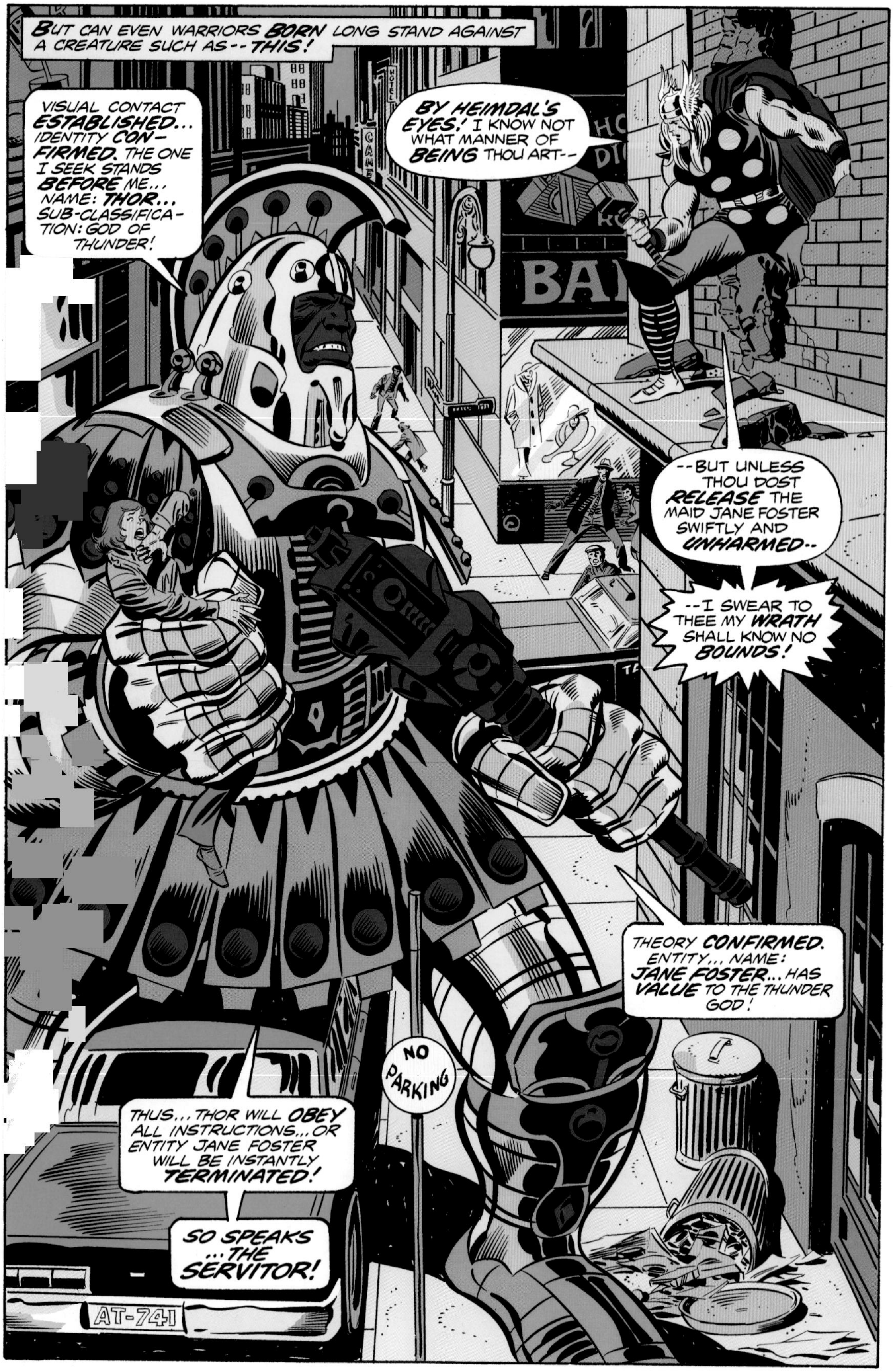
BUT CAN EVEN WARRIORS BORN LONG STAND AGAINST A CREATURE SUCH AS--THIS!
VISUAL CONTACT ESTABLISHED... IDENTITY CONFIRMED. THE ONE I SEEK STANDS BEFORE ME... NAME: THOR... SUB-CLASSIFICATION: GOD OF THUNDER!
BY HEIMDAL'S EYES! I KNOW NOT WHAT MANNER OF BEING THOU ART--
--BUT UNLESS THOU DOST RELEASE THE MAID JANE FOSTER SWIFTLY AND UNHARMED--
--I SWEAR TO THEE MY WRATH SHALL KNOW NO BOUNDS!
THEORY CONFIRMED. ENTITY... NAME: JANE FOSTER... HAS VALUE TO THE THUNDER GOD!
THUS... THOR WILL OBEY ALL INSTRUCTIONS... OR ENTITY JANE FOSTER WILL BE INSTANTLY TERMINATED!
SO SPEAKS ...THE SERVITOR!
NO PARKING
AT-741

THOU DOST SPEAK *CONFIDENTLY*, SERVITOR-- *TOO* CONFIDENTLY, METHINKS--

--FOR BE THOU FORMED OF PLIANT *FLESH* OR UNYIELDING *METAL*--

-- STILL SHALT THOU *FALL* BEFORE THE MYSTIC MIGHT OF *MJOLNIR!*

PERHAPS, THUNDER GOD... IF YOUR WEAPON CAN *REACH* ME...

...BUT MY *POWER-LANCE* SHALL SEE THAT IT DOES *NOT!*

NO--! HE *DEFLECTED* THOR'S HAMMER WITH A SINGLE *BLAST--!*

"IT'S FALLING TOWARDS THE *STREET*...

"...SMASHING THRU THAT POOR *CAR* AND...

SKRUMP!

"*WAIT--!* IT'S ARCING *UPWARD* AGAIN...

"...*RETURNING* TO MY DARLING'S *HAND!* THANK *HEAVEN!*"

NO, JANE FOSTER... THANK *ASGARD!* THANK *ODIN!*

THY *STAFF* HATH SAVED THEE *ONCE*, VILLAIN-- BUT 'PON MY WORD, 'TWILL BE *ONLY* ONCE!

SURRENDER MY *LADY*, SERVITOR-- OR SUR-RENDER THY *LIFE!*

13

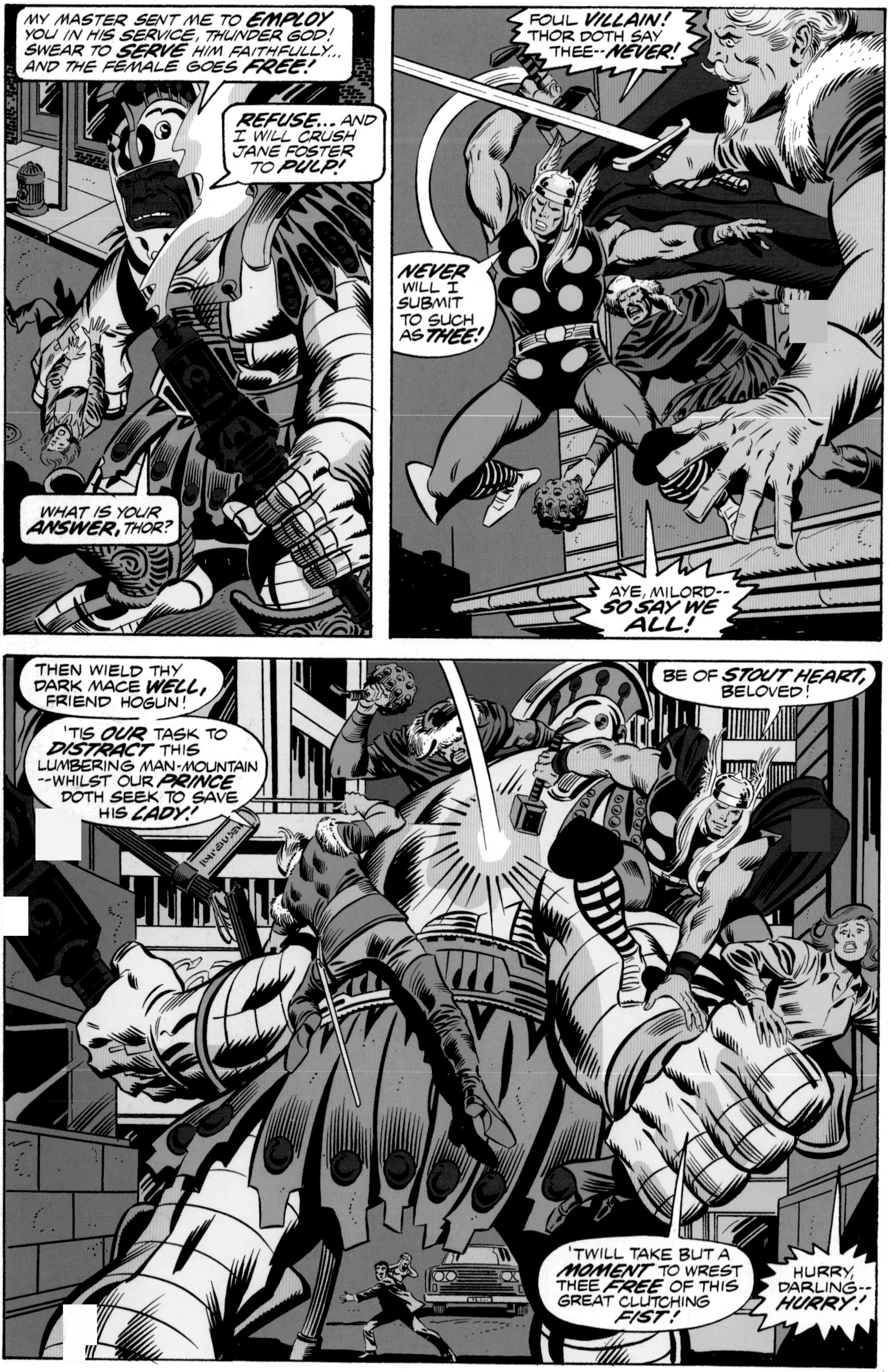

MY MASTER SENT ME TO EMPLOY YOU IN HIS SERVICE, THUNDER GOD! SWEAR TO SERVE HIM FAITHFULLY... AND THE FEMALE GOES FREE!
REFUSE... AND I WILL CRUSH JANE FOSTER TO PULP!
WHAT IS YOUR ANSWER, THOR?
FOUL VILLAIN! THOR DOTH SAY THEE--NEVER!
NEVER WILL I SUBMIT TO SUCH AS THEE!
AYE, MILORD-- SO SAY WE ALL!
THEN WIELD THY DARK MACE WELL, FRIEND HOGUN!
'TIS OUR TASK TO DISTRACT THIS LUMBERING MAN-MOUNTAIN --WHILST OUR PRINCE DOTH SEEK TO SAVE HIS LADY!
BE OF STOUT HEART, BELOVED!
'TWILL TAKE BUT A MOMENT TO WREST THEE FREE OF THIS GREAT CLUTCHING FIST!
HURRY, DARLING-- HURRY!

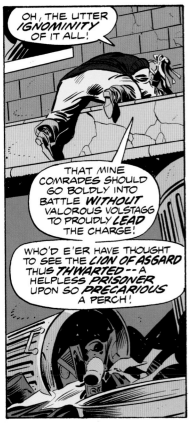

OH, THE UTTER *IGNOMINITY* OF IT ALL!

THAT MINE COMRADES SHOULD GO BOLDLY INTO BATTLE *WITHOUT* VALOROUS VOLSTAGG TO PROUDLY *LEAD* THE CHARGE!

WHO'D E'ER HAVE THOUGHT TO SEE THE *LION OF ASGARD* THUS *THWARTED*-- A HELPLESS *PRISONER* UPON SO *PRECARIOUS* A PERCH!

SURELY THE FICKLE FATES MUST *CHORTLE* AT THE IRONY-- THAT THE BOLDEST OF THE BOLD SHOULD BE *UNABLE* TO...

ZOUNDS!

CRRUMP

THE PRECIPICE DOTH *CRUMBLE*-- VALIANT VOLSTAGG DOTH *FALL*--!

BY ODIN! IT DOTH APPEAR I HATH *ACCOMPLISHED* MY DESCENT AS I DESIRED!

BUT PERHAPS I SHOULD-- ER-- *STAND BACK* FROM THE RAGING BATTLE FOR THE NONCE--

--UNTIL I HATH *ASCERTAINED* WHERE VIGOROUS VOLSTAGG'S MANY SKILLS MAY *BEST* BE EMPLOYED!

TWHUDD!

HAVE *FAITH*, MY LOVE!

THOUGH THESE MASSIVE *FINGERS* BE AS TIGHTLY CLENCHED AS THE BLAZING JAWS OF *FAFNIR* THE DRAGON--

--STILL SHALT THE RIGHTEOUS FURY OF THOR PRY THEM ASUNDER!

THEN PRAY *DO* SO WITH *HASTE*, THUNDER GOD!

METHINKS OUR *MIGHTIEST* BLOWS DOTH BE LITTLE MORE THAN AN *ANNOYANCE* TO THIS ARMORED BEHEMOTH!

CROOM!

15

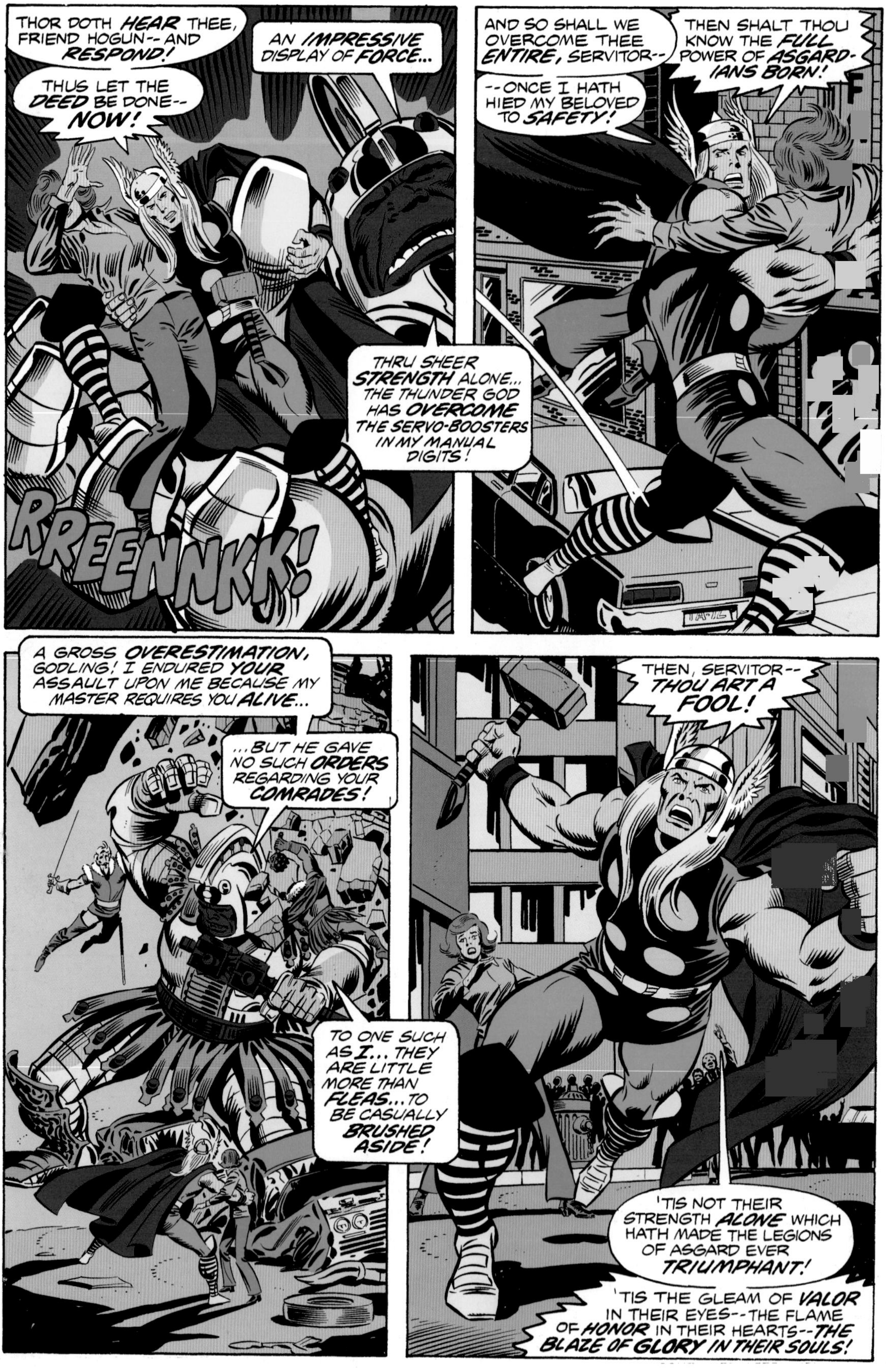
THOR DOTH HEAR THEE, FRIEND HOGUN-- AND RESPOND!
THUS LET THE DEED BE DONE-- NOW!
AN IMPRESSIVE DISPLAY OF FORCE...
THRU SHEER STRENGTH ALONE... THE THUNDER GOD HAS OVERCOME THE SERVO-BOOSTERS IN MY MANUAL DIGITS!
RREENNKK!
AND SO SHALL WE OVERCOME THEE ENTIRE, SERVITOR--
--ONCE I HATH HIED MY BELOVED TO SAFETY!
THEN SHALT THOU KNOW THE FULL POWER OF ASGARDIANS BORN!
A GROSS OVERESTIMATION, GODLING! I ENDURED YOUR ASSAULT UPON ME BECAUSE MY MASTER REQUIRES YOU ALIVE...
...BUT HE GAVE NO SUCH ORDERS REGARDING YOUR COMRADES!
TO ONE SUCH AS I... THEY ARE LITTLE MORE THAN FLEAS... TO BE CASUALLY BRUSHED ASIDE!
THEN, SERVITOR-- THOU ART A FOOL!
'TIS NOT THEIR STRENGTH ALONE WHICH HATH MADE THE LEGIONS OF ASGARD EVER TRIUMPHANT!
'TIS THE GLEAM OF VALOR IN THEIR EYES--THE FLAME OF HONOR IN THEIR HEARTS--THE BLAZE OF GLORY IN THEIR SOULS!

I DID NOT COME HERE TO TRADE *SPEECHES*, THUNDER GOD...BUT TO GAIN YOUR OATH OF *LOYALTY!*

SWEAR TO *SERVE* MY MASTER...OR MY POWER-LANCE WILL *BRING* YOU *PAIN* THAT EVEN A *GODLING* CANNOT LONG *ENDURE!*

ZZZKAK!

NEVER, THOU CHURL! THE PRINCE OF THE REALM ETERNAL WILL EVER SHOW *FEALTY* TO BUT *ONE* MASTER--ONE *LIEGE*--

--AND THOUGH, FOR THE NONCE, MY FATHER DOTH *DENY* ME--

--STILL SHALL THOR SERVE ONLY THE NOBLE *ODIN*--

--AYE--E'EN UNTO *DEATH!*

THOR? DARLING??

HE LIES SO *SILENT*--SO *STILL!*

I JUST CAN'T STAND BY AND WATCH HIM *TREATED* LIKE THIS! I'VE GOT TO...

NAY, MILADY!

THE THUNDER GOD ALREADY HATH *ENOUGH* TO CONCERN HIM--WITHOUT *ADDING* CONCERN FOR THEE *ANEW!*

I *BESEECH* THEE, MILADY--*STAY* THY HAND--

--AND LEAVE THE *BATTLE* TO THOSE WHO WERE *BRED* TO IT!

LET *GO* OF ME, VOLSTAGG! I WON'T LET YOU *STOP* ME FROM *HELPING* MY...

NAY, MY LOVE! VAST VOLSTAGG SPEAKS TRUE! THOU WOULDST AID ME BEST TO AID ME NOT AT ALL!

DARING HOGUN HATH GAINED ME TIME TO RECOVER MY SENSES--

--AND, IN TRUTH, THAT BE ALL I DOTH REQUIRE!

DARLING PLEASE--!

MILADY, PRAY LISTEN TO THE NOBLE THOR!

'TWOULD BE FOLLY TO DISPUTE HIS ORDERS NOW--

--WHEN LIVES HANG IN THE BALANCE!

ENTITY... NAME: HOGUN... STILL SEEKS TO DESTROY ME...

...BUT ONE WHO SERVES THE MASTER IS NOT EASILY DESTROYED!

BY ODIN! THE ARMORED ONE PLUCKS ME FROM HIS BACK LIKE A LEAF--

--THREATENS TO SNAP ME LIKE A TWIG--!

BUT LIKE THE MIGHTY OAK, FRIEND HOGUN -- THOU SHALT STAND!

THOU SHALT STAND!

THRANNGG!

MILORD THOR--!?!

18

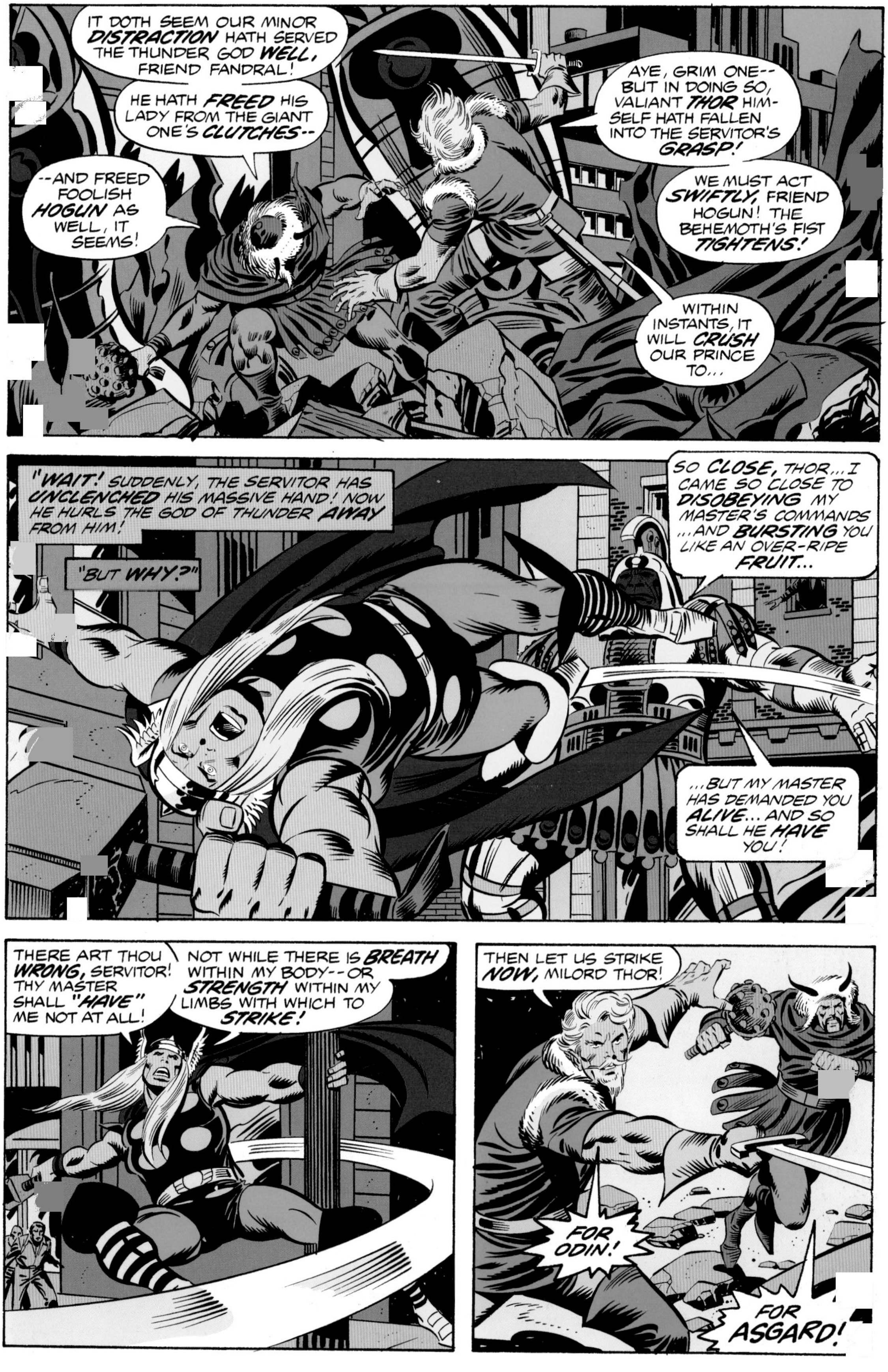
IT DOTH SEEM OUR MINOR DISTRACTION HATH SERVED THE THUNDER GOD WELL, FRIEND FANDRAL!
HE HATH FREED HIS LADY FROM THE GIANT ONE'S CLUTCHES--
--AND FREED FOOLISH HOGUN AS WELL, IT SEEMS!
AYE, GRIM ONE-- BUT IN DOING SO, VALIANT THOR HIMSELF HATH FALLEN INTO THE SERVITOR'S GRASP!
WE MUST ACT SWIFTLY, FRIEND HOGUN! THE BEHEMOTH'S FIST TIGHTENS!
WITHIN INSTANTS, IT WILL CRUSH OUR PRINCE TO...
"WAIT! SUDDENLY, THE SERVITOR HAS UNCLENCHED HIS MASSIVE HAND! NOW HE HURLS THE GOD OF THUNDER AWAY FROM HIM!
"BUT WHY?"
SO CLOSE, THOR... I CAME SO CLOSE TO DISOBEYING MY MASTER'S COMMANDS ...AND BURSTING YOU LIKE AN OVER-RIPE FRUIT...
...BUT MY MASTER HAS DEMANDED YOU ALIVE... AND SO SHALL HE HAVE YOU!
THERE ART THOU WRONG, SERVITOR! THY MASTER SHALL "HAVE" ME NOT AT ALL!
NOT WHILE THERE IS BREATH WITHIN MY BODY--OR STRENGTH WITHIN MY LIMBS WITH WHICH TO STRIKE!
THEN LET US STRIKE NOW, MILORD THOR!
FOR ODIN!
FOR ASGARD!

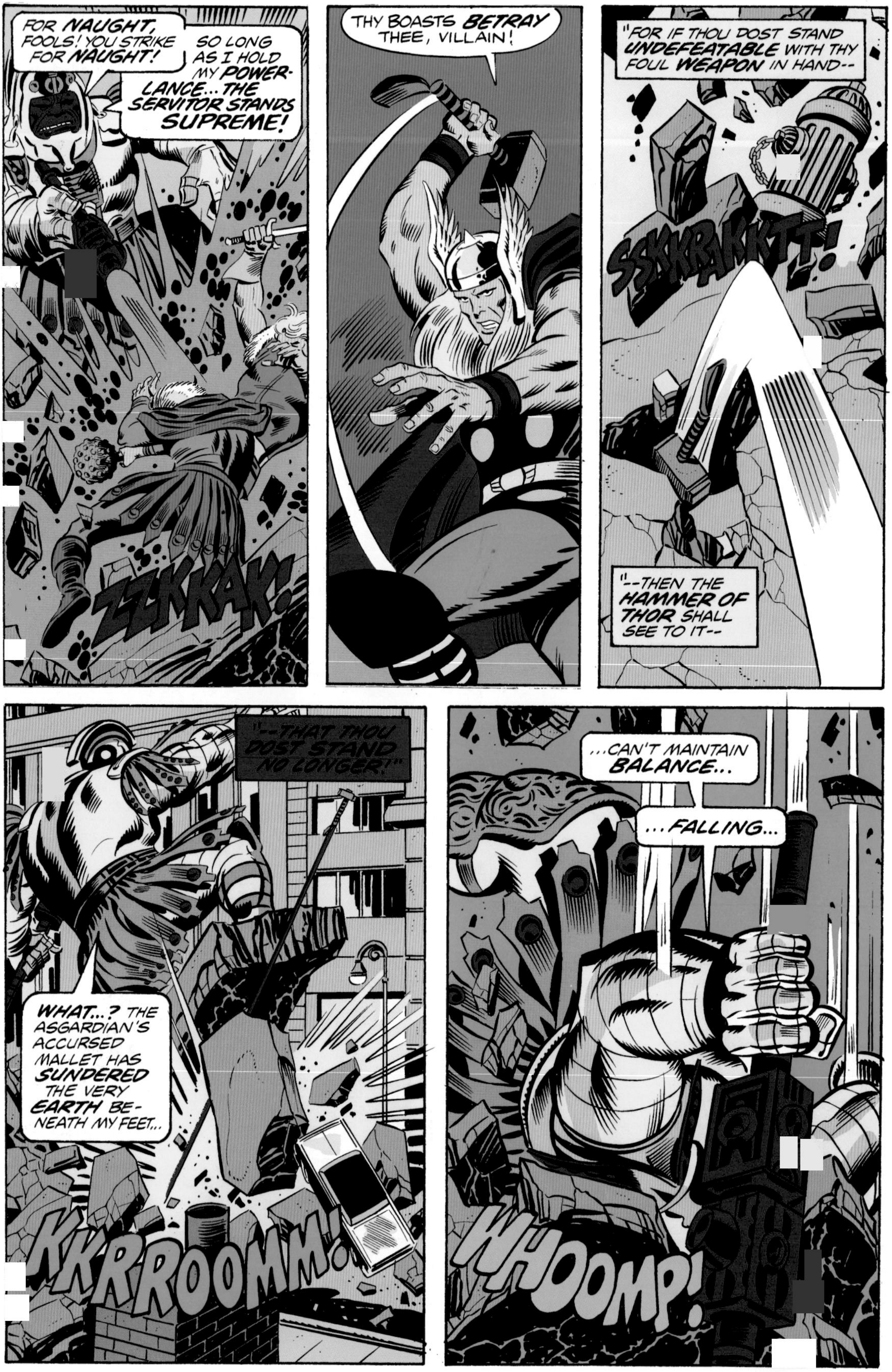
FOR NAUGHT, FOOLS! YOU STRIKE FOR NAUGHT!
SO LONG AS I HOLD MY POWER-LANCE... THE SERVITOR STANDS SUPREME!
ZZKKAK!
THY BOASTS BETRAY THEE, VILLAIN!
"FOR IF THOU DOST STAND UNDEFEATABLE WITH THY FOUL WEAPON IN HAND--
"--THEN THE HAMMER OF THOR SHALL SEE TO IT--
"--THAT THOU DOST STAND NO LONGER!"
WHAT...? THE ASGARDIAN'S ACCURSED MALLET HAS SUNDERED THE VERY EARTH BENEATH MY FEET...
KKRROOMM!
...CAN'T MAINTAIN BALANCE...
...FALLING...
WHOOMP!

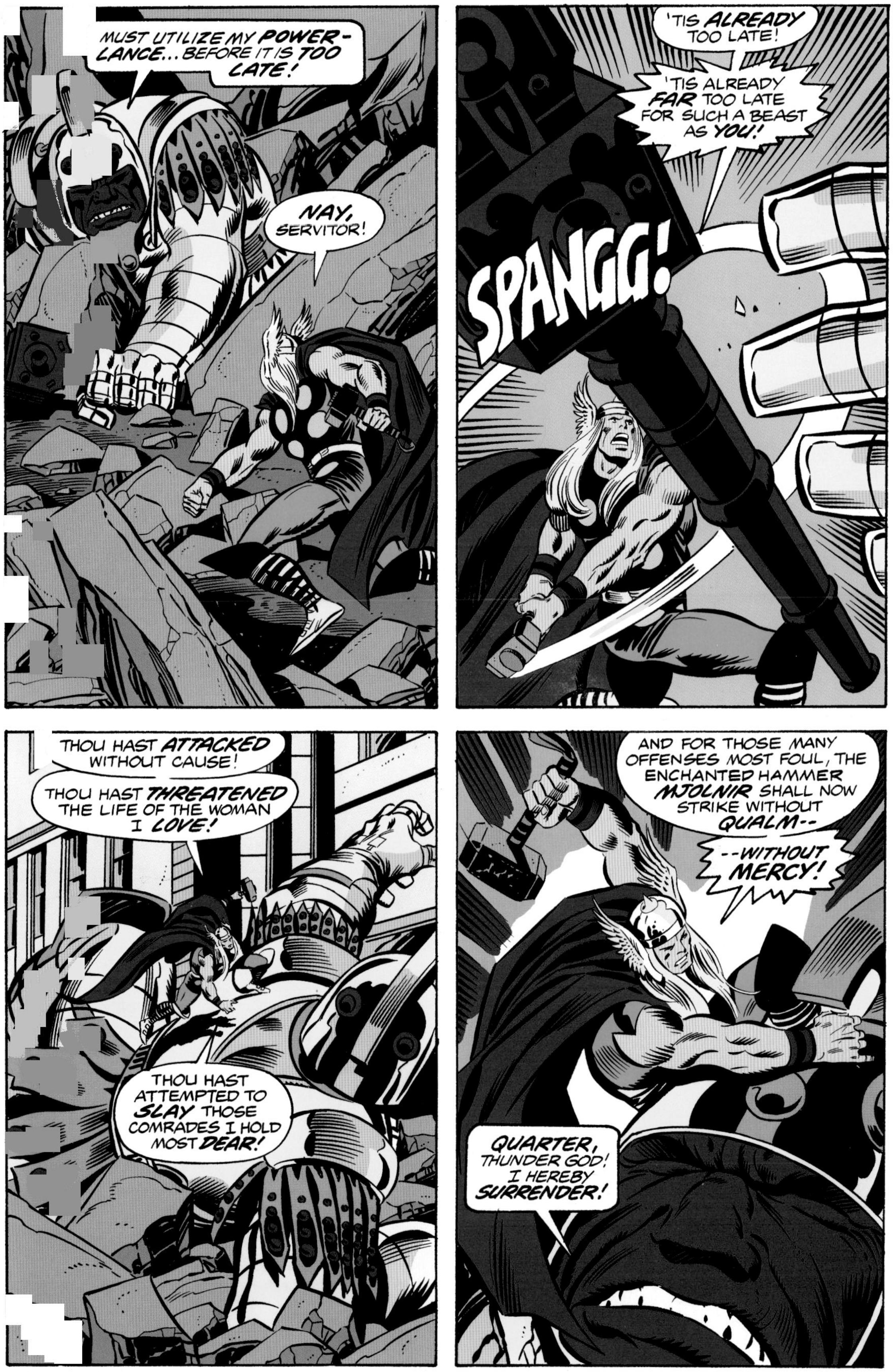
MUST UTILIZE MY POWER-LANCE... BEFORE IT IS TOO LATE!
NAY, SERVITOR!
'TIS ALREADY TOO LATE!
'TIS ALREADY FAR TOO LATE FOR SUCH A BEAST AS YOU!
SPANGG!
THOU HAST ATTACKED WITHOUT CAUSE!
THOU HAST THREATENED THE LIFE OF THE WOMAN I LOVE!
THOU HAST ATTEMPTED TO SLAY THOSE COMRADES I HOLD MOST DEAR!
AND FOR THOSE MANY OFFENSES MOST FOUL, THE ENCHANTED HAMMER MJOLNIR SHALL NOW STRIKE WITHOUT QUALM--
--WITHOUT MERCY!
QUARTER, THUNDER GOD! I HEREBY SURRENDER!

NAY, SERVITOR! 'TWILL NOT *HELP* THEE! NOW SHALT THOU FEEL THE RIGHTEOUS *WRATH* OF...

EH?

ENOUGH, THUNDER GOD! THE BATTLE IS *OVER!*

WHO--?

I AM HE WHOM THE SERVITOR CALLS *MASTER*, THOR! BUT *YOU* WOULD RECALL ME BY *ANOTHER* NAME--

ZARRKO--THE TOMORROW MAN!*

*AND *YOU* SHOULD RECALL ZARRKO TOO-- FROM *THOR #86, 101-102,* AND *MARVEL TEAM-UP # 9-11.* --LEN.

IF THOU HAST COME SEEKING *VENGEANCE* FOR THY PAST *DEFEATS* AT MY HAND, EVIL ONE--

--THOU SHALT FIND THE SON OF ODIN *READY!*

HOLD, THOR! THERE HAS BEEN AN UNFORTUNATE *MISUNDERSTANDING* HERE--

--A TRAGIC *FAILURE* TO *COMMUNICATE!*

"I DID NOT SEND MY SERVITOR HERE TO *BATTLE* YOU ALL--

--I SENT HIM BECAUSE-- *I NEED YOUR HELP!*

UNLESS YOU AGREE TO *AID* ME--*THE PLANET EARTH IS DOOMED!*

NEXT ISSUE: TURMOIL IN THE TIME-STREAM!

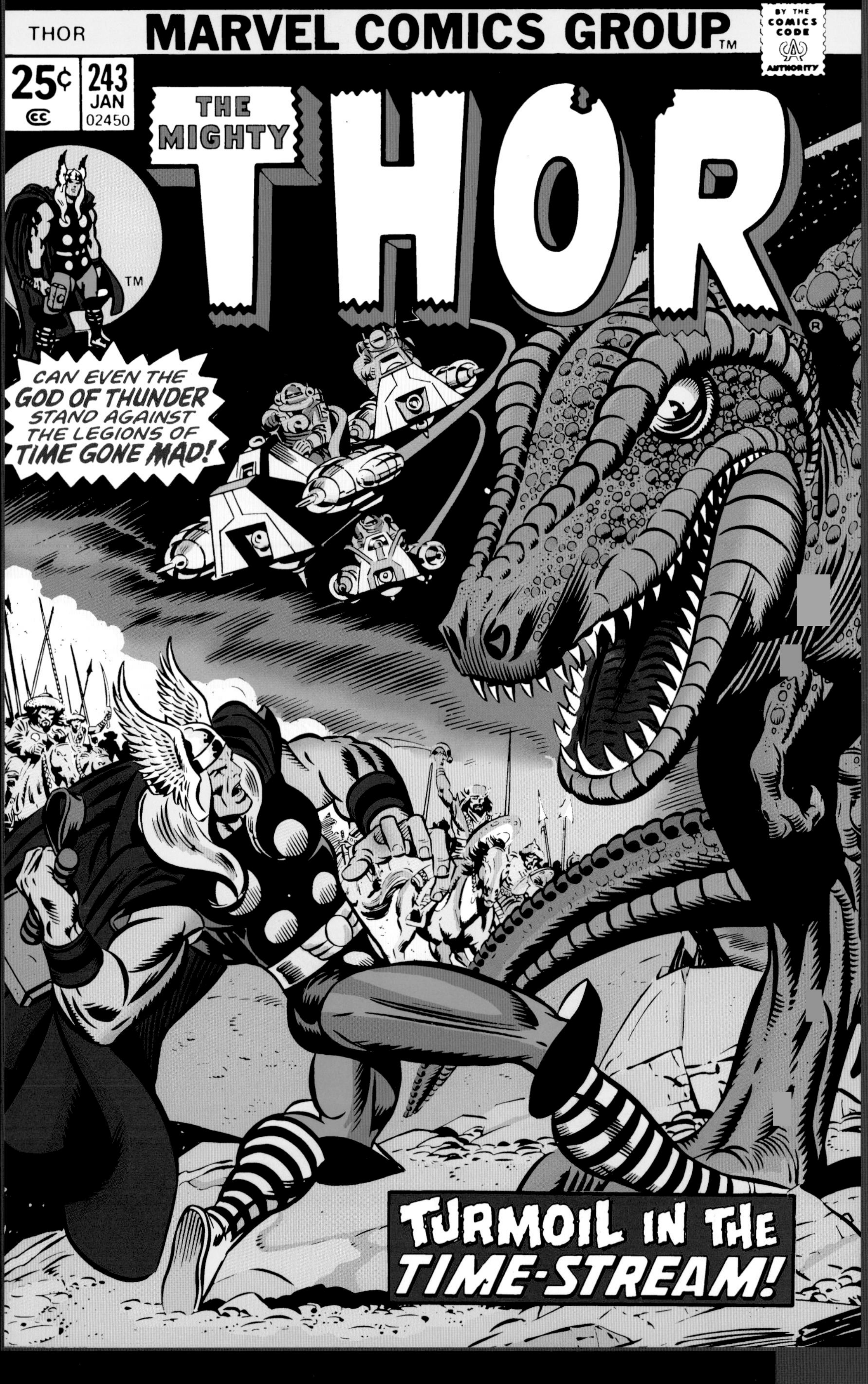
THOR
MARVEL COMICS GROUP™
BY THE COMICS CODE AUTHORITY
25¢
243
JAN
02450
THE MIGHTY
THOR
CAN EVEN THE GOD OF THUNDER STAND AGAINST THE LEGIONS OF TIME GONE MAD!
TURMOIL IN THE TIME-STREAM!

Stan Lee PRESENTS: THE MIGHTY THOR!
LEN WEIN WRITER / EDITOR
JOHN BUSCEMA + JOE SINNOTT ILLUSTRATORS
GLYNIS OLIVER WEIN COLORIST
JOE ROSEN LETTERER
WHAT HATH GONE BEFORE: THOR AND JANE FOSTER HAVE RETURNED TO NEW YORK-- WHERE THEY WERE GREETED BY THOSE BOLD ASGARDIANS NAMED FANDRAL, HOGUN AND VOLSTAGG--THEN ATTACKED BY A LIVING MONOLITH CALLED THE SERVITOR!
IN A BATTLE MOST BRUTAL, THE THUNDER GOD AND HIS COMPANIONS HAVE DEFEATED THE SERVITOR, BUT NOW FIND THEMSELVES FACING THE MECHANOID'S MASTER--THE EVIL GENIUS WHO CALLS HIMSELF ZARRKO THE TOMORROW MAN!
GOT ALL THAT, FAITHFUL ONE? SWELL--'CAUSE FROM HERE ON, YOU'RE ON YOUR OWN!
IF THOU DOST COME SEEKING BATTLE, ZARRKO--WE STAND READY!
NO, ASGARDIAN--I COME BECAUSE I NEED YOUR HELP!
UNLESS YOU AGREE TO AID ME--THE PLANET EARTH IS DOOMED!
TURMOIL IN THE TIME-STREAM

NAY, EVIL ONE! THOU DOST SEEK TO GAIN OUR *TRUST*-- ONLY SO THOU MAY *SLAY* US UNSUSPECTING!

IF I WANTED YOU ALL *DEAD*, ASGARDIAN-- MY *LASER-GUN* WOULD NOT HAVE *MISSED* MERE MOMENTS AGO!

NOW YOU *MUST* TRUST ME-- OR THE *DEATH* OF COUNTLESS WORLDS WILL BE ON *YOUR* HEADS!

FRIEND FANDRAL, MAYHAP THOU DOST ACT TOO *RASHLY!* LET US *HEAR* ZARRKO OUT!

AS THOU *WISH*, MILORD-- BUT METHINKS THIS TOMORROW MAN DOTH *SPEAK* WITH THE TONGUE OF A *TROLL!*

THE THUNDER GOD MIGHT HAVE *REASON* TO DISTRUST ME, ASGARDIAN-- BUT *YOU* DON'T EVEN *KNOW* ME--

--AND EVEN IF YOU *DID*-- YOU COULD *NOT* KNOW WHAT TRANSPIRED *AFTER* THOR AND I LAST *CLASHED!**

*BACK IN MARVEL TEAM-UP #11.-- LEN.

"LEFT TO WALLOW IN *DEFEAT* IN THE 23rd CENTURY-- THE ERA OF MY *BIRTH*-- I DWELLED FOR WEEKS UPON MY REPEATED *FAILURES*-- UNTIL, AT LAST, I HAD AN *INSPIRATION!*

"THE NEXT SEVERAL MONTHS WERE SPENT IN *ALTERING* ONE OF MY CENTURY'S INDESTRUCTIBLE *MINING ROBOTS* INTO A FITTING *SERVITOR* FOR ONE SUCH AS I INTENDED TO *BECOME!*

"THEN, FINALLY, MY SERVITOR AND I ENTERED THE *TIME CUBE* THAT WAS SO *NECESSARY* TO MY PLAN--

"--ACTIVATED THE CONTROLS--

"--AND LURCHED FORWARD INTO *TIME!*

"IN YOUR 20th CENTURY, I HAD BEEN CALLED THE *TOMORROW MAN!*

"NOW I HURTLED THRU THE AGES TO *FULFILL* THAT UNWITTING *PROPHESY!*

"THE CENTURIES SPED *BY* ME-- AN INCOMPARABLE *PANORAMA* OF MANKIND'S GREATEST *TRIUMPHS* AND *TRAGEDIES*--

"THE GREAT GLEAMING *SPIRES* OF TOWERING CITIES THAT COULD ONLY BE CALLED *PARADISE*--

"--WAR-RAVAGED *RUINS* THAT ONLY PROVED ONCE MORE MY *OWN* CENTURY'S *WISDOM* IN OUTLAWING ALL *WEAPONS!*

"ALL THIS I SAW AND *MORE*-- YET STILL I TRAVELED *ON*--

"--UNTIL, AT LENGTH, I REACHED EARTH'S *50TH CENTURY*--

"--AND DISCOVERED A WORLD SUBLIMELY *SUITED* TO MY NEEDS!

"I HAD *FOUND* THE TOMORROW I'D BEEN *SEARCHING* FOR!"

"WITH MY *SERVITOR* AT MY SIDE, IT DID NOT TAKE ME VERY LONG TO HAVE MYSELF PROCLAIMED *KING* AND MOST SOVEREIGN *RULER* OF THE ENTIRE *PLANET!*

26

YOUR TIME MIGHT NEVER HAVE **HEARD** FROM ME **AGAIN**--

--HAD I NOT LEARNED ABOUT THE **MENACE** OF-- **THE TIME-TWISTERS!**

TIME-TWISTERS, ZARRKO? WHAT MANNER OF BEINGS ARE **THEY?**

IF **BEINGS** THEY TRULY **ARE!**

THAT IS **DIFFICULT** TO EXPLAIN AT BEST, THUNDER GOD.

PERHAPS IT WOULD BE **SIMPLER** FOR ME TO **ILLUSTRATE!**

WE'RE DEALING WITH AN **ABSTRACT** CONCEPT HERE, ASGARDIANS --SO PAY **CLOSE ATTENTION!**

IMAGINE THAT THE **HUMAN RACE**-- AS A **RULE**--MOVES THRU TIME AS A **STRAIGHT LINE** IN ONE DIRECTION.

NOW IMAGINE THAT THE **TIME-TWISTERS** MOVE THRU TIME AS A **SPIRAL** IN THE **OPPOSITE** DIRECTION!

THE TIME-TWISTERS **APPEAR** UPON EARTH **ONLY** AT THOSE JUNCTURES WHERE THE TWO LINES **INTERSECT!**

THEIR STAY ON EARTH IS **BRIEF**--

--BUT THEIR **PASSING** CREATES A **COSMIC UPHEAVAL** THAT REDUCES THIS WORLD TO A **CINDER!**

THRU A **TIMESCOPE,** I WATCHED THE **DESTRUCTION** OF EARTH IN THE **80TH** CENTURY.

UNLESS YOU AGREE TO **HELP** ME, **50TH** CENTURY EARTH WILL BE THE **NEXT** TO FALL!

THY **CAUSE** INDEED SEEMS **NOBLE,** ZARRKO--BUT **WHY** HAST THOU TRAVELED THESE MANY CENTURIES TO SEEK **OUR** AID?

BECAUSE, FAT ONE, THE TIME-TWISTERS ONLY **TOUCH** THE EARTH EACH **THIRTY** CENTURIES.

IF THE **50TH** CENTURY FALLS, THE **20TH** CENTURY WILL **FOLLOW**--

--AND BY THEN, THE TWISTERS WILL HAVE GROWN **TOO STRONG** TO BE **DEFEATED!**

ZOUNDS.

NOW I MUST HAVE YOUR **ANSWER**, ASGARDIANS!

WILL YOU **HELP** ME SAVE THE **WORLD**?

ZARRKO, THOR DOTH SAY THEE... **AYE!** THE GOD OF THUNDER SHALL STAND **BESIDE** THEE!

THEN SO SAY WE **ALL**, TOMORROW MAN!

SO SAY WE **ALL!!**

SWIFTLY THEN, MY SERVITOR-- SUMMON THE **TIME CUBE!**

WE HAVE NO MORE TIME TO **WASTE!**

AS YOU **WISH**, MASTER... SO SHALL IT BE **DONE!**

WITHOUT ANOTHER **WORD**, A GREAT ARMORED FIST POINTS **SKYWARD**--

--A SINGLE BURST OF **ENERGY** SIZZLES FROM THE SERVITOR'S **POWER-LANCE**--

--AND, FROM ITS CLOUD-SWEPT **COVER**, A GLEAMING GOLDEN **OBJECT** SWOOPS SAVAGELY DOWN TOWARDS THE ISLE OF **MANHATTAN**--

--THEN WHISPERS TO A SUDDEN **STOP**, HOVERING SILENTLY ABOVE THE BENIGHTED CITY **STREETS**.

DON'T STAND ON **CEREMONY**, ASGARDIANS.

THE SOONER YOU **ENTER** THE CUBE, THE SOONER WE CAN BE **UNDERWAY!**

THEN *FARE-THEE-WELL*, JANE MY LOVE! I WILL *RETURN* TO THEE AS SWIFTLY AS...

NEVER MIND THE *GOOD-BYES*, DARLING. I'M COMING *WITH* YOU!

NAY, MILADY! 'TWOULD BE *FOLLY* TO...

FORGET THE *EXCUSES*, THOR-- I DON'T WANT TO *HEAR* THEM! I'M *COMING*-- AND THAT'S *FINAL!*

YOU'D NEVER HAVE LEFT BEHIND YOUR *LADY SIF* FOR FEAR OF HER *SAFETY* --AND I NEED NOT *REMIND* YOU THAT WHATEVER THERE REMAINS OF *HER* NOW DWELLS WITHIN *ME!*

BY MY FATHER'S THRICE-BLESSED BEARD-- METHINKS PERHAPS THOU ART *MORE* A GODDESS THAN ANY COULD HAVE *IMAGINED.*

AYE, JANE FOSTER, THOU MAY INDEED *COME*--

--AND MAY ODIN *PRESERVE* US *ALL!*

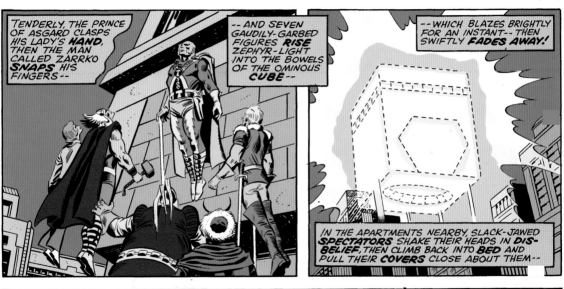

TENDERLY, THE PRINCE OF ASGARD CLASPS HIS LADY'S *HAND*, THEN THE MAN CALLED ZARRKO *SNAPS* HIS FINGERS--

--AND SEVEN GAUDILY-GARBED FIGURES *RISE* ZEPHYR-LIGHT INTO THE BOWELS OF THE OMINOUS *CUBE*--

--WHICH BLAZES BRIGHTLY FOR AN INSTANT-- THEN SWIFTLY *FADES AWAY!*

IN THE APARTMENTS NEARBY, SLACK-JAWED *SPECTATORS* SHAKE THEIR HEADS IN *DIS-BELIEF*, THEN CLIMB BACK INTO *BED* AND PULL THEIR *COVERS* CLOSE ABOUT THEM--

--WHILE IN THE THRONE ROOM OF THE REALM ETERNAL, TWO *OTHER* SPECTATORS WATCH THE TIME CUBE'S *DEPARTURE* IN TERRIBLE *SILENCE*, UNTIL...

TH-THOU SHOULDST BE *PROUD* OF THY MOST NOBLE SON, O REGAL *ODIN.*

THE FATE OF ALL *MIDGARD*[*] NOW RESTS IN HIS TWO *HANDS!*

I *HAVE* NO SON, VIZIER-- AND THOU WOULDST DO WELL TO *REMEMBER* THAT!

[*]THAT'S *EARTH* FOR ALL YOU LAYMEN OUT THERE.-- LEARNED LEN.

SO LONG AS THOR DOTH DEIGN TO KEEP COMPANY WITH THE MORTAL *JANE FOSTER* AGAINST MY WISHES--

SO LONG AS HE DOTH *DEFY* MY ROYAL *COMMAND*--

FOR SO LONG SHALL THE GOD OF THUNDER BE *NOT* MINE *HEIR!*

BUT, MY *LIEGE*...

DOTH NOT THE FACT THAT THE *SPIRIT* OF THE GODDESS *SIF* NOW POSSESSES THE MORTAL MAID'S BODY *SOFTEN* THY RESOLVE IN THE LEAST?

NAY, VIZIER--'TIS THE *PRINCIPLE* OF THE THING THAT DOTH SIT SO *ILL* WITH ME!

THOR WAS GIVEN A *COMMAND* MOST PLAIN--YET, OF HIS OWN ACCORD, THE THUNDER GOD CHOSE TO *IGNORE* IT!

SUCH *TEMERITY* MUST NOT GO *UNPUNISHED!*

SO THOU HAST *BANISHED* THINE OWN FLESH-AND-BLOOD FROM THE REALM ETERNAL UNTIL SUCH TIME AS HE *SUBMITS* TO THY *WILL!*

MILORD, THOUGH THOU DOST BE THE *WISEST* OF THE WISE-- STILL, AS THY MOST HUMBLE *ADVISOR* METHINKS PERHAPS THOU ART MAKING A *MISTAKE!*

NAY, VIZIER! I *ASSURE* THEE--

--I KNOW *EXACTLY* WHAT I AM *DOING!*

AND ON THAT **GRIM** NOTE, LET US RETURN TO THE **OBJECT** OF ODIN'S **IRE**...

THERE SEEMS TO BE **TURBULENCE** OF SOME SORT AHEAD IN THE **TIME-STREAM**, ASGARDIANS--

--BUT WE SHOULD **REACH** THE 50th CENTURY WITHOUT ANY **PROBLEMS!**

VERILY, I DO **HOPE** SO, ZARRKO!

NOT THAT THE **LION OF ASGARD** COULD E'ER KNOW **FEAR**, MIND YE--

--BUT WHILST A **WIZARD** SUCH AS THEE MAY **THRIVE** IN THIS SWIRLING VOID--

--A **WARRIOR** SUCH AS **I** DO FEEL FAR MORE **SECURE** WITH **BOTH** FEET PLANTED **FIRMLY** 'PON THE...

ZOUNDS!!

THE VERY **FLOOR** BENEATH ME DOTH **WRITHE--!**

INDEED IT **DOES**, VAST ONE-- FOR THIS VESSEL HATH LURCHED TO A **HALT!**

WHAT BE THE **MEANING** OF THIS, ZARRKO?

BY HEIMDALL'S EYES, IF THOU DOST SEEK TO **BETRAY** US, VILLAIN--

I **SWEAR** TO YOU, ASGARDIANS-- THIS IS **NONE** OF MY **DOING!**

SOME **UNKNOWN ELEMENT** IN THE TIME-STREAM SOMEHOW **IMPEDES** OUR PROGRESS--

--AND EVEN MY MOST SENSITIVE **SCANNERS** CANNOT TELL ME **WHAT** IT IS!

THOOMP! THOOMP!

WHATE'ER IT **IS**, ZARRKO-- IT DOTH SEEK TO GAIN **ENTRANCE** BY **FORCE!**

QUICKLY-- **OPEN** THE TIME CUBE'S **PORTAL**-- AND I WILL **INVESTIGATE** YON POUNDING'S **SOURCE!**

MYSTIC **MJOLNIR** CLENCHED TIGHTLY IN HIS FIST, THE GOD OF THUNDER STEPS BOLDLY FROM THE TIME-TOSSED **CUBE**--

--INTO A WORLD THAT IS REALLY **NOT** A WORLD AT ALL, BUT A BILLOWING **MIASMA** OF STIFLING MISTS THAT SWIRL IN FROM **OBLIVION** AND SWIRL AWAY INTO **DESPAIR**.

CAUTIOUSLY THE ODINSON STRIDES THRU THE SMOTHERING **FOG**, UNSURE OF EXACTLY **WHAT** TO EXPECT--

--BUT **NEVER** EXPECTING-- **THIS**!!

FAFNIR'S BLOOD! OUR VESSEL HATH BEEN ASSAULTED BY-- **A DRAGON!**

IN POINT OF FACT, IT'S A **DINOSAUR**--

SPECIFICALLY, **TYRANNOSAURUS REX**--

--THE **THUNDER LIZARD**--

--BUT THAT LITTLE BIT OF **IRONY** IS SOMEHOW **LOST** ON THE EMBATTLED ASGARDIAN!

RELEASE MINE **ARM**, BEHEMOTH! **RELEASE** ME, I SAY--

--OR KNOW THE **WRATH** OF **THOR**!!

THRAMM!

FOR AN INSTANT, THE SLICK-SCALED MONSTROSITY *TREMBLES* FROM THE FORCE OF THE THUNDER GOD'S *BLOW*--

--THEN, BELLOWING ITS RAGE, IT *FALLS*--

THOOM!

--BUT ITS *FURY* DOES NOT *DIMINISH!*

SO, BEHEMOTH-- STILL DOST THOU SEEK TO *DEVOUR* ME--

--BUT MINE HAMMER'S *NEXT* BLOW SHALL *SHUT* THINE GAPING *MAW!*

UNFORTUNATELY, THE BATTLE'S NEXT BLOW IS *NOT* STRUCK BY THE GOD OF THUNDER!

THRAKK!

VERILY, THOU ART AS *FEARSOME* AS THY LEGENDS HATH CLAIMED THEE, MONSTER--

--BUT THERE ARE *LEGENDS* TOLD AS WELL OF THE *SCION OF ODIN!*

I HATH NO REAL WISH TO *SLAY* THEE, MONSTER-- THOU ART ALMOST *NOBLE* IN THY FASHION--

--BUT IF THOU DOST SEEK TO *ATTACK* ME ANEW, THOU SHALT LEAVE ME NO *CHOICE!*

FOR THINE *OWN* SAKE, TURN THEE *BACK*, BEHEMOTH! I *BESEECH* THEE--

TURN THEE BACK-- OR PERISH!

I HATH GIVEN THEE FAIR **WARNING**, MONSTER-- BUT STILL DOST THOU LUMBER MADLY **TOWARD** ME!

THEN **SO BE IT!** THOU HAST MADE MY DECISION **FOR** ME, BEHEMOTH--

WHOMM!

--AND THY **FATE** HATH BEEN **SEALED!!**

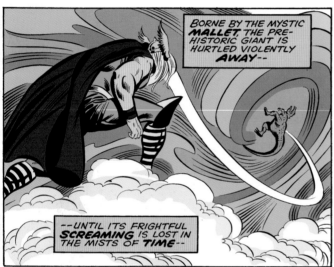

BORNE BY THE MYSTIC **MALLET**, THE PRE-HISTORIC GIANT IS HURTLED VIOLENTLY **AWAY**--

--UNTIL ITS FRIGHTFUL **SCREAMING** IS LOST IN THE MISTS OF **TIME**--

--AND ENCHANTED MJOLNIR **RETURNS** TO ITS MASTER--

--ALONE!

FRIEND THOR, WE COULD STAND IDLY BY **NO LONGER!**

SHOW US THE **FOE**-- AND IN ODIN'S NAME WE SHALL **STRIKE!**

THINE **AID** IS WELCOME ...BUT **UN-NECESSARY**, FRIEND HOGUN.

THE **DANGER** HERE HATH **PASSED!**

HAS IT, THOR?

THEN **LOOK** THEE TO YONDER **MISTS**, MILORD--

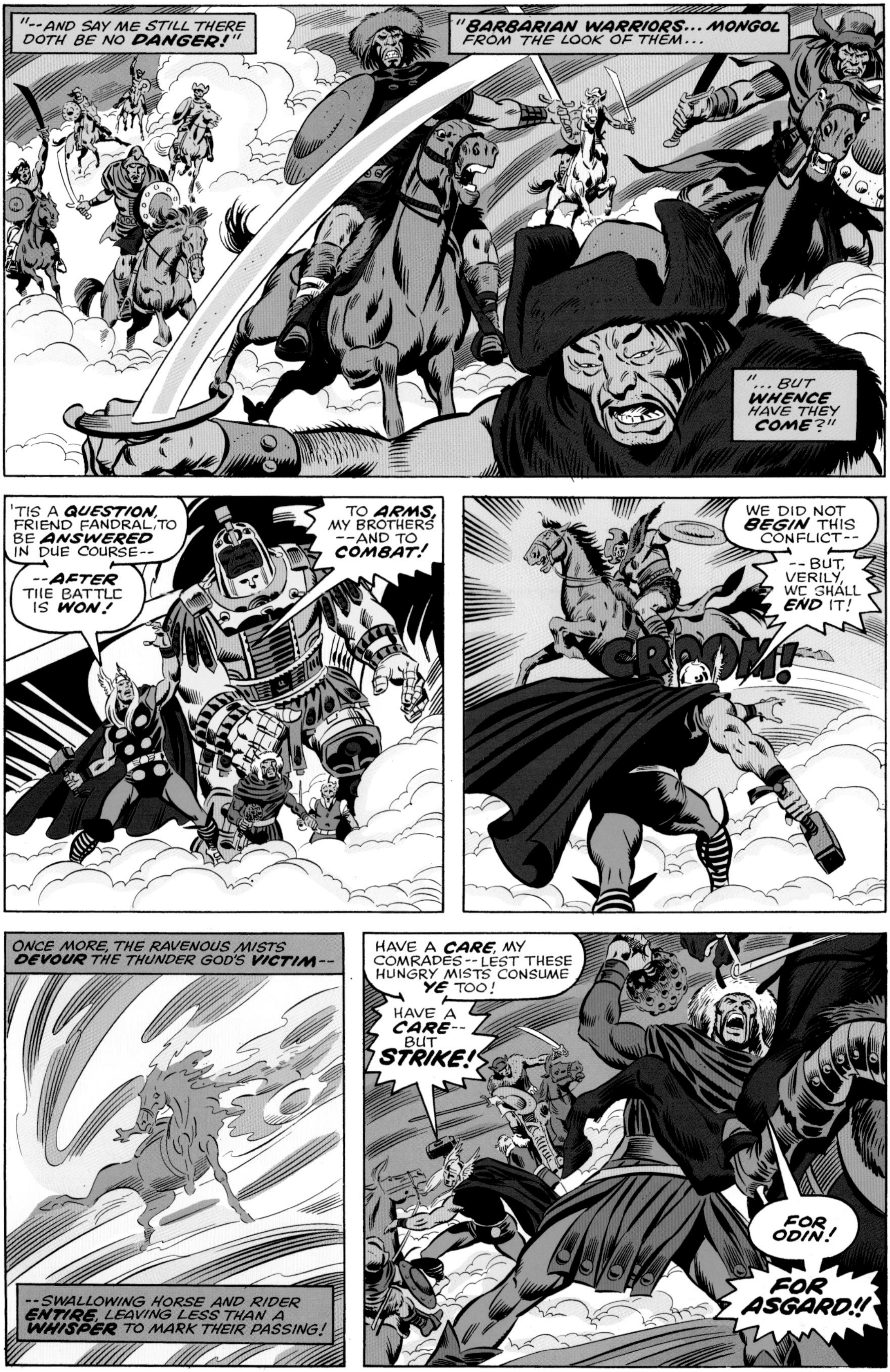
"--AND SAY ME STILL THERE DOTH BE NO DANGER!"
"BARBARIAN WARRIORS... MONGOL FROM THE LOOK OF THEM...
"...BUT WHENCE HAVE THEY COME?"
'TIS A QUESTION, FRIEND FANDRAL, TO BE ANSWERED IN DUE COURSE--
--AFTER THE BATTLE IS WON!
TO ARMS, MY BROTHERS --AND TO COMBAT!
WE DID NOT BEGIN THIS CONFLICT--
--BUT, VERILY, WE SHALL END IT!
CROOM!
ONCE MORE, THE RAVENOUS MISTS DEVOUR THE THUNDER GOD'S VICTIM--
--SWALLOWING HORSE AND RIDER ENTIRE, LEAVING LESS THAN A WHISPER TO MARK THEIR PASSING!
HAVE A CARE, MY COMRADES--LEST THESE HUNGRY MISTS CONSUME YE TOO!
HAVE A CARE-- BUT STRIKE!
FOR ODIN!
FOR ASGARD!!

NO, ASGARDIAN... FOR MY **MASTER**...

...AND FOR THE **FUTURE** OF HIS **WORLD!**

BY THY FATHER'S **BEARD**, FRIEND THOR-- HOW CAN VALIANT VOLSTAGG NOBLY DEFEND THE **REAR** IF THOU PERSIST IN DRIVING OUR ENEMIES **TO ME?**

AS EVER, VAST ONE, THY **COURAGE** KNOWS NO **END!**

BROK

BACK, THOU CHURLS!!

IN TRUTH, MILORD-- METHINKS 'TWOULD BE NIGH **IMPOSSIBLE** TO FIND SUCH VALOR'S **BEGINNING!** 'TWOULD REQUIRE A...

BY **ASGARD!** THAT **SOUND**... LIKE THE **GROWL** OF SOME **BEAST**...

"...OR THE **ROAR** OF AN ATTACKING **PLANE!**"

BHUD-UD-UD-UD-AH

YON AIRCRAFT DOTH SEEK TO **DESTROY** US, BROTHERS!

BUT MERE **MACHINE-GUN BULLETS** ARE AS **NOTHING**--

"-- WHEN COMPARED TO THE **HAMMER OF THOR!**"

THRO-M!

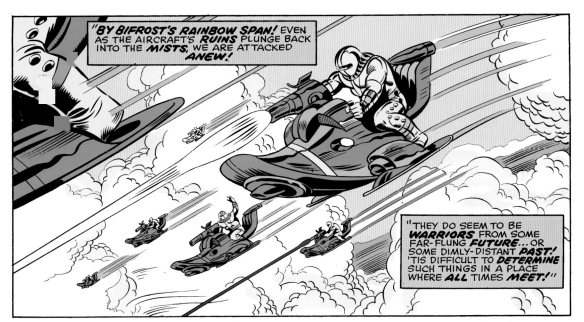

"BY BIFROST'S RAINBOW SPAN! EVEN AS THE AIRCRAFT'S *RUINS* PLUNGE BACK INTO THE *MISTS*, WE ARE ATTACKED *ANEW!*"

"THEY DO SEEM TO BE *WARRIORS* FROM SOME FAR-FLUNG *FUTURE*... OR SOME DIMLY-DISTANT *PAST!* 'TIS DIFFICULT TO *DETERMINE* SUCH THINGS IN A PLACE WHERE *ALL* TIMES *MEET!*"

BUT THERE CAN BE NO *DOUBT* AS TO THEIR EVIL *INTENT!*

THEY *TOO* DO SEEK TO *SLAY* US -- AND WELL THEY *MIGHT* --

-- WERE THOR NOT *GOD OF THUNDER!*

WERE THOR NOT *MASTER OF THE WIND* -- AND THE *STORM!*

TOOM!
TOOM!

TWICE THE MYSTIC MALLET IS STRUCK -- AND IN RESPONSE, THE TIMELESS MISTS ARE LACED WITH *LIGHTNING* --

-- WITH DARK, TORRENTIAL *RAINS* --

-- WITH HOWLING *WINDS* SO POWERFUL, THEY SWEEP ALL OPPOSITION WILDLY AWAY *BEFORE* THEM!

THE STORM IS *BRUTAL* IN ITS FURY, AND *NOTHING* MAY STAND AGAINST IT --

-- SAVE HE WHO HATH *SUMMONED* IT -- HE WHO ONCE *GLORIED* IN ITS MAJESTY, WITH THE *LADY SIF* STANDING STAUNCH AT HIS SIDE --

-- THE LADY *SIF*, WHO GAVE HER *ALL* THAT THOR'S BELOVED *JANE FOSTER* MIGHT *LIVE* --

--THAT THE THUNDER GOD MIGHT BE **REUNITED** ONCE MORE WITH THE ONE HE...

MILORD THOR, I PRITHEE-- **CEASE** THY HAMMER-WROUGHT **STORM**--

--LEST IT DOTH **CARRY OFF** THOSE IT WAS SUMMONED TO **SAVE!**

THY **PARDON**, FRIEND FANDRAL-- I GREW **LOST** IN THOUGHT!

AT ITS MASTER'S **COMMAND** THEN-- LET THE TEMPEST **BEGONE!**

IT HATH SERVED ITS PURPOSE **WELL!**

YOUR TALENTS ARE MOST **IMPRESSIVE**, ASGARDIAN! MY MASTER WAS **WISE** TO ENLIST YOU IN HIS **SERVICE!**

AS HE WAS WHEN HE CHOSE **THEE**, SERVITOR. THOU ART INDEED A MOST **ABLE** COMRADE-IN-ARMS!

I COULD BE NO **LESS**, THUNDER GOD... FOR AS SUCH WAS I **DESIGNED!**

COME, GIANT ONE-- LET US **RETURN** TO THE TIME-CUBE! THE BATTLE HERE BE **DONE!**

CONGRATULATIONS, THOR, I WITNESSED YOUR **VICTORY** ON MY VIEWSCREEN-- A CONFLICT NOBLY **WON!**

WE SEEK NOT **FLATTERY**, ZARRKO-- BUT **ANSWERS!**

WHENCE CAME THE **FOES** WE DEFEATED IN YON MISTS?

FROM **TIME** ITSELF, ASGARDIAN! THE SITUATION IS **WORSE** THAN I'D THOUGHT. EVEN NOW, THE TIME-TWISTERS **APPROACH** THE 50TH CENTURY--

--AND THEIR **PRESENCE** HAS CREATED **TURMOIL** IN THE TIME-STREAM!

YOU'VE **CLEARED** THE PATH BEFORE US, THOR-- BUT WE MUST **RETURN** TO MY ERA WITHOUT **DELAY!**

THEN, ZARRKO, LET US **PROCEED!**

NODDING GRIMLY, THE TOMORROW MAN RETURNS TO THE TIME-CUBE'S **CONTROLS**-- AND THE REST OF THE VOYAGE IS PASSED IN **SILENCE**--

--A **THOUGHTFUL**, FOREBODING **SILENCE.**

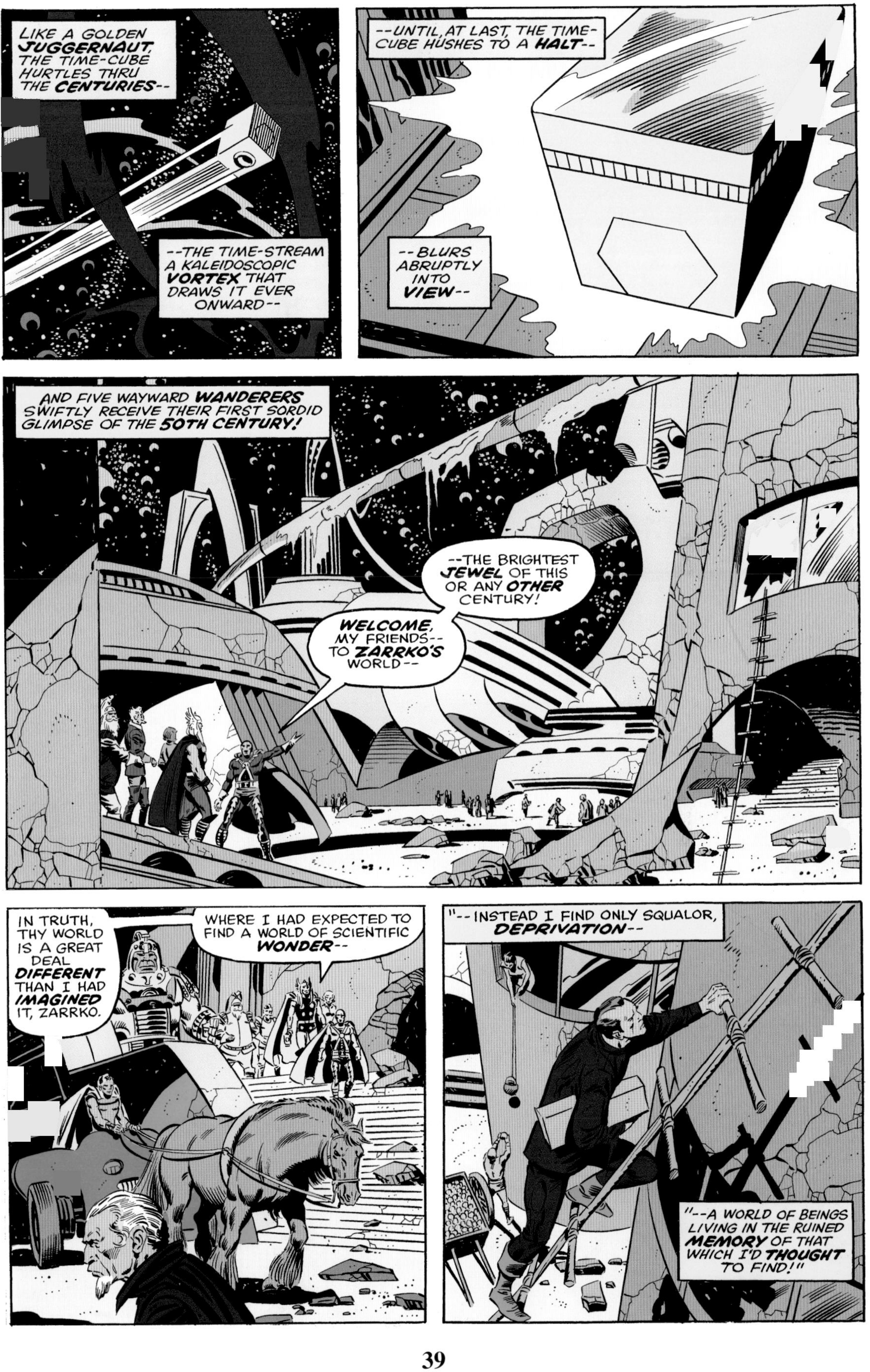
LIKE A GOLDEN JUGGERNAUT, THE TIME-CUBE HURTLES THRU THE CENTURIES--
--THE TIME-STREAM A KALEIDOSCOPIC VORTEX THAT DRAWS IT EVER ONWARD--
--UNTIL, AT LAST, THE TIME-CUBE HUSHES TO A HALT--
--BLURS ABRUPTLY INTO VIEW--
AND FIVE WAYWARD WANDERERS SWIFTLY RECEIVE THEIR FIRST SORDID GLIMPSE OF THE 50TH CENTURY!
WELCOME, MY FRIENDS--TO ZARRKO'S WORLD--
--THE BRIGHTEST JEWEL OF THIS OR ANY OTHER CENTURY!
IN TRUTH, THY WORLD IS A GREAT DEAL DIFFERENT THAN I HAD IMAGINED IT, ZARRKO.
WHERE I HAD EXPECTED TO FIND A WORLD OF SCIENTIFIC WONDER--
"--INSTEAD I FIND ONLY SQUALOR, DEPRIVATION--
"--A WORLD OF BEINGS LIVING IN THE RUINED MEMORY OF THAT WHICH I'D THOUGHT TO FIND!"

THAT'S NOT ENTIRELY **TRUE**, ASGARDIAN.

MY OWN **PALACE**, AS YOU CAN SEE, IS A GLOWING **TRIBUTE** TO ALL THAT THE 50th CENTURY HAS TO **OFFER**!

THE MOST MODERN **CONVENIENCES** WILL BE YOURS TO **ENJOY** ONCE... **EH**?

LORD **ZARRKO**, WE **BEG** YOU-- A **MOMENT** OF YOUR TIME-- **PLEASE**!

MY **TIME** AT THE MOMENT IS MOST **PRECIOUS**, CITIZEN-- BUT YOU MAY **SPEAK**!

WE'VE A **QUESTION** TO ASK, LORD ZARRKO. HOW STAND THE **ENER-GENERATORS**?

WHEN YOU GAINED THE **THRONE** YOU PROMISED THEY'D SOON BE **REPAIRED**-- YET THUS FAR WE'VE SEEN NO **RESULTS**!

LORD ZARRKO-- HOW MUCH LONGER MUST WE **WAIT**?

AS LONG AS IS **NECESSARY**, FOOLS!

YOU WILL HAVE **ENERGY** WHEN YOUR MASTER **DECREES** IT! UNTIL THEN-- **BEGONE**!

ZARRKO, METHINKS THINE IS A MOST **TARNISHED** JEWEL INDEED!

COME-- LET US HIE TO THY **PALACE**-- ERE MY STOMACH DOTH **TURN**!

SHORTLY...

ZARRKO, THOU DIDST ASK US TO HELP THEE **SAVE** THY CENTURY-- BUT MAYHAP 'TWOULD BE BETTER OFF **DEAD**!

WHAT ARE THE **ENER-GENERATORS** OF WHICH THY PEOPLE DOTH **SPEAK**?

WHY HAST THOU LEFT THY SUBJECTS WITHOUT **POWER**?

IT IS A VERY SIMPLE **EQUATION**, THUNDER GOD.

ENERGY PRODUCES **MOBILITY**... MOBILITY PRODUCES **COMMUNICATION**... COMMUNICATION PRODUCES **DISSENT**... AND DISSENT PRODUCES **REBELLION**!

BY WITHHOLDING ALL SOURCES OF **ENERGY**, I ELIMINATE THAT REBELLIOUS **TEMPTATION**-- AND INSURE MY SUBJECTS' **SAFETY**!

ALL THAT THREATENS THEM NOW IS-- THE **TIME-TWISTERS**!

IN SOOTH, ZARRKO-- I HATH BEGUN TO **WONDER** IF SUCH CREATURES TRULY **EXIST**!

AND AS IF IN **ANSWER** TO THE VAST ASGARDIAN'S **CHALLENGE**, THE VERY **SKIES** ARE ABRUPTLY SPLIT BY **LIGHTNING**--

--AND THE OMINOUS CLASH OF **THUNDER**!

WONDER NO LONGER, FAT ONE-- FOR THE **PROOF** OF MY CLAIMS DRAWS CLOSER EVEN **NOW**!

LOOK, ASGARDIANS-- DO YOU SEE THE GHOSTLY **NIMBUS** APPEARING ON THE STREET BEFORE US?

"DO YOU SEE THE MISSHAPEN **FIGURES** THAT MATERIALIZE WITHIN?

"THERE THEY **ARE**, ASGARDIANS!

"THE **TIME-TWISTERS** WALK AMONG US!"

AND UNLESS WE CAN SOMEHOW **DEFEAT** THEM--

--THIS ENTIRE PLANET IS **DOOMED**!

NEXT ISSUE: THE THRILLER YOU **NEVER** THOUGHT YOU'D SEE... **"THIS IS THE WAY THE WORLD ENDS!"**

41

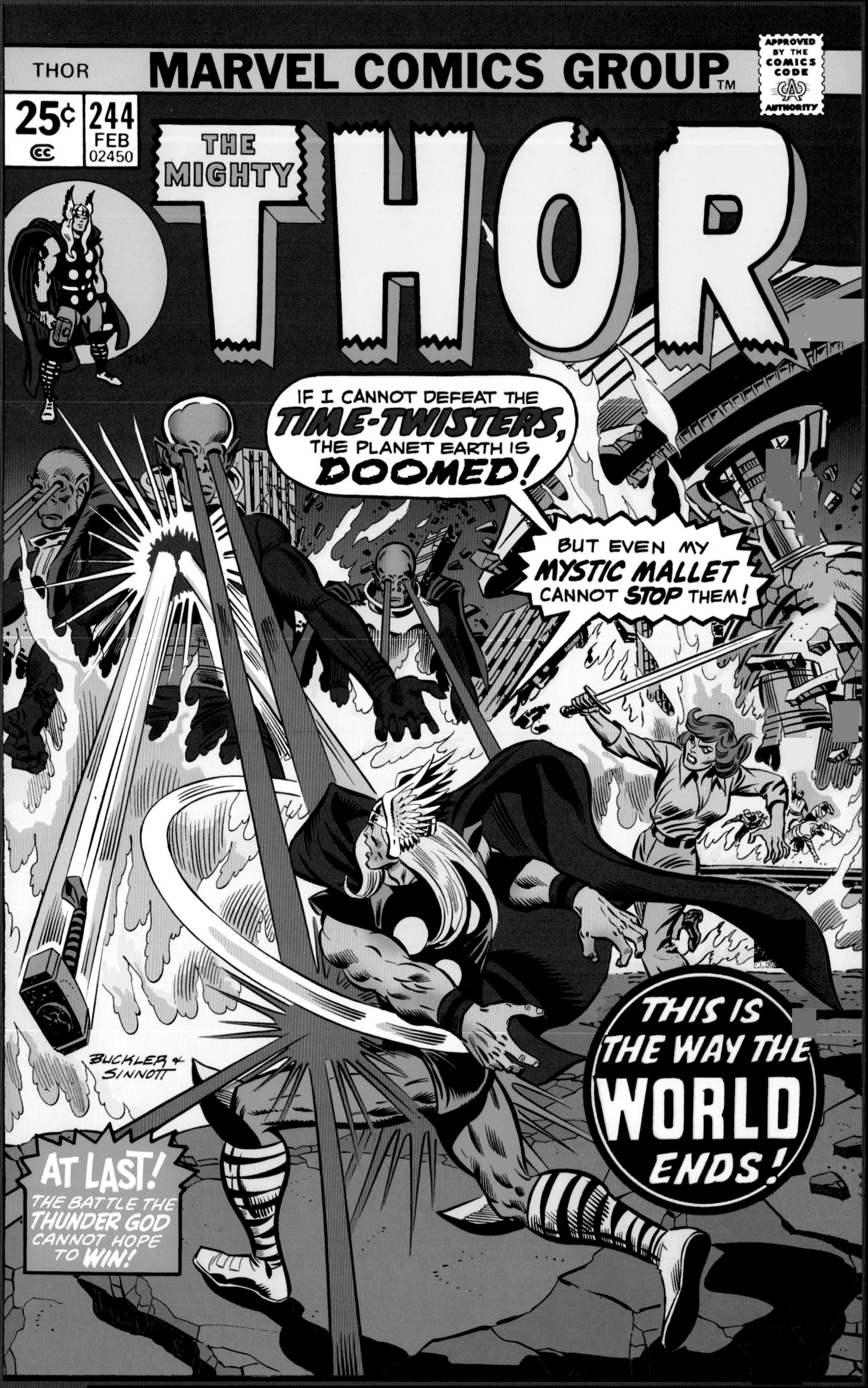
THOR
MARVEL COMICS GROUP
APPROVED BY THE COMICS CODE AUTHORITY
25¢
244 FEB 02450
THE MIGHTY THOR
IF I CANNOT DEFEAT THE TIME-TWISTERS, THE PLANET EARTH IS DOOMED!
BUT EVEN MY MYSTIC MALLET CANNOT STOP THEM!
BUCKLER & SINNOTT
THIS IS THE WAY THE WORLD ENDS!
AT LAST! THE BATTLE THE THUNDER GOD CANNOT HOPE TO WIN!

Stan Lee PRESENTS: THE MIGHTY THOR!™

LEN WEIN
WRITER/EDITOR | **JOHN BUSCEMA & JOE SINNOTT**
ILLUSTRATORS | **GLYNIS WEIN**
COLORIST | **JOE ROSEN**
LETTERER

THIS IS THE WAY THE WORLD ENDS!

IN THE **MONITOR ROOM** OF THE PALACE ROYAL OF THE VAST DECAYING CITY-STATE THAT RULES EARTH OF THE 50th CENTURY, FIVE FAMILIAR FIGURES STAND GRIMLY STUDYING THE SHIMMERING **IMAGES** PROJECTED UPON A BROAD **VIEWSCREEN** --

-- UNTIL, AT LENGTH, THE GOLDEN-HAIRED **GOD OF THUNDER** NARROWS HIS EYES, SETS HIS JAW FIRMLY, AND **SPEAKS**...

SO THESE BE THE **TIME-TWISTERS!** BUT FOR THEIR GREAT **SIZE**, THEY WOULD HARDLY SEEM A **THREAT** AT ALL --

--YET, AMONG THEM, THEY DO POSSESS THE POWER TO **DESTROY** THIS VERY **WORLD!**

...AND THE ENTIRE **PLANET** TREMBLES AT HIS **WORDS!**

JV179

COME, BROTHERS-- LET US CONFRONT YON CREATURES ERE THEY CAN ACCOMPLISH THEIR MAYHEM MOST FOUL!

DARLING, WAIT--!

YOU'D BE WISE TO HEED YOUR JANE FOSTER, THUNDER GOD.

AND IF I DO NOT CHOOSE TO HEED ZARRKO'?

ASGARDIAN, YOU WILL DO AS MY MASTER COMMANDS!

NAY, SERVITOR! THE SON OF ODIN BOWS TO THE WILL OF NO MAN!

NOR MUST YOU, THUNDER GOD. I FULLY ACKNOWLEDGE THAT YOU AND YOUR COMRADES HAVE COME TO THIS CENTURY AS MY ALLIES, NOT MY SLAVES!

THEN ORDER THY AUTOMATON TO REMOVE HIS PONDEROUS HAND FROM ME, ZARRKO-- ERE I REMOVE IT--

--FROM ITS WRIST!

YOUR PATIENCE SEEMS TO BE WANING, MY FRIEND. UNFORTUNATE.

A GENERAL WHO GOES INTO BATTLE WITHOUT KNOWING THE STRENGTH OF HIS ENEMY MAY SOON FIND HIMSELF LACKING AN ARMY!

BUT HE WHO IS ABSOLUTE MONARCH OF THE 50th CENTURY HAS WAYS OF DETERMINING THE TIME-TWISTERS' STRENGTHS... AND THEIR WEAKNESSES!

IF YOU'LL PERMIT ME A MOMENT AT THE PROJECTRON, I'LL GLADLY DEMONSTRATE!

BEFORE THE MIGHTY THOR CAN EVEN REPLY, THE MAD GENIUS CALLED THE TOMORROW MAN IS AT THE BIZARRE MACHINE, HIS FINGERS FLYING ACROSS THE CONTROLS--

--UNTIL A PULSATING AURA SPRINGS UP ABOUT HIS GREEN-CLAD FORM--

--AND HIS "FACE" IS FLUNG OUT OVER THE RUBBLE-STREWN STREET!

CITIZENS OF EARTH, ZARRKO COMES BEFORE YOU TODAY WITH A MOST GENEROUS OFFER--

--AND A MOST SERIOUS WARNING!

WHAT DOES THE TYRANT WANT NOW?

HE'S ALREADY STOLEN ALL OUR ENERGY SOURCES! WHAT MORE CAN HE TAKE FROM US?

44

FELLOW CITIZENS, A DIABOLICAL MENACE HAS SPRUNG UP IN OUR MIDST--THREE BEINGS WHO THREATEN THE **FUTURE** OF OUR WORLD!

I OFFER ONE MONTH OF UNLIMITED ENERGY **USAGE** TO ANY AND ALL CITIZENS WHO CAN DESTROY THE **TIME-TWISTERS**-- BEFORE THEY DESTROY US!

IS HE **SERIOUS**? HAS HE GONE **MAD**?

EVEN IF HE **HAS**, WE'D BE FAR **MADDER** TO TURN HIS OFFER **DOWN**!

THY TACTICS SIT **ILL** WITH ME, ZARRKO. I LIKE **NOT** USING HELPLESS MORTALS AS **PAWNS**!

NOT **PAWNS**, THOR-- **WARRIORS**!

MY SUBJECTS DESERVE THE **RIGHT** TO PROTECT THEIR OWN PLANET BEFORE **WE** DO BATTLE FOR THEM!

NONE OF THEM WILL RISK THEIR LIVES **UNWILLINGLY**, ASGARDIAN, THE CHOICE IS **THEIRS**!

BUT IN **SOME** OF THE DIMLY-LIT HOVELS, IT IS A CHOICE NOT EASILY **MADE**.

I **BEG** YOU, DEREK-- DON'T **DO** THIS THING! IT'S TOO **DANGEROUS**!

NO MATTER **WHAT** THE DANGER, GAYLA-- I **MUST** GO!

DON'T YOU REALIZE WHAT THIS COULD **MEAN** TO US?

ONE FULL **MONTH** OF UNLIMITED ENERGY--A CHANCE TO LIVE IN AN **ELECTRIC** WORLD AGAIN--TO GET **AWAY** FROM THE FILTH AND **SQUALOR** WE LIVE IN **NOW**!

I CAN'T **DENY** YOU THAT **OPPORTUNITY**, GAYLA.

DEREK, DON'T YOU **UNDER- STAND**? NONE OF THAT **MEANS** ANYTHING TO ME!

ALL THAT **MATTERS** TO ME IS... **YOU**.

AND ALL THAT **I** CARE ABOUT IS **YOU**, GAYLA MY LOVE.

THAT'S WHY I HAVE TO **GO**--

--OR I'LL NEVER BE ABLE TO **FACE** MYSELF AGAIN!

AND IT SEEMS DEREK HAS MADE THE CHOICE OF THE **MASSES**--

--FOR THE AVENUES ARE **FILLED** WITH FRIGHTENED, DESPERATE **FACES**--

--WITH MEN ARMED ONLY WITH MAKESHIFT **WEAPONS**--AND AN ALL- CONSUMING **NEED**!

45

THEIR **OBJECTIVE** IS SIMPLE:

TO **OVERCOME** THESE THREE STRANGE CREATURES WHO STRIDE, SEEMINGLY **UNCONCERNED**, THRU THE HEART OF THEIR DECLINING **CITY**--

--TO **DEFEAT** THESE MONSTROSITIES HOWEVER THEY **MUST**-- AND THUS GAIN THE GIFT OF **LIGHT!**

THE ODDS ARE ALMOST **EMBARRASSING**-- DOZENS TO **ONE**--

--YET CONQUERING SUCH AS THE **TIME-TWISTERS** MAY NOT BE ALL THAT **EASY** A TASK!

CURSE IT! THESE MONSTERS ARE **PROTECTED** BY SOME UNSEEN **FORCE-FIELD!**

OUR WEAPONS CANNOT EVEN **TOUCH** THEM!

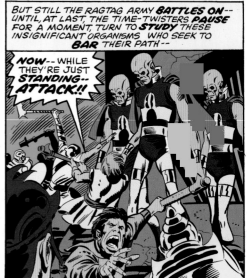

BUT STILL THE RAGTAG ARMY **BATTLES ON**-- UNTIL, AT LAST, THE TIME-TWISTERS **PAUSE** FOR A MOMENT, TURN TO **STUDY** THESE INSIGNIFICANT ORGANISMS WHO SEEK TO **BAR** THEIR PATH--

NOW-- WHILE THEY'RE JUST **STANDING**-- **ATTACK!!**

--AND, WITHOUT EVER UTTERING A **WORD,** ABRUPTLY **RAISE** THEIR MISSHAPEN **HANDS**--

--AND SEND SEETHING **ENERGIES** ERUPTING FROM THEIR SLENDER **FINGERS**--

--ENERGIES THAT SWEEP THE INEFFECTUAL OPPOSITION SAVAGELY **AWAY!**

AARRGGHH!!

UNFETTERED **FURY** RAGES IN THE FACES OF THOSE WHO REMAIN **ERECT.**

LOOK WHAT THESE MONSTERS HAVE **DONE** TO OUR **FRIENDS!**

ARE WE GOING TO LET THEM GET **AWAY** WITH THIS, CITIZENS?

ARE WE??

THE **ANSWER** RISES FROM THE CROWD AS A **SINGLE** VOICE...

NEVER! NEVER!!

AND ONCE MORE THEY SURGE TO THE **ATTACK!**

THE TIME-TWISTERS GREET THIS **NEW** AGGRESSION WITH BALEFUL **GLARES**--

--AND SIZZLING **POWER** THAT LANCES FORTH FROM THEIR STAR-DAPPLED **EYES!**

WRITHING IN **AGONY,** THE EARTHMEN STAND **ROOTED** TO THE SPOT--

--THEN FIND THEMSELVES PLUNGED **MADLY** INTO TIME'S DARK **ABYSS!**

IN THE SPACE OF A **HEARTBEAT,** STRONG VIRILE **MEN** BECOME SALLOW-FACED **ANCIENTS** AND ROSY-CHEEKED **YOUTHS**--

--ALL PANIC-STRICKEN **VICTIMS** OF BEINGS WHO CAN **CONTROL** THE RUSHING FLOW OF **TIME!**

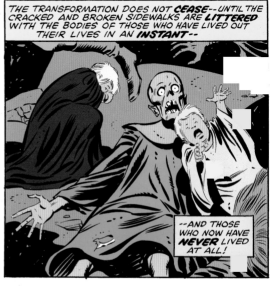

THE TRANSFORMATION DOES NOT **CEASE**--UNTIL THE CRACKED AND BROKEN SIDEWALKS ARE **LITTERED** WITH THE BODIES OF THOSE WHO HAVE LIVED OUT THEIR LIVES IN AN **INSTANT**--

--AND THOSE WHO NOW HAVE **NEVER** LIVED AT ALL!

47

WITHIN MOMENTS, BOTH ARE **GONE**-- THEIR PASSING MARKED ONLY BY BITS OF TATTERED **CLOTH** AND EDDYING PILES OF GRAY-WHITE **DUST**--

--AND SOON EVEN THE **DUST** HAS BLOWN AWAY.

SO **THIS** IS HOW THOU DOST **TEST** THINE **ENEMY**, ZARRKO-- BY SACRIFICING THY **SUBJECTS** LIKE SLAUGHTER-RIPE **LAMBS**?

STAND THEE **ASIDE**, ZARRKO! NOW SHALL THE **TIME-TWISTERS** FEEL THE **VENGEANCE** OF WARRIORS **BORN**!

PERHAPS 'TIS **THY** WAY, TOMORROW MAN-- BUT 'TIS NOT THE WAY OF **THOR**!

ANGRILY, THE THUNDER GOD AND HIS COMPANIONS **BOLT** FROM THE CHAMBER, THEIR **BATTLE CRY** STRONG ON THEIR LIPS-- "FOR **ODIN**! FOR **ASGARD**!"

AND ON THAT MOST **APPROPRIATE** NOTE, LET US SPAN TIME, SPACE, AND THE RAINBOW BRIDGE **BIFROST**, TO VISIT THE **REALM ETERNAL** AND A DIFFERENT **PALACE ROYAL**--

--WHERE A **VERY DIFFERENT MONARCH** ATTENDS TO AFFAIRS OF **STATE**.

MILORD **ODIN**, EVEN NOW THY **SON** AND HIS FELLOWS HAVE JOURNEYED TO THE 50th CENTURY TO **AVERT** THE DESTRUCTION OF **EARTH**--

--YET STILL HAST THOU **BANISHED** HIM FROM ASGARD FOR **LOVING** THE MORTAL **JANE FOSTER**!

ONCE AGAIN I MOST HUMBLY **BESEECH** THEE, MILORD-- MUST THY JUDGMENT BE SO **HARSH**?

THOU HAST BEEN MY **ADVISOR** ALMOST LONGER THAN THOUGHT CAN **RECALL**, VIZIER--

--THUS THY **WORDS** TROUBLE ME MOST **SORELY**!

THOU HAST **HEARD** MY ROYAL DECREE-- THOU HAST HEARD ME STATE THAT I WOULD **SPEAK** OF THE MATTER NOT AGAIN-- YET STILL DOST THOU **PERSIST** IN THY TIRESOME **PLEADING!**

BUT MY **LIEGE...**

SILENCE! I CAN DIVINE BUT **ONE** REASON FOR THY CONSTANT **DIS-OBEDIENCE!**

THOU HAST SERVED AT MY SIDE LOYALLY AND **LONG,** VIZIER-- MAYHAP **TOO** LONG!

METHINKS 'TIS TIME THOU DIDST TAKE THY **REST**-- AND RETIRED TO THE **TOWER OF SOLITUDE,** THERE TO STUDY THE ANCIENT SCROLLS, UNTIL SUCH TIME AS I DO **SUMMON** THEE ANEW!

MY LIEGE, THY WORDS DO **CUT** THRU ME LIKE **STEEL**-- BUT AS EVER SHALL I **DO** AS THOU HAST COMMANDED WITHOUT **QUESTION**-- WITHOUT **HESITATION.**

I SHALL **GO** TO YON TIMELESS TOWER TO AWAIT THY **SUMMONS**-- AND WHILE I WAIT, I SHALL **PRAY** THOU HAST CHOSEN **A'RIGHT!**

FARETHEEWELL, MILORD-- UNTIL WE DO MEET **AGAIN.**

WELL, BRAVE **BALDER,** THY LIEGE DOTH SEEM WITHOUT **COUNSEL.** THUS I HAVE CHOSEN A **TASK** FOR THEE.

GO THEE TO THE **DUNGEONS** 'NEATH THE PALACE ROYAL-- AND BRING TO ME THE ONE CALLED **IGRON,** HE WHO WAS ONCE **ADVISOR** TO THE **EVIL LOKI!**

'TIS **HE** WHO SHALL STAND AT MY **SIDE.**

ALL-FATHER, THY WILL IS MY **LIFE**-- BUT **IGRON...?**

DOST **THOU** TOO DOUBT MY **WISDOM,** BALDER?

METHINKS SLY IGRON HATH SUFFERED PUNISHMENT **ENOUGH!** 'TIS TIME HIS **REHABILITATION** WAS BEGUN!

AND WHERE **BETTER** TO LEARN THE WORD AND THE WAY, THAN AT THE FOOT OF HE WHO **IS** IMMORTAL ASGARD?

NOW GET THEE **GONE,** BALDER-- AND DARE NOT RETURN **WITHOUT** HIM I DO **SEEK!**

BY THY **LEAVE,** MY LIEGE-- I **GO.**

BUT, IN TRUTH, I DO INDEED BEGIN TO **DOUBT** THY FABLED **WISDOM!**

DARLING, **MUST** YOU BATTLE THESE TIME-TWISTERS?

THOU CANST **ASK** SUCH A THING, BELOVED-- AFTER THOU HAST **WITNESSED** WHAT THEY HAVE **DONE**?

THEY WERE **MET** BY FORCE, SO THEY **RETURNED** FORCE-- BUT BEINGS SUCH AS THEY CANNOT BE **MONSTERS**!

LOOK AT THEIR **CLOTHING**, THEIR **FACES**-- LOOK INTO THEIR **EYES**, THOR! THESE ARE CREATURES OF VAST **INTELLIGENCE**!

SPEAK TO THEM, DARLING-- **REASON** WITH THEM! TRY TO MAKE THEM **UNDERSTAND** WHAT THEY ARE **DOING**!

SUCH IS **NOT** THE WARRIOR'S **WAY**, MY LOVE--

-- BUT STILL THY WORDS HAVE **WISDOM**. VERY **WELL**, MILADY-- FOR ONCE THE THUNDER GOD SHALL **WITHHOLD** HIS ANGRY HAMMER--

-- UNTIL ALL ELSE HATH **FAILED**!

ALIENS! THOU WHO DOST TREAD THE MYRIAD PATHWAYS OF **TIME**! IN THE NAME OF **REASON**-- IN THE NAME OF **PEACE**-- THE PRINCE OF GOLDEN **ASGARD** DOTH BID THEE **HALT**!

I SAY THEE, **AGAIN**, TIME-TWISTERS-- **HALT**!

BUT WITHOUT SO MUCH AS A **GLANCE**, THEY STRIDE ON.

AGAIN AND AGAIN, THE GOD OF THUNDER **BECKONS** TO NO **AVAIL**--UNTIL, AT LAST, HE HAS HAD...

ENOUGH! THE SON OF ODIN WILL NOT BE SO CALLOUSLY **IGNORED**!

NO, DARLING,-- YOU **PROMISED**--!

AND THOR'S **PLEDGE** DOTH BE HIS **BOND,** MY LOVE!

VERILY, UNTIL FIRST I HAVE **SPOKEN** TO THE TIME-TWISTERS, I SHALL NOT SEEK THEIR **BLOOD**--

"--BUT, BY ALL THE MATCHLESS POWER OF MINE MYSTIC MALLET **MJOLNIR,** I **SHALL** HAVE THEIR **ATTENTION**!

"**ZOUNDS!** MY ENCHANTED BARRIER DOTH SEEM TO **STAY** THEM NOT AT ALL! WHAT MANNER OF CREATURES **ARE** THESE?"

A QUESTION.

AT OUR **INCEPTION**, IT WAS **DECREED** ALL QUESTIONS MUST BE **ANSWERED**--

--FOR IN ANSWERS **ALONE** MAY THE QUEST FOR **KNOWLEDGE** BE FULFILLED.

THUS **SPEAK**, WORLDLING. VOICE YOUR QUESTION **ANEW**.

WHAT **KNOWLEDGE** DO YOU SEEK FROM WE WHO ARE **KNOWLEDGE INCARNATE**?

KNOWLEDGE OF THY **PURPOSE**... THINE **ORIGINS**. WHENCE DOST THOU **COME**? WHERE DOST THOU **GO**?

WHY DOST THOU SUNDER ENTIRE **PLANETS** IN THY WAKE?

WE ARE **PILGRIMS**-- ON A JOURNEY FROM THE **END** OF TIME, TO FIND TIME'S **BEGINNINGS**.

OUR SEARCH HAS CARRIED US ACROSS A THOUSAND THOUSAND **WORLDS**-- YET STILL WE SEEM NO **CLOSER** TO OUR GOAL.

THOU HAST LEFT **ONE** QUESTION **UNANSWERED**, TIME-TWISTER.

THOU WHO DOST CLAIM TO BE THE **PERSONIFICATION** OF **WISDOM**...

DOST THOU KNOW WHAT THY **PASSING** HATH **DONE** TO THOSE **MYRIAD** WORLDS?

ONE WOULD ASSUME THEY ARE SO MUCH THE **BETTER** FOR THE GIFT OF **LEARNING** WE HAVE GRANTED THEM.

NAY, ALIEN-- THOU HAST **DESTROYED** THEM!

THE **ENERGIES** UNLEASHED WHENE'ER THOU DOST **REND** THE VERY FABRIC OF TIME DOTH CREATE **COSMIC UPHEAVALS** WHICH HAVE REDUCED EACH WORLD TO A BLACKENED **CINDER**!

FOR THE SAKE OF **THIS** WORLD AND COUNTLESS WORLDS **BEYOND**, TIME-TWISTERS-- **THOU MUST ABANDON THY QUEST!**

51

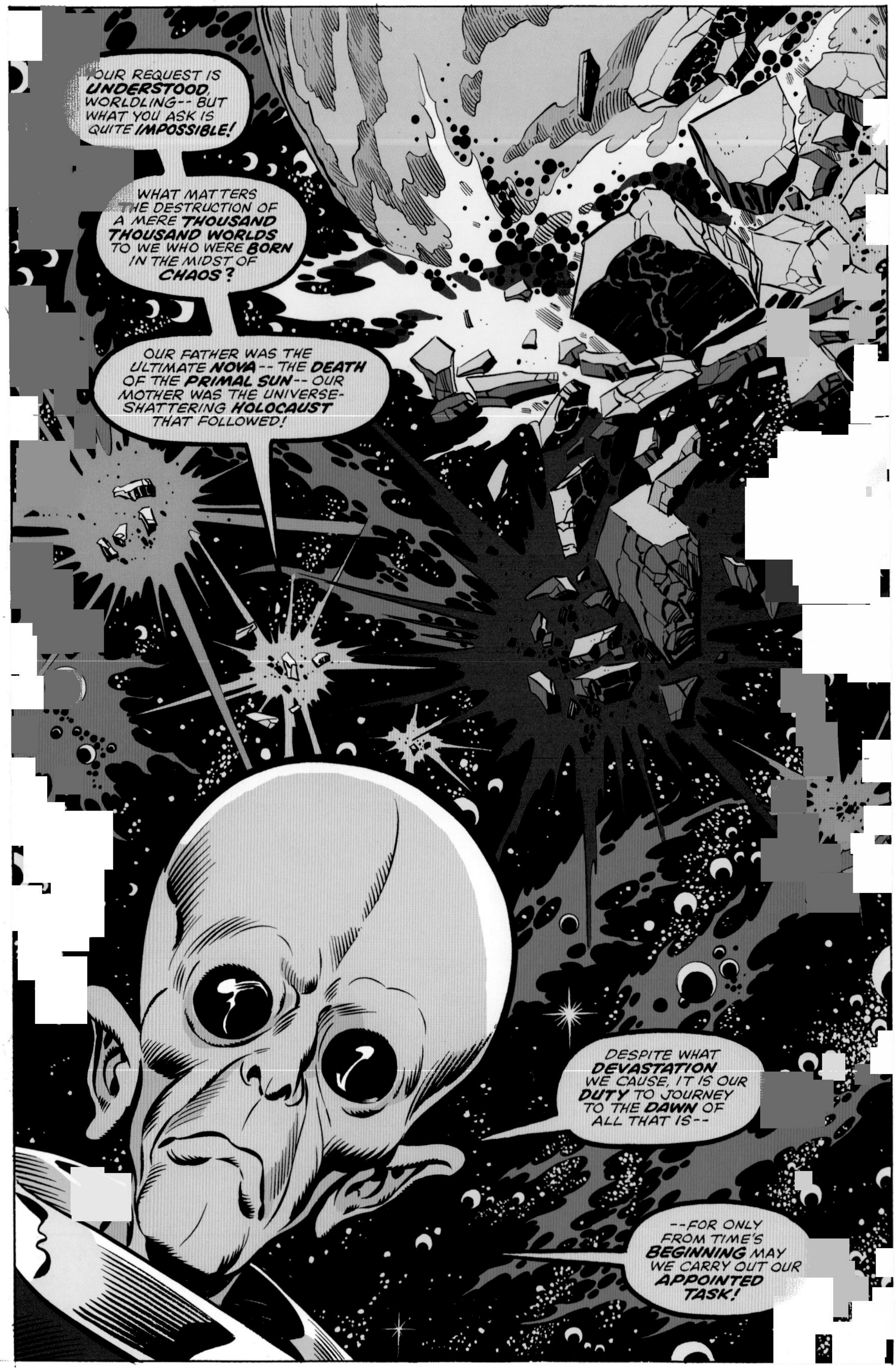
YOUR REQUEST IS UNDERSTOOD, WORLDLING-- BUT WHAT YOU ASK IS QUITE IMPOSSIBLE!
WHAT MATTERS THE DESTRUCTION OF A MERE THOUSAND THOUSAND WORLDS TO WE WHO WERE BORN IN THE MIDST OF CHAOS?
OUR FATHER WAS THE ULTIMATE NOVA-- THE DEATH OF THE PRIMAL SUN-- OUR MOTHER WAS THE UNIVERSE-SHATTERING HOLOCAUST THAT FOLLOWED!
DESPITE WHAT DEVASTATION WE CAUSE, IT IS OUR DUTY TO JOURNEY TO THE DAWN OF ALL THAT IS--
--FOR ONLY FROM TIME'S BEGINNING MAY WE CARRY OUT OUR APPOINTED TASK!

ABANDON OUR **QUEST,** WORLDLING?

WE WOULD SOONER ABANDON OUR **LIVES!**

THEN-- **SO BE IT!**

I HAVE TRIED TO **REASON** WITH THESE CREATURES AS THOU HADST **ASKED,** JANE.

NOW I SHALL DEAL WITH THEM **MY** WAY!

AMIDST THE RUINS, A FIGURE **STIRS**--

--A FIGURE WHO'D BEEN **LOST** BENEATH THE RUBBLE DURING THE FIRST CATASTROPHIC **ASSAULT** UPON THE TIME-TWISTERS--

--AND THUS HAD BEEN **SPARED** AN "UNTIMELY" **DEMISE.**

HE STAGGERS TO HIS **KNEES**--

--STARES **DUMBFOUNDED** AT THE MOUNDS OF DUST AND TATTERS THAT ARE ALL THAT **REMAIN** OF THOSE WHO HAD BEEN HIS **NEIGHBORS**--

--HIS **FRIENDS**--

--AND THE MAN CALLED DEREK... **DESPAIRS!**

ZARRKO DID THIS!

HE SENT US ALL ON THIS **FOOL'S ERRAND...** THIS **SUICIDE CHASE!**

ZARRKO IS **RESPONSIBLE** FOR THIS CARNAGE--

--AND HE'S GOING TO **PAY** FOR IT!

THUS SAYING, THE BEDRAGGLED FIGURE STUMBLES AWAY DOWN THE CRACKED AND BROKEN **STREET**--

--AND IS SOON **SWALLOWED** BY THE SHADOWS OF THE **PALACE.**

NEARBY, A STRIDENT **BATTLE CRY** RINGS OUT!

FOR ODIN!

FOR **ASSGGARRD!!**

AND FOUR GRIM-VISAGED **GODS** CHARGE FORTH--

--STRAIGHT INTO A BARRAGE OF AWESOME **POWER** THAT LEAPS FROM THE TIME-TWISTERS' **EYES!**

SCINTILLATING **ENERGY** PLAYS AROUND THE MUSCULAR FORMS--

--ENERGY THAT SHORTLY BEFORE HAD **DESTROYED** MANY **OTHER** BRAVE MEN--

--BUT NOW LEAVES THE ASGARDIANS REMARKABLY **UNTOUCHED!**

BY THY **FATHER'S EYES**, THOR-- YON ALIENS' LIFE-DEVOURING **RAYS** HAVE CONSUMED US **NOT AT ALL!**

NOR **SHALL** THEY, FRIEND FANDRAL. WHAT MATTER THE **RAVAGES** OF TIME--TO WE WHO ARE **IMMORTAL?**

FASCINATING. NEVER BEFORE HAVE WORLDLINGS **WITHSTOOD** OUR CHRONAL CHARGES.

NEVER BEFORE HAST THOU FACED **ASGARDIANS BORN**--

--OR THE POWER OF THE MYSTIC MALLET **MJOLNIR!**

54

THE POWER OF YOUR WEAPON BECOMES QUITE *ACADEMIC*, WORLDLING--

--IF IT CANNOT *PENETRATE* THE EVER-PRESENT *ENERGY-SHIELD* THAT SURROUNDS US.

BUT WE *WASTE* FAR MORE PRECIOUS *TIME* HERE THAN YOU *DESERVE*.

IF IT IS *COMBAT* YOU DESIRE, THEN YOU SHALL *HAVE* IT--

--THUS!

THEY ERUPT FROM THE RAVAGED PAVEMENT LIKE *SMOKE*--

--SAVAGE *APPARITIONS* TORN INSANELY FROM THE WINE-DARK DEPTHS OF *TIME*--

--BATTLE-HUNGRY WARRIORS GIVEN *SUBSTANCE* BY CREATURES TO WHOM TIME IS BUT A *PATHWAY* TO A FAR GREATER *GOAL*.

THY MINIONS WILL NOT LONG *STAY* US, ALIENS.

IN MOMENTS, THEY SHALL *FALL*--

--AND *THOU* SHALT SWIFTLY *FOLLOW!*

ZOUNDS! THE BATTLE DOTH *RAGE* ABOUT ME.

STAND YE *ASIDE*, WARRIORS!

HOW CAN VALIANT *VOLSTAGG* ESTABLISH A *REAR DEFENSE* IF THOU DOST CLUMSILY STAND IN HIS...

OOOPS.

WHUMPP!

I DUNNO WHAT'S *GOIN' ON* AROUND HERE, BUT I GOT ME MY *ORDERS*--

BUD-UD-UD-AH!

--AND THEM ORDERS SAY-- *SHOOT TO KILL!*

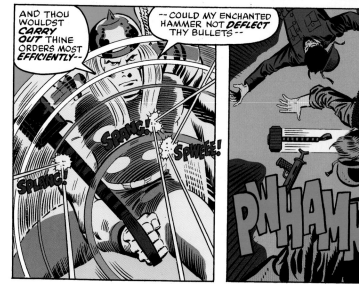

AND THOU WOULDST *CARRY OUT* THINE ORDERS MOST *EFFICIENTLY*--

-- COULD MY ENCHANTED HAMMER NOT *DEFLECT* THY BULLETS --

SPLING! SPANG! SPWEEE!

"--THEN FLY FORTH TO *DISMISS* THEE ENTIRE!"

PNHAMM!

56

THOR AND THE OTHERS ARE HOLDING THEIR OWN-- BUT THEY'LL *NEVER* STOP THE TIME-TWISTERS BEFORE IT'S *TOO LATE!*

I JUST CAN'T STAND BY AND *WATCH* ANYMORE.

THE SOUL OF A *WARRIOR-GODDESS* DWELLS WITHIN ME--

--AND IT'S TIME I STARTED TO *ACT* LIKE IT!

MILADY JANE FIGHTS LIKE A TRUE *ASGARDIAN*--

--BUT WHILE *WE* DO BATTLE, YON *ALIENS* MAKE GOOD THEIR *ESCAPE!*

'TIS TIME I PUT A *STOP* TO THIS SENSELESS *CONFLICT*--

--AS ONLY HE WHO CONTROLS THE RAGING TEMPEST *CAN!*

TOOM! TOOM!

TWICE ENCHANTED MJOLNIR IS STRUCK--

--AND AS *LIGHTNING* CRASHES SAVAGELY ABOUT THE SUDDENLY *STORMSWEPT* BATTLEFIELD, THE THUNDER GOD GLANCES AT *JANE FOSTER*-- AND FOR AN *INSTANT* SEES HER IN A WHOLLY *DIFFERENT* LIGHT--

--BUT *ONLY* FOR AN INSTANT!

'TWAS NAUGHT BUT A *TRICK* OF THE LIGHTNING, HE TRIES TO *CONVINCE* HIMSELF-- IT COULD HAVE BEEN NOTHING *MORE.*

THEN HE *RETURNS* TO THE RAIN-DRENCHED *DONNYBROOK*--

--AND, HIS COMPANIONS AT HIS SIDE, SWIFTLY *ENDS* IT!

BUT HAS HE ENDED IT IN *TIME?*

ALIENS, *STOP* WHERE THOU ART--

--OR, BY ODIN, I SHALL STOP YE-- *ONCE AND FOR ALL!*

WORLDLING, YOU ARE BECOMING MOST *TIRESOME.* SIMPLY *ACCEPT* YOUR FATE-- AND BE *DONE* WITH IT.

YOU WAGED YOUR BATTLE *ADMIRABLY*-- BUT YOU HAVE *LOST!*

AN *OATH* ON HIS LIPS, THE THUNDER GOD VAULTS *FORWARD*--

--TO FIND HIS PATH SUDDENLY *BARRED* BY THE *PAVEMENT* THAT HEAVES UP BEFORE HIM.

THWAMM!

THE EARTH *GROANS* IN PROTEST-- AND, FOR AN INSTANT, IT SEEMS TO THOR THAT THE *END OF THE WORLD* IS AT HAND!

UNFORTUNATELY... HE IS *RIGHT!*

THE VERY STREET *WRITHES* BENEATH ME!

I CANNOT KEEP MY *FOOTING!*

IT'S THE SAME ALL *AROUND* US! THE TIME-TWISTERS MUST HAVE *REACHED* THEIR POINT OF *DEPARTURE*--

--AND THE *COSMIC UPHEAVAL* HAS *BEGUN!*

METHINKS I SHOULD--AH--HIE ME *BACK* TO OUR ALLY *ZARRKO* AND--ER-- *ALERT* HIM TO THIS *PERIL!*

AND SO I *SHALL*-- CAN I BUT *CEASE* MY STOMACH'S *CHURNING!*

58

BUT ZARRKO ALREADY **UNDERSTANDS** THE SITUATION ALL TOO **WELL!**

I **TRUSTED** THOSE ASGARDIANS, SERVITOR-- AND THEY HAVE **FAILED** ME!

THERE IS ONLY **ONE** PATH OF ACTION LEFT **OPEN** TO US!

THEN LET US **TAKE** SAID PATH WITH **HASTE**, MASTER-- BEFORE THIS PALACE BECOMES OUR **TOMB!**

AND ALL **AROUND** THE PALACE, A CITY WHICH-- DEPRIVED OF ITS **RESOURCES**-- HAD BEEN DYING BY **DEGREES**, NOW PERISHES FAR MORE **SWIFTLY**--

--WITH A **DIGNITY** THAT HAD LONG BEEN **DENIED** IT BY HE WHO WAS ITS ABSOLUTE **RULER!**

A RULER WHO, AT THE MOMENT, IS CONCERNED SOLELY WITH **HIMSELF!**

SWIFTLY, SERVITOR-- TO THE **TIME CUBE!**

WE CAN STILL MAKE GOOD OUR **ESCAPE!**

WHILE, IN THE **MIDST** OF THE **DEVASTATION**...

THE PROTECTIVE **SHIELD** ENCHANTED MJOLNIR HATH WOVEN ABOUT US CANNOT ENDURE **FOREVER!**

OUR ONLY **HOPE** WAS TO **HALT** THE ACCURSED **TIME-TWISTERS**--

--BUT 'TIS FAR **TOO LATE** FOR THAT **NOW!**

"EVEN AS WE **SPEAK**, YON ALIENS **RETURN** TO THEIR TIME-TOSSED **PILGRIMAGE**, UNMINDFUL OF THE **DESTRUCTION** THEY HAVE WROUGHT!

"AND THERE IS **NAUGHT** WE CAN DO TO **STOP** THEM!"

59

IS THERE THEN NO *HOPE*, MILORD?

NAY, DASHING FANDRAL-- *NONE.*

I FEAR 'TIS *FAREWELL*, MY BROTHERS-AT-ARMS-- NO MAN NOR *GOD* COULD EVER KNOW *FRIENDS* MORE TRUE THAN *YE.*

AND FARE-*THEE*-WELL, MILADY JANE. KNOW THAT I HAVE *LOVED* THEE.

NO! IT CAN'T JUST ALL BE *OVER*-- IT *CAN'T!!*

I WON'T LET IT END LIKE THIS!!

THEN JANE FOSTER'S PLAINTIVE VOICE IS DROWNED OUT BY THE *DEATH-CRY* OF THE PLANET *EARTH*--AS IT CONVULSES IN VOLCANIC *AGONY* AND CONSUMES ITSELF IN *COSMIC FIRE.*

THIS IS THE WAY THE *WORLD* ENDS--

--NOT WITH A *BANG*--

--NOT WITH A *WHIMPER*--

--BUT WITH AN OVERWHELMING *SIGH OF RELIEF!*

THEN AT LAST THE HOLOCAUST IS *OVER*-- AND REMARKABLY FIVE WEARY *FIGURES* ARE FOUND STANDING AMID THE SMOLDERING *SOLITUDE.*

BY HELA'S GRIM HAND-- WE STILL *LIVE!?!*

BUT HOW CAN THIS *BE*, MILORD THOR?

I KNOW *NOT*, FRIEND HOGUN-- NOR DOTH THE ANSWER TRULY *MATTER* NOW.

ALL THAT BE *IMPORTANT* IS THAT WE HAVE *FAILED* IN OUR APPOINTED *TASK*--

--AND *BECAUSE* OF US--

--THE PLANET *EARTH* IS *DEAD!!*

NEXT ISSUE: "*The TEMPLE AT THE END OF TIME!*"

NEED WE SAY... *BE HERE!*

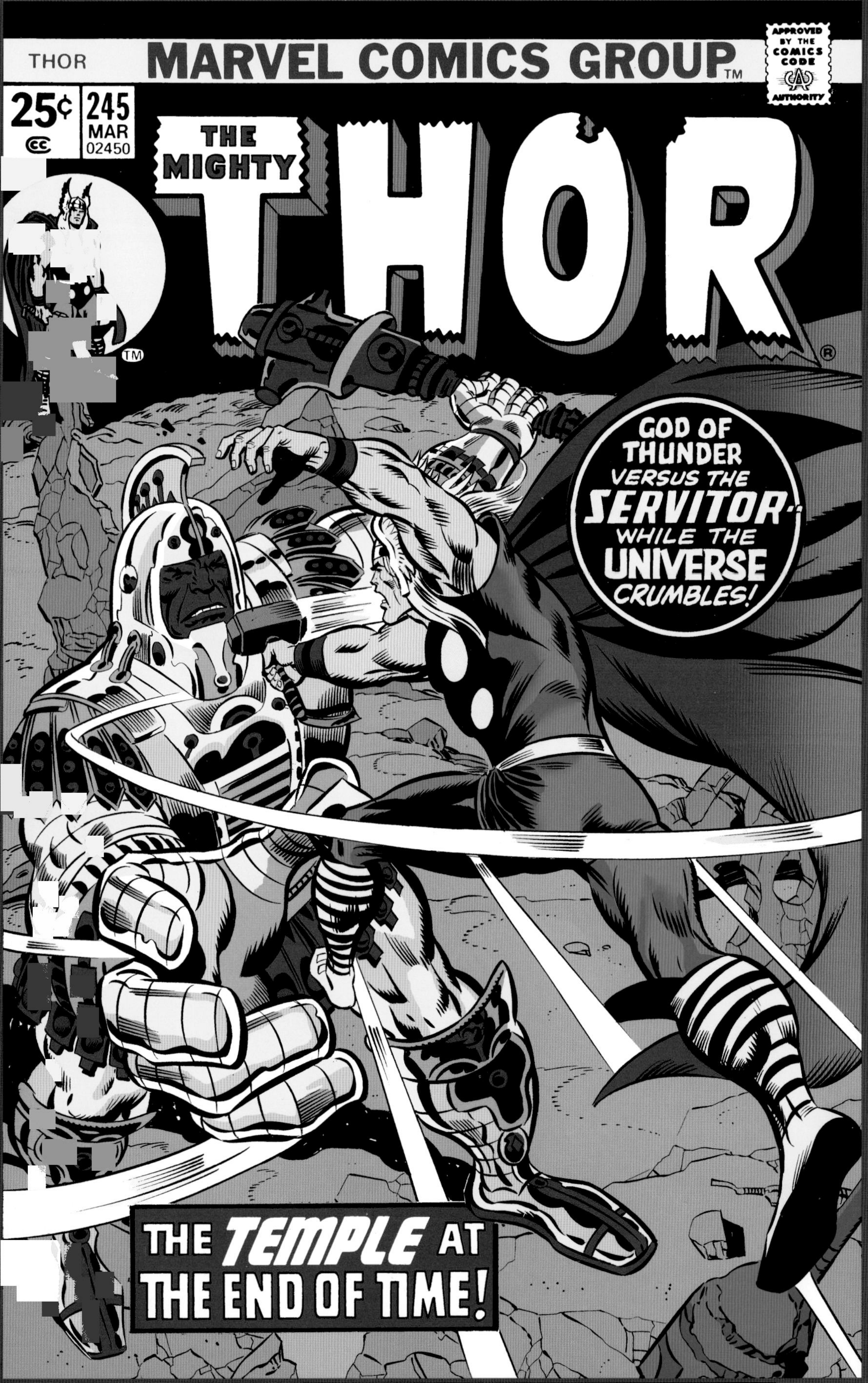
THOR
MARVEL COMICS GROUP™
APPROVED BY THE COMICS CODE AUTHORITY
25¢
245 MAR 02450
THE MIGHTY THOR®
GOD OF THUNDER VERSUS THE SERVITOR-- WHILE THE UNIVERSE CRUMBLES!
THE TEMPLE AT THE END OF TIME!

Stan Lee PRESENTS: THE MIGHTY THOR!

LEN WEIN
WRITER/EDITOR

JOHN BUSCEMA • JOE SINNOTT
ILLUSTRATORS

GLYNIS WEIN
COLORIST

JOE ROSEN
LETTERER

THE TEMPLE AT THE END OF TIME!

ARMAGEDDON PLUS ONE: THERE REALLY ISN'T MUCH TO DO AFTER THE END OF THE WORLD--AND THE FIVE SORROWFUL FIGURES WHO, REMARKABLY, SOMEHOW SURVIVED THE PLANETARY HOLOCAUST DON'T EVEN BOTHER TO TRY!

YOU SEE, THEY BLAME THEMSELVES FOR THE STILL-SMOLDERING DE-VASTATION THAT SURROUNDS THEM--BY FAILING TO STOP THE MYSTERIOUS TIME-TWISTERS BEFORE THEY COULD DESTROY THE WORLD THAT HAD BEEN 50TH CENTURY EARTH!

THEY DID THEIR BEST, BUT IT JUST WASN'T ENOUGH--AND NOW ALL THAT'S LEFT FOR THEM TO DO IS--

--MOURN!

MILORD THOR, MY POOR MIND FAIRLY **REELS** WITH QUESTIONS!

WHY, PRITHEE, DID WE **FIVE** ALONE **SURVIVE** THE FLAMING STORM THAT **CONSUMED** ALL ELSE?

WHY WERE WE FIVE SO SINGLY **BLESSED?**

IN TRUTH, FRIEND VOLSTAGG, I KNOW **NOT**-- BUT METHINKS THE **ANSWER** DOTH LIE WITH WITH MILADY **JANE**--

--SHE WITHIN WHOM THE SPIRIT OF THE GODDESS **SIF** DOTH DWELL--

--FOR SIF'S WAS THE POWER TO **BYPASS TIME AND SPACE!** *

I--I DON'T **UNDERSTAND,** DARLING.

*IF YOU DON'T BELIEVE **US,** JUST CHECK **THOR** #139 & 143 AMONG OTHERS. --LEN.

'TIS **SIMPLE,** MY LOVE. SOMEHOW, WHEN THE MOMENT OF CATACLYSM WAS **UPON** US, THOU DIDST **SUMMON** THAT POWER FROM THE VERY DEPTHS OF THY **SOUL**--

--AND HIED US **AWAY** UNTIL THE MOMENT **PASSED!**

FOR ALL OUR **POWER,** 'TWAS **THEE** ALONE, JANE FOSTER, WHO... **EH?**

BY HEIMDAL'S EYES! THE VERY AIR BEFORE US DOTH **SHIMMER** AND **GLOW**--

--AND A GREAT GOLDEN **OBJECT** DOTH APPEAR--

"--THE **TIME CUBE** OF-- **ZARRKO, THE TOMORROW MAN!**"

SO, ASGARDIANS-- IT SEEMS YOU **ALSO** ESCAPED THE DISASTER!

A **PITY,** MASTER. IT IS MORE THAN THEY **DESERVE!**

MY SERVITOR'S WORDS ARE **JUSTIFIED,** THUNDER GOD! I BROUGHT YOU AND YOUR FRIENDS FROM THE 20th CENTURY TO HELP ME **SAVE** MY WORLD--

-- BUT WHEN THE **CHIPS** WERE DOWN, YOU **FAILED** ME--

--AND **BECAUSE** OF YOU, AN ENTIRE PLANET IS **DEAD!**

WE DO NOT **DENY** OUR GUILT, ZARRKO, SHOULDST **THOU** NOT DO THE **SAME?**

IN THINE OWN **WORDS,** THOU DIDST SUMMON US ONLY TO **HELP** THEE--

--YET WHERE WERT **THOU** WHEN THE MOMENT OF **TRUTH** ARRIVED?

MY **MASTER** WILL ASK ALL THE **QUESTIONS** HERE, ASGARDIAN!

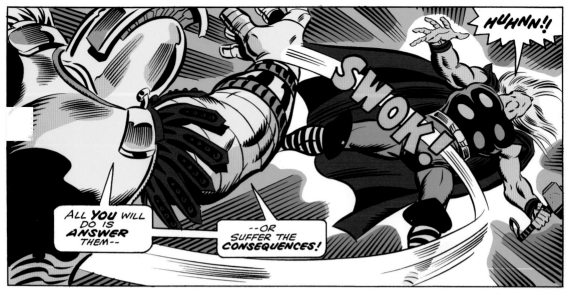

HUHNN!!

SWOK!

ALL *YOU* WILL DO IS *ANSWER* THEM--

--OR SUFFER THE *CONSEQUENCES!*

THOU HADST NO CALL TO *DO* THAT, SERVITOR!

I HAD LOOKED ON THEE AS AN ABLE *COMRADE-IN-ARMS*-- MAYHAP EVEN AS A *FRIEND!*

BUT, IF THOU DOST CHOOSE TO SET THYSELF *AGAINST* ME--

--SO BE IT!

THOU DIDST STRIKE ME FROM *BEHIND*-- WITHOUT *QUALM*, WITHOUT *WARNING!*

"THUS SO SHALL MINE ENCHANTED HAMMER *MJOLNIR* STRIKE--

BWHOOM!

"--*WITHOUT MERCY!*"

BUT HAVING STRUCK *ONCE*, IT NEED STRIKE *NO MORE*--

--FOR I HAVE NO WISH TO *BATTLE* THEE, SERVITOR!

THOU DIDST STRIKE *ME* AND THOU WERT *STRUCK* IN TURN! THE SCALES ARE *BALANCED!*

64

KROOM!

WRONG, THUNDER GOD! YOU HAVE **SHAMED** ME BEFORE MY **MASTER!**

THE SCALES CANNOT BE **BALANCED** UNTIL I HAVE WASHED THAT SHAME **AWAY**-- WITH YOUR **BLOOD!**

THEN THOU DOST LEAVE ME LITTLE **CHOICE**, SERVITOR!

I STRIKE NOW WITH **RELUCTANCE**--

PROK!

"--BUT, NONETHELESS, I **STRIKE!**"

ONCE **BEFORE**, WE **CLASHED** LIKE THIS *--

--BUT **THEN** THY MASTER **SAVED** THEE!

*IN **THOR** #242. --LEN.

THIS TIME ONLY **ONE** OF US SHALL **SURVIVE!**

AND SINCE ALL EYES ARE ON THE TWO **COMBAT-ANTS**, NOBODY EVEN **NOTICES** A TATTERED FIGURE STAGGER NUMBLY FROM THE **TIME CUBE**--

--A FIGURE NO ONE HAD EVEN **KNOWN** WAS ABOARD!

HIS **NAME**-- NOT THAT IT REALLY **MATTERS** NOW-- IS **DEREK!** JUST BEFORE THE **CATACLYSM**, HE HAD STOLEN INTO ZARRKO'S **CASTLE** TO MAKE THE TOMORROW MAN **PAY** FOR THE DEATHS OF HIS **FRIENDS!***

HE NEVER CAME **CLOSE** TO GETTING THE **CHANCE!**

*LAST ISSUE, RIGHT? --L.

NOW, HIS MIND *AWHIRL* WITH THE THINGS HE HAS WITNESSED DURING ZARRKO'S TIME-FLIGHT TO ESCAPE THE *HOLOCAUST*--

--DEREK SHAMBLES AIMLESSLY THRU THE MISSHAPEN *SLAG* THAT ONCE HAD BEEN THE CITY HE CALLED *HOME!*

GRANTED, A CITY WITHOUT *ENERGY,* WITHOUT *HOPE*--

--BUT *HIS* CITY, NONETHELESS.

FOR DEREK'S *WIFE* HAD LIVED HERE!

AAAAAA

OUT OF MY *WAY,* WOMAN!

NO, SERVITOR-- THIS *INSANITY* HAS GONE ON *LONG ENOUGH!*

MILADY, GET THEE *BACK!* GET THYSELF TO *SAFETY!*

NOW *STOP* THIS STUPIDITY, *BOTH* OF YOU -- AND *LISTEN* TO ME!

IT'S NOT *MY* SAFETY I'M WORRIED ABOUT, DARLING!

MAYBE WE *DID* FAIL TO SAVE THE *EARTH* -- BUT ONLY IN *THIS* CENTURY!

THE *TIME-TWISTERS* ARE STILL ON THE *LOOSE* -- AND UNLESS WE *PURSUE* THEM --

-- THE *20TH CENTURY* WILL BE THE *NEXT* TO FALL!

WHAT DOES THAT MATTER TO *ME,* WOMAN? *MY* WORLD HAS *ALREADY* BEEN DESTROYED!

WHY SHOULD MY *SERVITOR* AND I EVEN *BOTHER* TO FACE THE TIME-TWISTERS NOW?

TO GAIN THY *VENGEANCE* PERHAPS, ZARRKO?

THE DASHING FANDRAL SPEAKS *TRULY,* ZARRKO. WHAT IF I WERE TO SAY TO THEE THY WORLD MIGHT YET BE *SAVED?*

THEN I'D CALL YOU A RAVING *LUNATIC,* ASGARDIAN!

HOW DOES ONE GO ABOUT RESTORING *LIFE* TO A SMOLDERING *RUIN?*

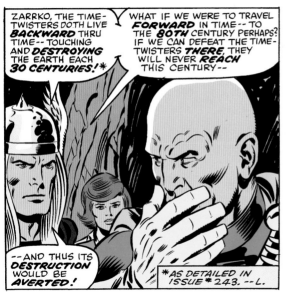

ZARRKO, THE TIME-TWISTERS DOTH LIVE **BACKWARD** THRU TIME-- TOUCHING AND **DESTROYING** THE EARTH EACH **30 CENTURIES!** *

WHAT IF WE WERE TO TRAVEL **FORWARD** IN TIME-- TO THE **80TH** CENTURY PERHAPS? IF WE CAN DEFEAT THE TIME-TWISTERS **THERE**, THEY WILL NEVER **REACH** THIS CENTURY--

--AND THUS ITS **DESTRUCTION** WOULD BE **AVERTED!**

* AS DETAILED IN ISSUE #243. --L.

AN **INTRIGUING** IDEA, THUNDER GOD-- BUT LET ME GO YOU ONE **FURTHER!**

SUPPOSE INSTEAD OF THE **80TH** CENTURY, WE WENT TO THE VERY **END** OF TIME-- AND PREVENTED THE TIME-TWISTERS FROM EVER COMING INTO **BEING**?

IS SUCH A JOURNEY **POSSIBLE**, ZARRKO?

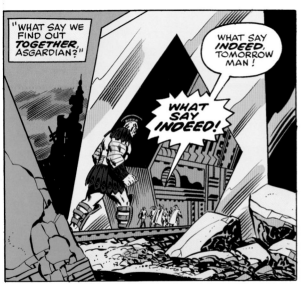

"WHAT SAY WE FIND OUT **TOGETHER**, ASGARDIAN?"

WHAT SAY **INDEED**, TOMORROW MAN!

WHAT SAY INDEED!

WITHIN MOMENTS, THE SEVEN DETERMINED FIGURES ARE SAFELY **INSIDE** THE GREAT GLEAMING **MECHANISM**-- AND ZARRKO SITS ONCE MORE AT THE **CONTROLS!**

LIKE A MASTER **PIANIST**, HIS HANDS **FLY** ACROSS THE DIALS-- AND THE **TIME-CUBE** BLURS SOFTLY **OUT** OF THE RUINED 50th CENTURY--

--AND HURTLES HEADLONG **THRU** THE AGES--

-- LEAVING BEHIND ONLY BITTER **MEMORIES**--

-- AND THE FORGOTTEN MAN CALLED **DEREK!**

WILL THE JOURNEY TAKE **LONG**, ZARRKO?

DEFINE "**LONG**" FOR ME, THUNDER GOD. IS IT A **MINUTE**? AN **HOUR**? AN **EON**?

HOW DOES ONE **MARK** TIME, ASGARDIAN-- WHEN ONE TRAVELS SO EASILY **THRU** IT?

THINE IMPERIOUS TONE IS **UNNECESSARY**, ZARRKO! 'TWAS A **SIMPLE** ENOUGH QUESTION TO...

ZOUNDS!

DARLING, WH--WHAT'S **HAPPENING?**

"THE TIME-CUBE DOTH **SHUDDER**, MILADY-- IT DOTH **TREMBLE** AS IF SORELY **AFRAID!**

"ZARRKO, I SAY THEE-- **WHY?**

"ARE WE **BESET** ONCE MORE BY CREATURES TORN FROM TIME-- OR ART THOU MERELY UNABLE TO **COMMAND** THY VESSEL AS ITS MASTER **SHOULD?**

THIS IS **BEYOND** MY POWER TO **CONTROL**, THOR! I'VE NEVER **PUSHED** THE TIME-CUBE THIS **HARD** BEFORE!

IT'S BEING **BUFFETED** BY FORCES WE COULD NOT BEGIN TO **COMPREHEND!**

AYE, TOMORROW MAN-- ALREADY THY CRAFT STARTS TO **BUCKLE** 'NEATH THE **STRAIN!**

DARLING, IF THAT BULKHEAD **RUPTURES**, WE'RE **LOST** BEFORE WE EVEN **BEGIN!**

FEAR **NOT**, MILADY-- THE WALL SHALL **STAND!**

IN THE **NAME** OF ALL THAT HATH EVER **BEEN** AND ALL THAT MAY EVER **BE**-- IT SHALL **STAND!!**

YOU NEED NOT STRUGGLE **ALONE,** ASGARDIAN!

THE SERVITOR STANDS **BESIDE** YOU!

AND NO MORE **ABLE** ALLY COULD ANY MAN **DESIRE!**

THE SERVITOR DOES NOT **RESPOND**-- BUT MERELY **CLENCHES** HIS TEETH, AND PRESSES THAT MUCH **HARDER** AGAINST THE DANGEROUSLY BUCKLING **WALL.**

THE TIME-CUBE HURTLES **ONWARD**-- AND FORCES LOCKED IN **CONFLICT** ABRUPTLY REACH **ACCORD.**

METHINKS THE TURBULENCE HATH FINALLY **PASSED!**

I AM **OBLIGED** TO THEE, SERVITOR. THINE AID WAS MOST **WELCOME** INDEED.

YOUR **GRATITUDE** IS ILL-SPENT, ASGARDIAN.

I ACTED NOT TO HELP **YOU**-- BUT TO INSURE MY MASTER'S **SAFETY!**

THIS TIME, 'TIS THE **THUNDER GOD** WHO OFFERS NO **REPLY.** INSTEAD HE TURNS TO HIS **COMPANIONS** AND SADLY **SHAKES** HIS HEAD --

--THEN SNAPS HIS GAZE TOWARDS **ZARRKO** AS THE TIME-CUBE SUDDENLY **WHINES** IN EFFORT--

--THEN BEGINS TO **WIND DOWN!**

WHAT **NEW** TROUBLE ASSAILS THY VESSEL, ZARRKO?

NONE WHATSOEVER, THOR. WE'RE SIMPLY APPROACHING OUR **DESTINATION!**

WITHIN MOMENTS, WE SHALL BE THE FIRST IN **HISTORY** TO WITNESS HISTORY'S **END!**

IF YOU WISH, YOU MAY **OBSERVE** OUR TARGET THRU THE **VIEWSCREEN!**

'TIS TRULY **BREATHTAKING,** IS IT NOT? THE **PRIMAL SUN** DOTH **HEAVE** IN FUTILE **EFFORT**--

--AS IF IT **KNEW** EACH MOMENT COULD BE ITS VERY **LAST!**

BUT WHAT'S THAT STRANGE **BUILDING** ON THAT OUTCROPPING OF **ROCK?**

"IT'S A *TEMPLE* OF SOME SORT," ZARRKO REPLIES GRIMLY. "THE ONLY *LIFE ENERGIES* RECORDED IN THIS TIME PERIOD BY MY INSTRUMENTS EMANATE FROM *THERE!*"

"ART THOU *CERTAIN,* TOMORROW MAN?" QUERIES THE *DASHING* FANDRAL. "METHINKS MAYHAP THINE INSTRUMENTS HATH *SUFFERED* FOR OUR JOURNEY."

"AYE, ZARRKO," OFFERS HOGUN THE GRIM. "LOOK THEE AT YON *STATUARY* STANDING STAUNCH BEFORE THE DWELLING'S *PORTALS!*"

"WOULD SUCH NOBLE *SCULPTURES* BE LEFT IN SUCH *ILL REPAIR* WERE THERE ANYONE *ABOUT?*"

FRANKLY, ASGARDIAN-- YOUR QUESTION HARDLY DESERVES AN *ANSWER!*

I WOULD ASSUME WHO-EVER HAS *SURVIVED* HERE TO AWAIT THE FINAL HOLOCAUST WOULD HAVE MORE *IMPORTANT* THINGS TO WORRY ABOUT!

BUT I SUGGEST THAT WE FIND OUT FOR *OURSELVES!*

FORTUNATELY, THIS CRUMBLING PLANETOID HAS RETAINED ITS *GRAVITY* AND A *BREATHABLE ATMOSPHERE,* SO WE NEEDN'T *WORRY* ABOUT... *EH?*

THE ENTIRE *TEMPLE AREA*--IT'S SURROUNDED BY AN UNSEEN *FORCE FIELD!*

WE CAN'T GET *THRU!*

ONCE AGAIN, ZARRKO-- THOU DOST RECKON WITHOUT THE *POWER* OF MINE *ENCHANTED HAMMER!*

BY GEIRRODUR'S **FLAMING FURNACES!** MYSTIC MJOLNIR HATH **NO EFFECT** 'PON YON BARRIER!

IT SEEMS YOUR MUCH-VAUNTED **POWER** IS NOT ALL IT'S **SUPPOSED** TO BE, GODLING!

BUT PERHAPS, MASTER, IF MY **POWER-LANCE** WAS **JOINED** WITH THE ASGARDIAN'S **HAMMER**, THE FORCE FIELD COULD BE **BREACHED!**

THE CHOICE IS **YOURS**, THOR!

HAVE I EVER **REFUSED** THINE AID, SERVITOR?

STAND THEE BESIDE ME **SWIFTLY**--

BENEATH THE SAVAGE **ENERGY ONSLAUGHT**, THE SHIMMERING FORCE FIELD **PULSES** AND **WRITHES**--

--AND LET BE DONE WHAT **MUST** BE DONE--

NOW!

-- THEN ABRUPTLY **ERUPTS** IN A BLINDING **PAROXYSM**--

--AND IS **GONE!**

YOU'VE **DONE** IT! NOW **NOTHING** STANDS BETWEEN US AND OUR **GOAL!**

MAYHAP THOU DOST SPEAK TOO **SOON**, ZARRKO!

FOR IT SEEMS YON **STATUES** ARE FAR **MORE** THAN MERE **GRAVEN IMAGES!**

VERILY THEY ARE ALIVE!

INTRUDERS, YOU HAVE VIOLATED **SACRED GROUND!** TURN BACK-- OR **PERISH!**

SO SPEAK-- THE **PROTECTROIDS!**

DEFEND THYSELVES, MY COMRADES! THE BATTLE HATH BEEN **JOINED** AND WE MUST **TRIUMPH**--

--OR ALL THAT TIME HATH EVER **SPAWNED** WILL GO FOR **NAUGHT!**

ZZAAKK

ZOUNDS! METHINKS 'TWOULD BE WISE FOR VALOROUS VOLSTAGG TO BRAVELY ATTEND THE **REAR**--

--AND **SWIFTLY!**

RRAAKK!

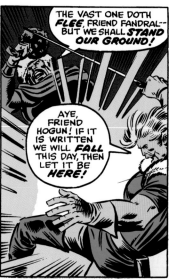

THE VAST ONE DOTH **FLEE,** FRIEND FANDRAL-- BUT WE SHALL **STAND OUR GROUND!**

AYE, FRIEND HOGUN! IF IT IS WRITTEN WE WILL **FALL** THIS DAY, THEN LET IT BE **HERE!**

THEN FALL YOU **WILL,** FOOLS! OUR SOLE PURPOSE IN **BEING** IS TO PROTECT **THOSE WHO SLEEP**--

--AND NOTHING THAT LIVES MAY **STAY** US FROM OUR SACRED **TRUST!**

I'M NOT EQUIPPED TO **BATTLE** THOSE CREATURES! BETTER GET TO **COVER** -- AND LET THE **ASGARDIANS** HANDLE...

NO!?!

KKRRAAKK!

NOW, INTRUDER-- YOU WILL SUFFER THE FATE OF **ALL** WHO DARE TO **THREATEN** THOSE WHO SLEEP!

N-NO-- YOU **MUSTN'T**--!

I CAN'T HAVE COME THIS FAR ONLY TO **DIE!**

FEAR **NOT,** MASTER! I WILL...

AARRGH!

VVRRAK!

THE **SERVITOR!** HE TOOK THE **FULL BRUNT** OF THE BLAST MEANT FOR **ME!**

"HIS INNER CIRCUITRY IS ALL BUT **DESTROYED**-- YET STILL HE MOVES TO **DEFEND** ME--!"

"HE'S **ATTACKING** THE PROTECTROID-- WASTING HIS **LAST IOTA** OF ENERGY ON **MY** BEHALF--"

"--**STRAINING** HIMSELF TO THE POINT OF **SELF-DESTRUCTION**--"

KWA-VOOM!

"-- AND **BEYOND!**"

BUT THY SERVITOR'S **SACRIFICE** HATH NOT BEEN IN **VAIN,** ZARRKO!

HIS NOBLE **DEED** HATH **DISTRACTED** THE REMAINING **PROTECTROIDS**--

KKKRAK! SKRAK!

--AND E'ER THEY CAN **REGAIN** THEIR **WITS**--

--MINE AVENGING HAMMER DOTH **STRIKE!**

COME, ZARRKO-- THERE IS NOTHING MORE WE CAN **DO** HERE.

THY SERVANT HATH PASSED **BEYOND** OUR POWER TO **ATTEND** HIM!

HE WAS **MORE** THAN JUST MY **SERVANT,** ASGARDIAN.

HE WAS... MY **FRIEND.**

THEN **JOIN** US, ZARRKO-- AND HELP TO MAKE WHAT **NEXT** WE DO A **SHRINE** TO THY COMRADE'S **MEMORY!**

THE SERVITOR HATH **GIVEN** US HIS LAST **FULL** MEASURE OF **DEVOTION.**

'TIS UP TO **US** TO DO WHAT **REMAINS!**

73

A HOLLOW **HUM** FILLS THE TEMPLE HALL AS THE ANXIOUS BAND **ENTERS**, TO FIND...

THE ENTIRE CHAMBER IS FILLED WITH **MACHINERY**--!

AND ALL DEDICATED TO **ONE** END, METHINKS--

"--**PRESERVING** THOSE WHO DOTH **SLEEP** WITHIN YON SHIMMERING **EGGS!**

"MY FRIENDS, VERILY WE HAVE FOUND THE **TIME-TWISTERS!**"

THEN WHAT ARE YOU **WAITING** FOR?

DESTROY THEM-- **NOW!**

THE SON OF ODIN DOTH NOT TAKE LIFE **LIGHTLY,** ZARRKO--

--BUT 'TWOULD SEEM I HAVE NO **CHOICE!**

FOR THE UNIVERSE TO **LIVE**, THE TIME-TWISTERS MUST...

INTRUDER-- **HOLD!**

SMASH THOSE **NURTURE-PODS** AND YOU CONDEMN **UNTOLD GENERATIONS** TO THE BLACK PITS OF **IGNORANCE!**

YOU WILL DEPRIVE A **FUTURE** YET UNBORN OF THE PRICELESS **KNOWLEDGE** OF THE **PAST!**

COULD YOU BE THAT **CRUEL?**

OLD ONE, THOU KNOWEST **NOT** WHAT THOU DOST **SAY!**

I KNOW ALL THAT I **NEED** TO KNOW, STRIPLING.

I AM... HE WHO **REMAINS!**

I ALONE, OF ALL MY RACE, AM LEFT TO **GUARD** THOSE WHO SHALL **SURVIVE** ETERNITY'S **ENDING!**

I ALONE AM LEFT TO SOW **DESTINY'S SEEDS!**

BUT IF THY BITTER SEEDS BEAR **FRUIT**, WORLDS WITHOUT NUMBER WILL **PERISH!**

THUS, THOUGH IT DOTH SORELY **GRIEVE** ME, MINE ENCHANTED **HAMMER** MUST...

STRIPLING-- **STOP!** COULD YOU STILL NOT **UNDER-STAND?**

MY **STRENGTH--!**

IT DOTH **DRAIN** FROM MY VERY **LIMBS!**

AS I **INTENDED.** NOW YOU WILL **LISTEN** AS I **EXPLAIN.**

YOU SEE, STRIPLING-- **TIME** IS BUT A **CIRCLE.** FROM THE ASHES OF THE **FINAL HOLOCAUST,** THE UNIVERSE WILL BEGIN **ANEW.**

THOSE WHO SLEEP ARE OUR **GIFT** TO THE FUTURE-- THREE BEINGS WHO ARE **KNOWLEDGE INCARNATE**-- AND WILL **TEACH** THOSE OF THE NEXT CYCLE TO **AVOID** THE ERRORS **WE** MADE.

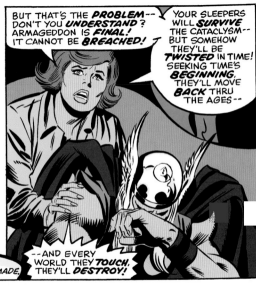

BUT THAT'S THE **PROBLEM**-- DON'T YOU **UNDERSTAND?** ARMAGEDDON IS **FINAL!** IT CANNOT BE **BREACHED!**

YOUR SLEEPERS WILL **SURVIVE** THE CATACLYSM-- BUT SOMEHOW THEY'LL BE **TWISTED** IN TIME! SEEKING TIME'S **BEGINNING,** THEY'LL MOVE **BACK** THRU THE AGES--

--AND EVERY WORLD THEY **TOUCH,** THEY'LL **DESTROY!**

WOMAN, YOU SPEAK **NONSENSE!**

I ONLY WISH I **DID**--BUT WITH MY OWN EYES I **SAW** YOUR PRECIOUS SLEEPERS **DEVASTATE** 50th CENTURY **EARTH!**

THAT'S WHY WE'VE **COME** HERE-- TO **PREVENT** SUCH WANTON DESTRUCTION FROM EVER **HAPPENING!**

BUT ALL OUR **HOPES**-- OUR DREAMS OF A **UNIVERSAL UTOPIA**--?

ARE YOU WILLING TO **MURDER** COUNTLESS TRILLIONS OF **LIVING BEINGS** TO MAKE THOSE DREAMS COME **TRUE?**

THAT'S WHAT IT COMES **DOWN** TO, YOU KNOW.

CAN **YOU** BE THAT **SELFISH?**

BUT BEFORE THE WIZENED FIGURE CAN VOICE A *REPLY*, THERE COMES A *ROAR* LIKE THE BELLOW OF SOME WOUNDED *BEAST*--

--AND THE TEMPLE IS *SHAKEN* TO ITS VERY *FOUNDATIONS*.

BY THE BEARD OF MY *FATHER!* WHAT DOTH BE THE *MEANING* OF THIS?

THAT WAS THE FIRST *SHOCK-WAVE* FROM THE ERUPTING *PRIMAL SUN!*

THEY WILL GET *WORSE* AS THEY GO *ON!*

THEN-- *THE CATACLYSM HAS BEGUN!!*

QUICKLY, EVERY-ONE-- TO THE *TIME-CUBE!* IT'S OUR ONLY HOPE OF LEAVING HERE *ALIVE!*

WE DO NOT *LIKE* LEAVING HERE, ZARRKO-- WITH OUR *MISSION* NOT YET *COMPLETE!*

BUT NONETHELESS, TOMORROW MAN-- WE *GO!*

WE *GO!*

GO *SWIFTLY* THEN, STRIPLINGS. TIME GROWS *SHORT.*

THEN COMEST THOU *WITH* US, OLD ONE. THOU HAST *DISCHARGED* THY DUTY MOST *NOBLY.*

LEAVE THY SLEEPERS TO THE SPINNING *FATES*-- AND *FLEE!*

I APPRECIATE YOUR *OFFER,* STRIPLING-- BUT I *CANNOT!*

THERE ARE THINGS LEFT TO BE *DONE* HERE--THAT ONLY *I* CAN DO.

SAVE *YOURSELF* WHILE YOU CAN-- AND KNOW THAT YOU TAKE WITH YOU AN OLD MAN'S *GRATITUDE*--

--FOR MORE THAN YOU COULD EVER *REALIZE.*

FOR A MOMENT, THE THUNDER GOD *HESITATES*--THEN A *SECOND* TREMOR ROCKS THE TEMPLE-- AND SADLY NODDING HIS HEAD AT THE ANCIENT GUARDIAN'S *WISDOM,* THOR RACES FROM THE CHAMBER--

--AND STRAIGHT INTO CONVULSING *CHAOS!*

COME *QUICKLY,* MILORD THOR! METHINKS THE *END* DOTH DRAW *NIGH!*

MAKE **HASTE**, COMRADES. THE TIME-CUBE CANNOT **LINGER**.

A **MOMENT**, VOLSTAGG-- WHILE I BID A FINAL **FARE-WELL** TO ONE FAR **NOBLER** THAN **WE**.

THE PRINCE OF ASGARD GAZES ONE LAST TIME UPON THE TEMPLE OF **SLEEPERS**, AND BOWS HIS HEAD SLOWLY IN SILENT **SALUTE**--

--THEN THE MASSIVE METAL **PORTAL** HUSHES SHUT **BEHIND** HIM--

--AND THE GREAT GLEAMING CUBE **VANISHES** BACK INTO THE MISTS OF **TIME**.

WITHIN THE TEMPLE, HE WHO REMAINS AWAITS THE CATACLYSM **QUIETLY**.

HE SHUFFLES ABOUT THE **CHAMBER**, MAKING CERTAIN THAT ALL IS IN ITS **PROPER PLACE**--

--AND JANE FOSTER'S PLAINTIVE **WORDS** WHIRL WILDLY THRU HIS **MIND**.

THE NURTURE-PODS BEFORE HIM STILL PULSATE AND **GLOW**, THEIR SOFT INCANDESCENCE GLINTING BLINDLY OFF THE SINGLE **BEAD OF MOISTURE** THAT CURLS FROM THE OLD ONE'S **EYE**.

THEN A WITHERED **HAND** REACHES TREMBLING ACROSS THE **CONTROL CONSOLE**--

TERMINATE LIFE-SUPPORT SYSTEMS

--AND DOES WHAT **MUST** BE DONE!

THE JOURNEY BACK THRU THE CENTURIES IS TINGED WITH AN ATMOSPHERE OF **ANTICIPATION**--

-- AND **DREAD**.

FOR, WHATEVER THE TIME-TRAVELLERS HAD EXPECTED TO **FIND** UPON THEIR RETURN TO THE 50th **CENTURY**--

--IT CERTAINLY HAD NOT BEEN-- **THIS!**

TH-THIS ISN'T *MY* WORLD! THERE IS *TECHNOLOGY* EVIDENT HERE THAT I'D NEVER HAVE *PERMITTED!*

CITIZEN *ZARRKO?* WE WERE TOLD TO *EXPECT* YOU SOMEDAY,

FIRST CITIZEN *DEREK* WISHES TO *SPEAK* WITH YOU, YOU WILL *ACCOMPANY* US PLEASE?

THE GUARDS ARE POLITE BUT *PERSISTENT*, THUS SHORTLY...

WHO *ARE* YOU? WHAT HAVE YOU *DONE* TO MY WORLD?

I AM THE *LEGACY* THAT YOU LEFT *BEHIND*, ZARRKO;-- --AND THIS WORLD IS *YOURS* NO LONGER!

WHEN YOU *AVERTED* THE TRAGEDY THAT BEFELL US AND THE TIMESTREAM *RESTORED* ITSELF, YOU WERE TRAVELLING *BETWEEN* THE AGES --

--FOR ALL INTENTS AND PURPOSES, YOU DID NOT *EXIST*--

-- AND THUS THE EARTH WAS REBORN *WITHOUT* YOU!

AS FIRST CITIZEN, I *WELCOME* YOU TO THE *FREE FEDERATION OF EARTH!* YOU ARE INVITED TO DWELL AMONG US IN *PEACE*--

--OR YOU ARE FREE TO *DEPART!*

THE CHOICE, ZARRKO, IS ENTIRELY *YOURS!*

NO! YOU CAN'T *DO* THIS TO ME! I WON'T LET YOU *STEAL* MY WORLD!

ASGARDIANS, YOU'VE GOT TO *HELP* ME REGAIN MY...

EH?

EVEN IF WE WOULD *WANT* TO HELP THEE, ZARRKO-- WE *CANNOT!*

MILORD THOR, W-WE GROW MOST *PALE* --!

NO--*STOP!* YOU CAN'T *LEAVE* ME LIKE THIS!

BUT WE *MUST*, ZARRKO! THE TIME-TWISTERS WERE *DEFEATED* ERE THEY COULD E'EN BE *BORN!*

-- THUS THERE WAS NO *CAUSE* FOR THEE TO HAVE *SUMMONED* US TO THIS CENTURY--

"--AND SINCE THOU DIDST NOT *SUMMON* US--

"--WE WERE NEVER *HERE!*"

78

THE TIMESTREAM *RIPPLES,* THEN GROWS *CALM* ONCE MORE--AND IN THE APARTMENT OF *JANE FOSTER...*

I HOPE I HAVEN'T KEPT YOU ALL *WAITING* VERY LONG?

FOR *THEE,* LADY JANE--WE WOULD GLADLY WAIT *FOREVER.*

IS THE REPAST *SERVED,* MILADY?

I'M AFRAID YOU GENTS WILL HAVE TO SETTLE FOR *LEMON-ADE.* THAT'S ALL THAT'S *LEFT* IN THE REFRIGERATOR.

'TWAS ALMOST--ER--*EMPTY* WHEN WE *ARRIVED,* MILADY.

THOU ART A MOST *GRACIOUS* HOSTESS, JANE FOSTER.

THY COLD BEVERAGE IS *MORE* THAN ENOUGH.

MORE THAN ENOUGH FOR DOUR *HOGUN,* MAYHAP--

--BUT *NOT* SO FOR FANDRAL THE *CONNOIS-SEUR!*

HAST THOU NOTHING *STRONGER,* LADY JANE?

WELL,...THERE'S A WARM BOTTLE OF *PEPSI* IN THE KITCHEN.

'TWAS NOT--AH--*QUITE* WHAT I HAD IN *MIND,* LADY JANE. COULDST THOU...

BY ODIN!

IF THOU DOST NOT PLAN TO *DRINK* THY LEMON NECTAR, FRIEND FANDRAL--

--PRAY OFFER IT TO SOMEONE WHO *WILL!*

CARE FOR THAT *PEPSI* NOW, FANDRAL?

THE MOMENT *PASSES.*

NO GREAT GOLDEN *HAND* BURSTS IN THRU THE WALL TO *ABDUCT* JANE FOSTER.

NO *TIME-TRAVELLER* APPEARS TO SUMMON THE ASGARDIANS FORTH TO *WAR!*

IT IS AN EVENING NOT UNLIKE A THOUSAND *OTHERS*--

--AND IT PASSES IN GOOD *HUMOR*--AND *PEACE.*

NEXT ISSUE: BECAUSE YOU *DEMANDED* IT... **THE FURY OF FIRELORD!**

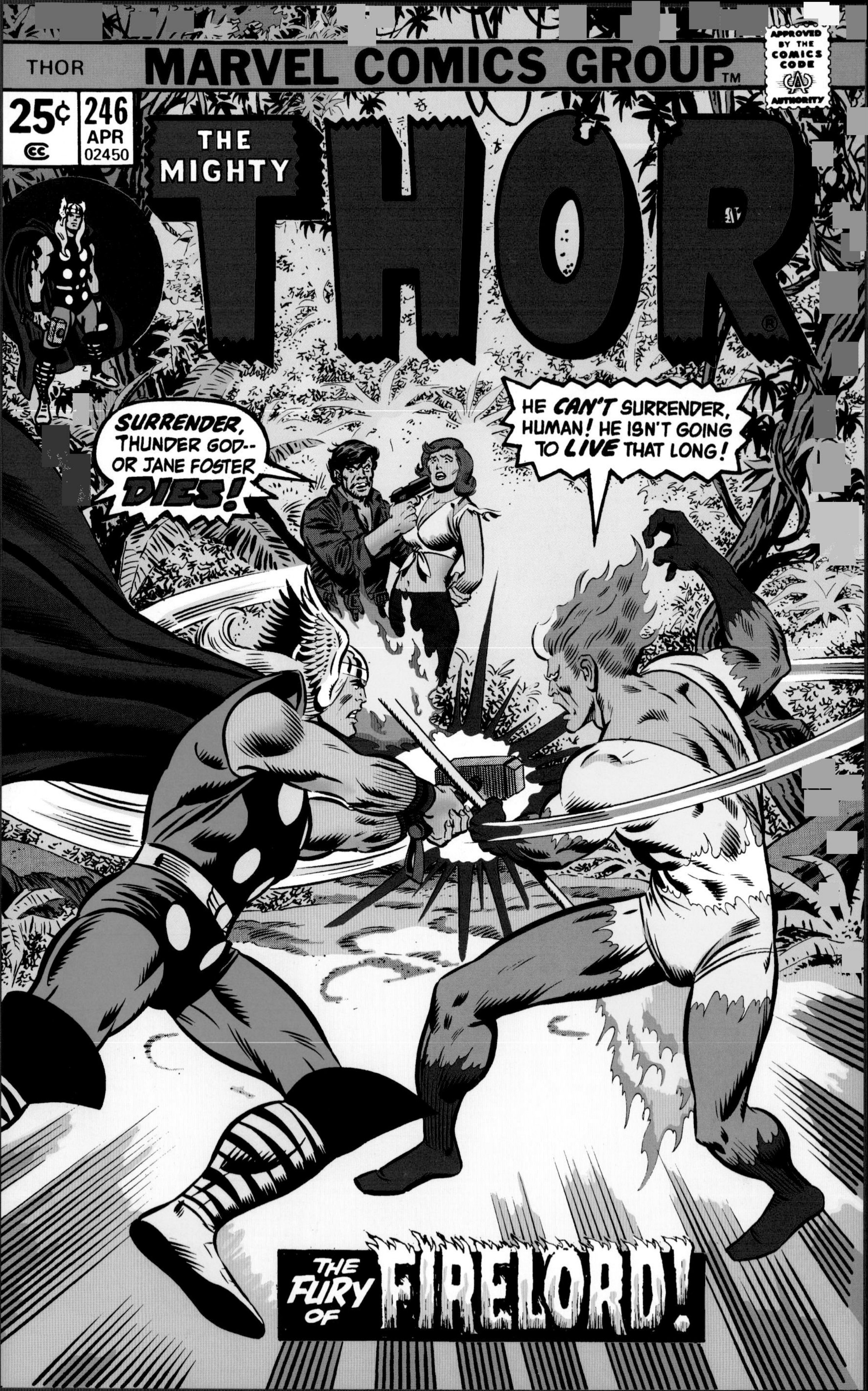
THOR
MARVEL COMICS GROUP
APPROVED BY THE COMICS CODE AUTHORITY
25¢
246
APR
02450
THE MIGHTY
THOR
SURRENDER, THUNDER GOD-- OR JANE FOSTER DIES!
HE CAN'T SURRENDER, HUMAN! HE ISN'T GOING TO LIVE THAT LONG!
THE FURY OF FIRELORD!

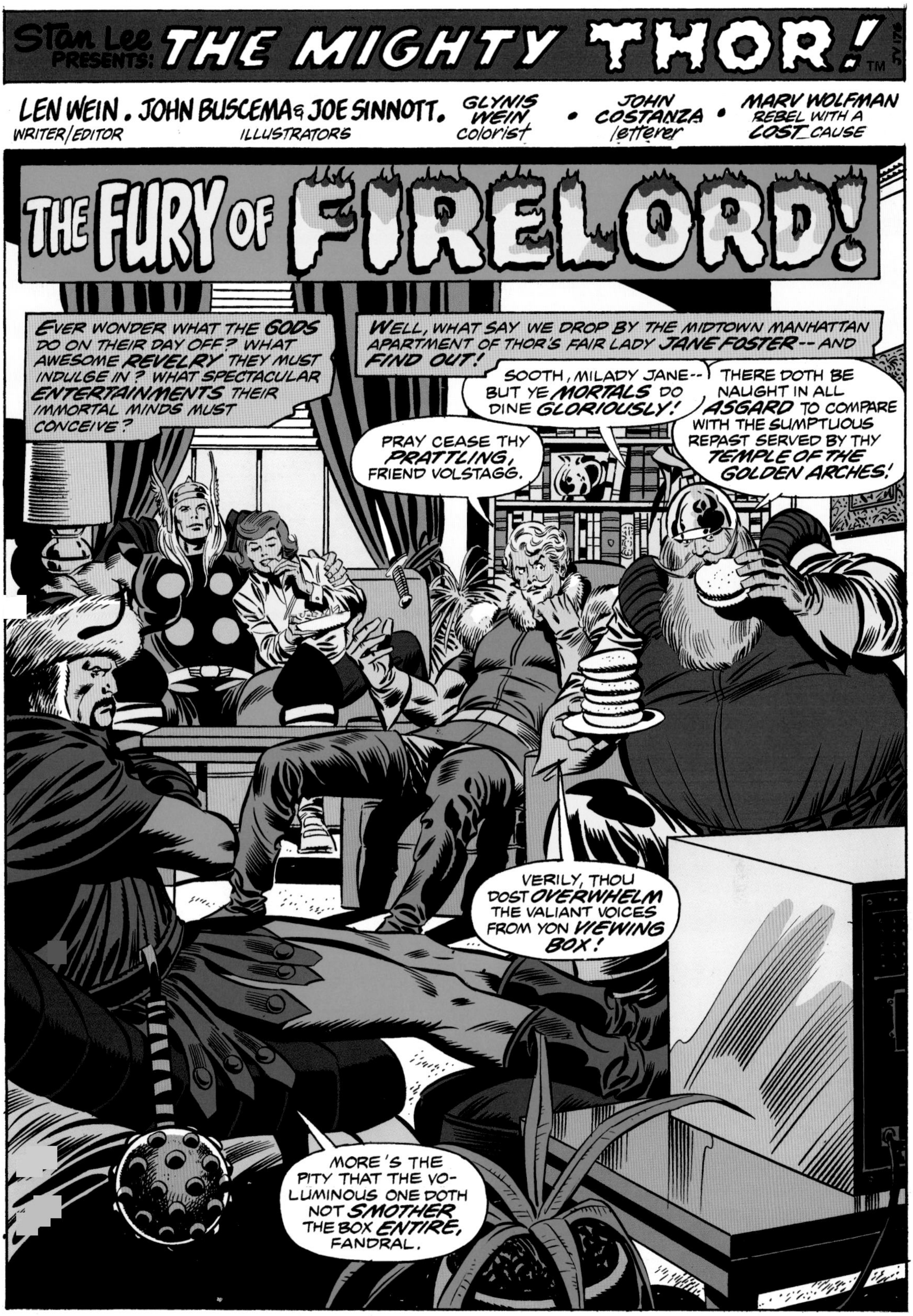
Stan Lee PRESENTS: THE MIGHTY THOR!
LEN WEIN . WRITER/EDITOR
JOHN BUSCEMA & JOE SINNOTT . ILLUSTRATORS
GLYNIS WEIN colorist
JOHN COSTANZA letterer
MARV WOLFMAN REBEL WITH A LOST CAUSE
THE FURY OF FIRELORD!
EVER WONDER WHAT THE GODS DO ON THEIR DAY OFF? WHAT AWESOME REVELRY THEY MUST INDULGE IN? WHAT SPECTACULAR ENTERTAINMENTS THEIR IMMORTAL MINDS MUST CONCEIVE?
WELL, WHAT SAY WE DROP BY THE MIDTOWN MANHATTAN APARTMENT OF THOR'S FAIR LADY JANE FOSTER-- AND FIND OUT!
SOOTH, MILADY JANE-- BUT YE MORTALS DO DINE GLORIOUSLY!
THERE DOTH BE NAUGHT IN ALL ASGARD TO COMPARE WITH THE SUMPTUOUS REPAST SERVED BY THY TEMPLE OF THE GOLDEN ARCHES!
PRAY CEASE THY PRATTLING, FRIEND VOLSTAGG.
VERILY, THOU DOST OVERWHELM THE VALIANT VOICES FROM YON VIEWING BOX!
MORE'S THE PITY THAT THE VO-LUMINOUS ONE DOTH NOT SMOTHER THE BOX ENTIRE, FANDRAL.

GRIM HOGUN SPEAKS ALL TOO *TRULY,* FRIEND FANDRAL.

HOW CANST THOU *WASTE* HOURS ON END, OBSERVING THE TIRING *ANTICS* OF THE TINY BEINGS WHO DO *DWELL* WITHIN YON BOX--

--WHEN RATHER THOU COULDST BE CARVING NEW *LEGENDS* OF THINE *OWN?*

'TIS NO LIFE FOR A *FIGHTING* MAN, TO SIT *IDLE* WHILST...

EH?

THE BATTLE HATH *ENDED,* DASHING ONE -- AND AS EVER, THINE ILLUSTRIOUS ERROL FLYNN HATH *TRI-UMPHED!*

THIS IS *EMORY LEWIS,* WITH THE *SIX O'CLOCK REPORT.*

THE TOP STORY IN THE *NEWS* TONIGHT IS THE VIOLENT *REVO-LUTION* RAGING IN THE SMALL LATIN AMERICAN REPUBLIC OF *COSTA VERDE!*

LED BY *THIS* MAN, WHO CALLS HIMSELF *EL LOBO* -- THE *WOLF* -- THE REBELS HAVE STRUGGLED FOR MONTHS IN AN *UNSUCCESSFUL* ATTEMPT TO OVER-THROW THE DEMOCRATIC GOVERNMENT OF *PRESIDENT JUAN ELMIREZ* --

--BUT IN THE PAST SEVERAL DAYS, SOMETHING HAS *OCCURRED* IN COSTA VERDE THAT MAY TURN THE TIDE IN THE *REBELS'* FAVOR AT LAST!

THAT'S ABOUT ENOUGH OF *THAT!* I'LL TURN THIS OFF SO WE CAN...

WAIT, MILADY-- A MOMENT *LONGER.* I WOULD HEAR *MORE.*

SEEMINGLY FROM OUT OF *NOWHERE,* A BIZARRE BEING WHO CALLS HIMSELF *FIRELORD* HAS BECOME A BLAZING *FIGUREHEAD* FOR THE REBEL CAUSE!

WITH THIS STRANGE CREATURE URGING THE REBELS *ONWARD,* IT SEEMS DOUBTFUL THE GOVERNMENT OF PRESIDENT ELMIREZ CAN LONG *SURVIVE!*

SO! WHAT I HAVE LONG *FEARED* HATH FINALLY COME TO *PASS!*

'TIS *MY* RESPON-SIBILITY THAT FIRELORD DOTH NOW DWELL AMONG *MEN* --

--THUS 'TIS *I* WHO MUST NOW *SMITE HIM DOWN!*

* BACK IN *THOR* #228, FOOTNOTE-FOLLOWERS. -- LEN.

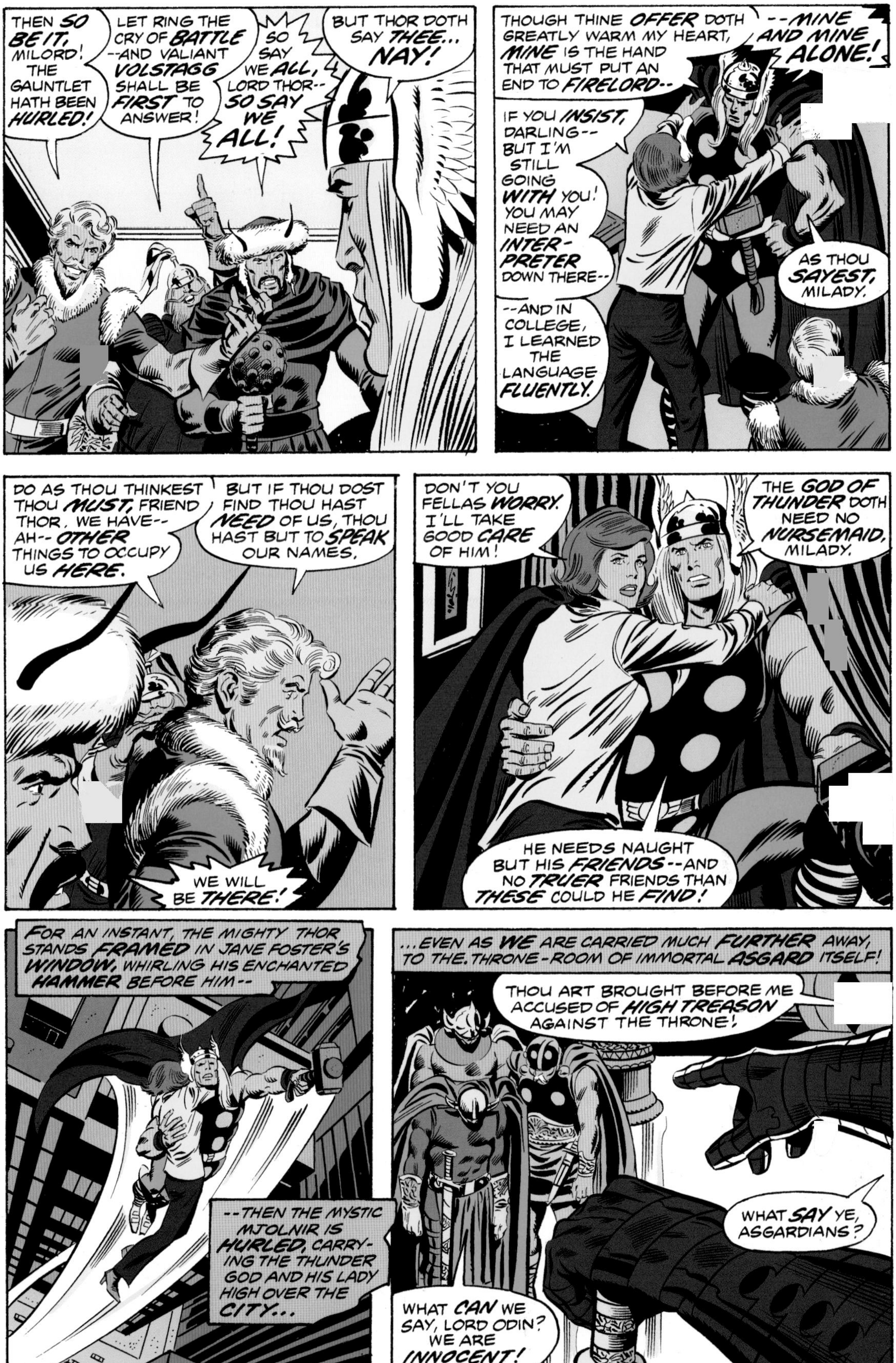
THEN SO BE IT, MILORD! THE GAUNTLET HATH BEEN HURLED!
LET RING THE CRY OF BATTLE --AND VALIANT VOLSTAGG SHALL BE FIRST TO ANSWER!
SO SAY WE ALL, LORD THOR-- SO SAY WE ALL!
BUT THOR DOTH SAY THEE... NAY!
THOUGH THINE OFFER DOTH GREATLY WARM MY HEART, MINE IS THE HAND THAT MUST PUT AN END TO FIRELORD--
--MINE AND MINE ALONE!
IF YOU INSIST, DARLING-- BUT I'M STILL GOING WITH YOU! YOU MAY NEED AN INTER-PRETER DOWN THERE--
--AND IN COLLEGE, I LEARNED THE LANGUAGE FLUENTLY.
AS THOU SAYEST, MILADY.
DO AS THOU THINKEST THOU MUST, FRIEND THOR, WE HAVE-- AH-- OTHER THINGS TO OCCUPY US HERE.
BUT IF THOU DOST FIND THOU HAST NEED OF US, THOU HAST BUT TO SPEAK OUR NAMES.
WE WILL BE THERE!
DON'T YOU FELLAS WORRY. I'LL TAKE GOOD CARE OF HIM!
THE GOD OF THUNDER DOTH NEED NO NURSEMAID, MILADY.
HE NEEDS NAUGHT BUT HIS FRIENDS--AND NO TRUER FRIENDS THAN THESE COULD HE FIND!
FOR AN INSTANT, THE MIGHTY THOR STANDS FRAMED IN JANE FOSTER'S WINDOW, WHIRLING HIS ENCHANTED HAMMER BEFORE HIM--
--THEN THE MYSTIC MJOLNIR IS HURLED, CARRY-ING THE THUNDER GOD AND HIS LADY HIGH OVER THE CITY...
...EVEN AS WE ARE CARRIED MUCH FURTHER AWAY, TO THE THRONE-ROOM OF IMMORTAL ASGARD ITSELF!
THOU ART BROUGHT BEFORE ME ACCUSED OF HIGH TREASON AGAINST THE THRONE!
WHAT SAY YE, ASGARDIANS?
WHAT CAN WE SAY, LORD ODIN? WE ARE INNOCENT!

STILL DOST THOU PROTEST THINE *INNOCENCE* -- WHEN THINE ACCUSER IS THE NOBLE *IGRON*, ADVISOR TO THE *ALL-FATHER* HIMSELF?

THOU DOST *DARE?*

MY LIEGE, THOUGH I AM BUT THY HUMBLE *ADVISOR*, MIGHT I OFFER A *SUGGESTION?*

PUT AN *END* TO THIS CHARADE -- AND *SWIFTLY!*

NAUGHT WILL BE GAINED BY *CONTINUING* IT -- SAVE THE FERMENTING OF FURTHER *UNREST.*

AS EVER, GOOD IGRON -- THOU SPEAKEST A 'RIGHT.

THUS TO THE *MOLTEN MIRE-PITS* DO I BANISH YE -- UNTIL I DO DECREE THY LESSON HATH BEEN *LEARNED!*

FOR I AM THE WISDOM, THE WILL, AND THE *WAY* -- AND TO SET THYSELF AGAINST *ODIN* IS TO SET THYSELF AGAINST *ASGARD!*

WITHOUT EVEN A *SCREAM*, THE THREE CONDEMNED IMMORTALS *VANISH* -- AND ALL THE GATHERED NOBLES OF THE REALM ETERNAL STAND IN SILENT AWE OF THEIR MONARCH'S *JUSTICE* --

-- ALL, THAT IS, SAVE *ONE!*

SICKENED TO HIS VERY SOUL BY WHAT HE HAS SEEN, BALDER THE BRAVE, MOST *BELOVED* OF ALL THE GODS, TURNS TO *LEAVE* THE PALACE ROYAL --

-- ONLY TO BE *HALTED* IN MID-STRIDE BY A GRIM COMMANDING *VOICE!*

HAST THOU BEEN GRANTED *LEAVE* TO DEPART THY MASTER'S *COURT*, BRAVE BALDER?

THERE WAS A LESSON MOST *GRIM* TO BE TAUGHT HERE TODAY!

I HOPE THAT THOU HAST *LEARNED* FROM IT!

INDEED I *HAVE*, MILORD -- INDEED I *HAVE!*

I HAVE LEARNED THAT OMNIPOTENT *ODIN*, THE LIVING *HEART* OF THE GOLDEN REALM, HATH GONE *INSANE!*

AND ON THAT RATHER *OMINOUS* NOTE, LET'S RETURN TO *EARTH*-- AND TWO FAMILIAR *FIGURES*, WHO EVEN NOW APPROACH THE CAPITAL CITY OF BATTLE-TORN *COSTA VERDE*...

THE PRESIDENT'S PALACE DOTH LIE *AHEAD*, MILADY.

WELL, I SUPPOSE IF YOU'RE GOING TO START YOUR ONE-MAN COUNTER-CRUSADE *ANYWHERE*--

--IT MIGHT AS WELL BE *THERE*!

PRESIDENT ELMIREZ MIGHT BE ABLE TO HELP US *LOCATE* FIRELORD!

BUT REGARD- LESS, WE OUGHT TO LET HIM *KNOW* WE'RE ON *HIS* SIDE!

MAYHAP WE SHOULD HAVE INFORMED HIM *BEFORE* WE ARRIVED, JANE.

THE PALACE *GUARDS* DO SEEM SORELY AT OUR *PERTURBED* COMING!

MADRE DE DIOS! WHAT SORT OF *DEMON* DO THE REBELS SEND AT US *NOW*?

BLAM!
BLAM!
BLAM!

WHATEVER HE IS, FERNANDO-- WE MUST *KILL* HIM BEFORE HE CAN *SLAY* EL PRESIDENTE!

VERILY, IT DOTH SEEM 'TWILL NOT BE *EASY* TO AID THE OPPRESSED *PEOPLE* OF COSTA VERDE!

SPANG
SPWEE!
SPAK!

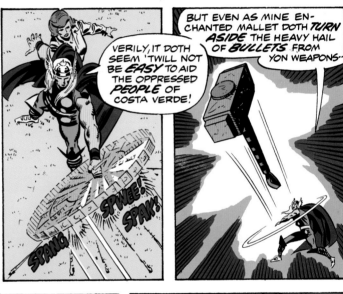

BUT EVEN AS MINE EN- CHANTED MALLET DOTH *TURN ASIDE* THE HEAVY HAIL OF *BULLETS* FROM YON WEAPONS--

"--SO TOO SHALL IT TURN ASIDE THOSE WHO DO *WIELD* THOSE WEAPONS--

SPOOM!

"--UNTIL SUCH TIME AS THEY CAN LEARN TO *REASON* ERE THEY BLINDLY *REACT*!"

YOU CERTAINLY HAVE A WAY OF MAKING YOUR *POINT*, DARLING.

SOMETIMES, MILADY--THERE DOTH BE NO *OTHER* WAY.

NOW *COME*. LET US *INTRODUCE* OURSELVES TO THE *MASTER* OF THIS SORROWFUL MANOR.

THUS, MOMENTS LATER...

WHO *KNOCKED* ON MY DOOR? WHOEVER IT IS, GO *AWAY* BEFORE I... *MADRE DE DIOS!*

WH-WHO ARE *YOU?* WH-WHAT DO YOU *WANT* HERE?

HONORED MORTAL, *THOR,* GOD OF THUNDER, SON OF ODIN, PRINCE OF ASGARD, DEFENDER OF THE REALM ETERNAL, DOTH GIVE THEE *GREETINGS!*

I HAVE COME TO *RID* THY NOBLE COUNTRY OF THE VILLAINOUS *EL LOBO* -- AND THE ALIEN MENACE CALLED *FIRELORD!*

Y-YOU *WHAT?* B-BUT HOW DO I KNOW Y-YOU'RE TELL-ING THE *TRUTH?*

H-HOW DO I KNOW THIS ISN'T JUST ANOTHER OF EL LOBO'S *TRICKS?*

THOR DOTH GIVE THEE HIS MOST *SACRED* WORD, MORTAL -- AND NO MAN MAY ASK FOR *MORE.*

NOW *SPEAK,* MAN! TELL ME WHERE I MIGHT *FIND* THOSE I DO SEEK!

Y-YOU REALLY *DO* WANT TO *HELP* MY BELOVED COSTA VERDE?

THEN *GO,* AMIGO -- WITH MY BLESSINGS!

EL LOBO AND HIS REBELS ARE HIDDEN IN THE *JUNGLE* THAT SURROUNDS THE CAPITAL CITY.

IT IS *THERE* YOU WILL *FIND* HIM... OR *HE* WILL FIND *YOU!*

WHATEVER THE MANNER OF OUR MEETING, MORTAL, I DO *ASSURE* THEE--

--'TIS *EL LOBO* WHO WILL SURELY *REGRET* IT!

NOW, MILADY --LET US *BEGONE!*

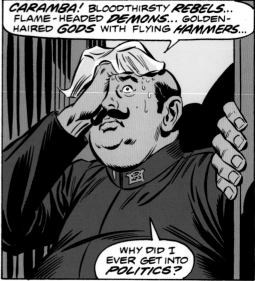

CARAMBA! BLOODTHIRSTY *REBELS...* FLAME-HEADED *DEMONS...* GOLDEN-HAIRED *GODS* WITH FLYING *HAMMERS...*

WHY DID I EVER GET INTO *POLITICS?*

THE JUNGLE AIR IS *HUMID,* HEAVY, THICK ENOUGH TO *CUT*--

--AND FILLED WITH THE *CHATTER* OF ANIMALS, THE *SINGING* OF BIRDS, THE *MONOTONOUS DRONE* OF INSECTS--

--ALL SOUNDS THAT SUDDENLY *CEASE,* AS THE GOD OF THUNDER AND HIS BELOVED JANE FOSTER DROP LIGHTLY INTO THE CENTER OF AN OVERGROWN *CLEARING.*

WE ARE *HERE,* MILADY.

ONE *QUESTION,* DARLING.

EXACTLY WHERE IS *"HERE"*?

DOES IT TRULY MAKE A *DIFFERENCE,* JANE?

'TIS NOT WHERE OUR QUEST DOTH *START* THAT MATTERS--BUT WHERE IT DOTH FIND ITS *ENDING!*

THEN LET'S GET *AT* IT, DARLING.

IT'S STARTING TO GROW *HOT!*

AND IT GROWS HOTTER *STILL* AS THE HOURS WEAR ON--

--UNTIL...

HANG ON A MINUTE, THOR, I'VE GOT A FEW *ADJUSTMENTS* TO MAKE!

MILADY?

I JUST DID *NOT* COME DRESSED FOR TRAIPSING AROUND *DANTE'S INFERNO,* DARLING.

KKRRIIIPP!

MY CLOTHING IS STICKING TO ME LIKE A CLAMMY *SECOND SKIN*--

--SO I FIGURE THE *LESS* OF IT I'M WEARING, THE MORE *COMFORTABLE* I'LL BE!

THERE YOU *ARE!* I MAY NOT EXACTLY BE *SHANNA THE SHE-DEVIL*-- BUT I GUESS I'LL DO!

THEN LET US *CONTINUE,* MILADY. 'TWOULD BE BEST TO FIND OUR *QUARRY* ERE THEY CAN FIND *US!*

UNFORTUNATELY, THE ODINSON'S *ADMONITION* COMES A TRIFLE *TOO LATE!*

FOR SEVERAL MINUTES, A KHAKI-CLAD FORM *FOLLOWS* THESE STRANGE INTRUDERS INTO HIS DOMAIN--

--THEN, AND RACES OFF INTO THE *UNDER-BRUSH.*

WHILE, IN A HIDDEN *ENCAMPMENT* NOT TOO TERRIBLY FAR *AWAY...*

HOW GOES THE *REVOLUTION,* EL LOBO?

BETTER THAN *EXPECTED,* GYPSY-- BUT NOT NEARLY AS WELL AS *PLANNED.*

THE ACCURSED *FEDERALES* DO NOT GIVE GROUND *EASILY!*

BUT THEY CANNOT STAND *AGAINST* US MUCH *CONGER*-- NOT WITH MY BELOVED *FIRELORD* LEADING OUR PATRIOTIC TROOPS INTO *BATTLE!*

SOON WE WILL STAND ON THE VERY *STEPS* OF THE *PRESIDENTIAL PALACE*--

--AND THE OPPRESSOR *ELMIREZ* WILL *GROVEL* AT OUR FEET!

IF HE IS INDEED THE *MONSTER* YOU SAY HE IS, GYPSY--IT IS A FATE HE WELL *DESERVES!*

SWEET GYPSY HAS DONE VERY *WELL.* THE LOCO *ALIEN* IS COMPLETELY UNDER HER *SPELL.*

AS LONG AS FIRELORD BELIEVES THE WITCH *LOVES* HIM, THERE IS *NOTHING* HE WILL NOT *DO* AT HER COMMAND...

...INCLUDING *DELIVERING* COSTA VERDE TO US ON A *STOLEN* SILVER PLATTER!

EL LOBO-- COME *QUICKLY!* WE ARE UNDER *ATTACK!*

WHAT *IS* IT, LUIS? DO THE FEDERALES MARCH ON US *AGAIN?*

NO, MI GENERALE-- THERE ARE ONLY *TWO.* ONE IS JUST A *WOMAN,* BUT THE *OTHER...*

THE OTHER IS MORE LIKE A *GOD* THAN A MAN! H-HE CARRIES A FLYING *HAMMER*--

--AND THE WOMAN, SHE CALLED HIM--*THOR!*

FOR A LITTLE THING LIKE *THIS,* YOU *BOTHER* ME?

LUIS, ARE YOU NOT A *SOLDIER* IN THE ARMY OF THE *REVOLUTION?*

SI, MI GENERALE.

AND ARE YOU NOT MY *SECOND-IN-COMMAND?*

S-SI, MI GENERALE.

THEN GO *DO* WHAT SUCH A MAN IS *SUPPOSED* TO DO!

TAKE SOME *MEN*, ESTUPIDO, AND *KILL* THE TWO INTRUDERS--

--BEFORE I THROW YOU BACK INTO THE *CESSPOOL* WHERE I *FOUND* YOU!

S-S-SI, MI GENERALE!

THOR? WHY DOES THAT NAME SOUND SO *FAMILIAR?* I FEEL I SHOULD *KNOW* THIS THOR, AND YET...

WHY IS THE *PAST* SUCH A *BLUR* TO ME?

DON'T LET IT *BOTHER* YOU, DARLING. THE PAST IS NOT *IMPORTANT!*

ALL THAT MATTERS IS THE *FUTURE*-- THE FUTURE OF *COSTA VERDE!*

AND WITH ME *BESIDE* YOU, I PROMISE YOU, DARLING--

--IT WILL BE A MOST *GLORIOUS* FUTURE INDEED!

WHILE, IN A DARKENED *MEADHALL* ON THE VERY *OUTSKIRTS* OF IMMORTAL *ASGARD*...

I SAY THEE *AGAIN*, GOOD HILDEGARDE-- OUR LIEGE IS NOT *HIMSELF!*

SINCE THE EVIL *IGRON* HATH REPLACED THE WISE *VIZIER* AS THE ALL-FATHER'S *ADVISOR,* LORD ODIN HATH GROWN EVER *ANGRIER,* EVER MORE *CRUEL*--

--AS IF DRIVEN BY SOME *DEMON* DEEP WITHIN!

COULD IT NOT MERELY BE *ANGUISH* O'ER HIS *BANISHMENT* OF THE MOST NOBLE *THOR* THAT DOTH *COLOR* ODIN'S THOUGHTS?

NAY, WOMAN-- 'TIS FAR *MORE,* I TELL THEE!

NE'ER BEFORE HATH THE ALL-FATHER ALLOWED HIS *PERSONAL* GRIEF TO TEMPER HIS ACTIONS AS *LORD* OF THE REALM ETERNAL!

SLY IGRON HATH SOMEHOW *TWISTED* NOBLE ODIN TO HIS *WILL,* AND IF OUR LIEGE CANNOT *FREE* HIMSELF FROM IGRON'S *GRASP*--

SLAM!

--THEN HE MUST BE OUR LIEGE *NO LONGER!*

SO... NOW EVEN BRAVE *BALDER* DOTH SPEAK OF *INSURRECTION*, AY?

SUCH A *DIRTY* OCCUPATION FOR ONE WITH SO *NOBLE* A HEART!

AH, WELL... TO EACH HIS *OWN*, METHINKS.

SOME, LIKE GOOD BALDER, ARE BORN TO BE *HEROES*--AND OTHERS, LIKE *SNAYKAR THE SKULKER*, MUST EARN THEIR KEEP IN *OTHER* WAYS.

I WONDER HOW MUCH SLY *IGRON* WILL *PAY* FOR MY INFORMATION *THIS* TIME?

AND AS THE SITUATION IN ASGARD SLOWLY GROWS HOTTER, LET'S RETURN TO WHERE IT'S ALREADY BROILING...

DARLING, HOW MUCH *LONGER* ARE WE GOING TO KEEP GOING AROUND IN *CIRCLES*?

FORGIVE ME, JANE--I SHOULD HAVE *REALIZED*--!

THOUGH THY *SPIRIT* IS TRULY THAT OF A *GODDESS BORN*, STILL THY *FLESH* IS ALL TOO *MORTAL*.

WE WILL *REST* FOR THE NONCE--UNTIL THOU HAST *REGAINED* THY... *EH?*

SOMETHING DOTH *MOVE* IN YONDER *BUSHES*--!

GET THEE *DOWN*, MILADY-- *SWIFTLY!*

WH-WHAT *IS* IT, DARLING?

IN A *WORD*, BELOVED--

SPLANG

--WE ARE *BESIEGED!*

ONWARD, MI COMPANEROS!

SLAY THOSE WHO WOULD *OPPOSE* US!

BHUD-UD-UD-AH!

VIVA LA REVOLUTION!

IS *MADNESS* A WAY OF *LIFE* IN THIS LAND?

SPAK AK AK AK AK!

ONCE AGAIN, UNTHINKING MORTALS DO SPRAY THE AIR WITH THEIR BELOVED *BULLETS*--

"--AND ONCE AGAIN, THE POWER OF MINE EN-CHANTED URU HAMMER DOTH *RETURN* THE LEADEN PELLETS WHENCE THEY *CAME!*"

SPWEEE SPWEEE

MADRE DE MI! STOP *SHOOTING,* AMIGOS-- BEFORE WE KILL *OURSELVES!*

THEN PUT YOUR RIFLES *ASIDE,* AMIGOS--

--AND LET US TEAR THE GOLDEN-HAIRED ONE *APART* WITH OUR BARE *HANDS!*

FOOLISH MORTALS, HAST THOU NOT YET *LEARNED?*

"*BULLETS...FISTS...*ALL ARE AS *NOTHING* COMPARED TO THE RAGING FURY OF *MJOLNIR!*"

THWAMM!

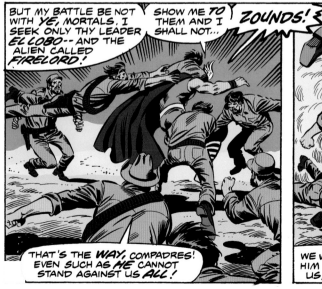

BUT MY BATTLE BE NOT WITH *YE,* MORTALS, I SEEK ONLY THY LEADER *EL LOBO--* AND THE ALIEN CALLED *FIRELORD!*

SHOW ME *TO* THEM AND I SHALL NOT...

ZOUNDS!

THAT'S THE *WAY,* COMPADRES! EVEN SUCH AS *HE* CANNOT STAND AGAINST US *ALL!*

SEE HOW HE *FALLS* BEFORE OUR SHEER *WEIGHT OF NUMBERS?*

WE WILL *CRUSH* HIM BENEATH US, THEN...

91

CARAMBA! IT IS NOT *POSSIBLE*--!

THE GOLDEN-HAIRED ONE *BUCKS* BENEATH US LIKE A HERD OF WILD *STALLIONS!*

WE CANNOT HOLD HIM *DOWN!*

AWAY, MORTALS! AWAY, I SAY YE--

--LEST THOU DOST *SEAL* THINE OWN *FATES!*

FOR 'TIS ODIN'S *ENCHANTMENT* THAT MINE MYSTIC MALLET MUST EVER *RETURN* TO MINE HAND--

--NO MATTER *WHAT* MIGHT STAND IN ITS WAY!

HADST THOU STOOD *BETWEEN* US, MIGHTY MJOLNIR WOULD HAVE CRUSHED YE ALL TO *PULP!*

--A FATE I WOULD WISH ON *NO* MAN!

THEN THROW YOUR WEAPON *DOWN*, AMIGO--

--OR MY PISTOL WILL DO *WORSE* TO YOUR WOMAN THAN YOUR *HAMMER* COULD EVER HAVE DONE TO *US!*

HUH?

WHAMM

IN A PURPLE *PIG'S EYE* YOU WILL, MISTER!

I CAN TAKE CARE OF *MYSELF,* DARLING! YOU DO WHAT YOU *HAVE* TO DO!

HE WILL NOT *LIVE* THAT LONG, CHIQUITA!

I AM *MANUEL*-- AND I WILL *SNAP* THE GRINGO'S SCRAWNY *NECK!*

ENOUGH, MORTAL!

I GROW MOST *TIRED* OF THIS CHILDISH *GAME*--

--BUT THY *COMRADES,* IT DOTH SEEM, HAVE *NOT!*

N-NOOO!

"THEN *CONTINUE* THINE INFANTILE ENTERTAINMENT IF THOU *MUST,* FOOLISH MORTALS--"

PLOW!

"--BUT CONTINUE IT BY *THYSELVES!*"

ENOUGH, BLONDHAIR-- WE KNOW WHEN WE ARE *BEATEN!*

T-TAKE YOUR WOMAN AND *GO!* WE WILL NOT TRY TO *STOP* YOU!

EVEN *WE* ARE NOT THAT *INSANE!*

THEN TELL ME WHERE I WILL *FIND* THOSE I DO *SEEK,* AND WE SHALL *LEAVE* THEE IN...

EH?

IF YOU ARE LOOKING FOR *FIRELORD,* INTRUDER--YOU NEED LOOK NO *FURTHER!*

FOR YOU HAVE *FOUND* HIM!

BE *CAREFUL,* DARLING! THE GOLDEN-HAIRED ONE IS *DANGEROUS!*

SO AM I, MY DEAR GYPSY... *SO AM I!*

FIRELORD, WE HAVE MET *BEFORE...* AS *FRIENDS!** I WOULD HAVE IT THUS *AGAIN!*

TURN *AWAY* FROM THOSE WHO SEEK TO *CONQUER* COSTA VERDE! STAND *BESIDE* ME IN THE NAME OF *FREEDOM!*

* SEEN AS RECENTLY AS *THOR #234.* --LEN.

93

DON'T *LISTEN* TO HIM, FIRELORD! HE ONLY TRIES TO *CONFUSE* YOU-- AS ELMIREZ HAS CONFUSED OUR POOR OPPRESSED *PEOPLE!*

KILL HIM *QUICKLY*, MY DARLING-- BEFORE IT IS *TOO LATE!*

NOT SO LONG AS MY CRIMSON BATTLE CLOAK CAN *SHIELD* ME FROM THINE ANGRY *FLAMES!*

VERILY, I HAD HOPED TO *TURN* THEE FROM THE PATH OF *MADNESS,* FIERY ONE--

SPOOM!

FOR A MOMENT, I THOUGHT... BUT *NO!* AS ALWAYS, GYPSY-- YOU ARE *RIGHT!*

FOR THE GLORY OF *COSTA VERDE,* THE ONE CALLED *THOR* MUST--*DIE!*

--BUT IF *BATTLE* THOU DOST *WANT*-- --THEN *BATTLE* THOU SHALT *HAVE!*

THEN YOUR DEATH IS *ASSURED,* FOOL-- --FOR NOTHING THAT LIVES CAN *STAND* BEFORE THE COSMIC ENERGY OF MY *FIRESTAFF!*

NOR IS THE POWER OF ENCHANTED *MJOLNIR* SOMETHING TO BE LIGHTLY *RECKONED* WITH, ALIEN!

BUT OUR POWERS ARE TOO EVENLY *MATCHED!*

A *STALEMATE* SUCH AS THIS COULD RAGE FOR *HOURS*--

--LEST *ONE* OF US DOTH TAKE THE *INITIATIVE*-- --AND DOTH SWIFTLY *STRIKE!*

BY ALL THE STARS OF SPACE!

YOU MUST BE *MAD!*

NAY, FIRELORD-- NOT *MAD!*

I--AM-- *ENRAGED!*

PWAM!

WHEN I SEE SUCH AS *THEE,* WHO ONCE SOARED THRU SPACE AS FAITHFUL *HERALD* TO THE WORLD-DEVOURING *GALACTUS,** REDUCED TO *USURPING* A PITIFUL LITTLE *NATION* SUCH AS THIS--

* UNTIL GOLDI-LOCKS AND HERCULES *RELEASED* HIM BACK IN *THOR #228.--*L.

--THE RIGHTEOUS ANGER OF THE GOD OF THUNDER DOTH KNOW NO *BOUNDS!*

SILENCE, THOR-- I WILL HEAR *NO MORE!*

BRAK

WHY DO YOU *TORMENT* ME SO WITH THINGS THAT HAVE NO *MEANING* TO ME?

DOST THOU NOW SEEK TO *DENY* THY PAST, FIRELORD?

HAST THOU SUNK SO *LOW?*

I *HAVE* NO PAST, THUNDER GOD-- NO *MEMORIES!*

WHAK!

I HAVE ONLY THE *LOVE* OF THE WOMAN CALLED *GYPSY*--

--AND I *NEED* NOTHING *ELSE!*

CHOOM! CHOOM! CHOOM!

THEN THE *ANSWER* DOTH AT LAST BECOME *CLEAR!*

'TIS NOT OF THINE OWN *WILL* THAT THOU DOST SEEK TO *CONQUER* COSTA VERDE!

METHINKS THE WOMAN CALLED *GYPSY* HATH SOMEHOW *BEWITCHED* THEE, FIERY ONE--

--AND BY THE *BEARD* OF MY *FATHER*, I SHALL *FREE* THEE FROM HER *ENCHANTMENT*--

CHOK!

--OR *PERISH* IN THE *TRYING!*

THWAM!

MADRE DE DIOS! IT CANNOT *BE*--! THE *GOLDEN-HAIRED* ONE IS *DEFEATING* THE *FIRELORD!* BUT *HOW*--?

PERHAPS THE *FLAMING* ONE CANNOT FULLY CONTROL HIS *POWERS* WHILE UNDER YOUR *SPELL!*

BUT *WITHOUT* MY *SPELL*, FIRE-LORD WILL NOT *FOLLOW* US!

THEN THERE IS NOTHING WE CAN *DO*, WOMAN-- BUT *PRAY!*

NO--WE'RE NOT FINISHED *YET!* THE GOLDEN-HAIR *TOO* HAS A *WEAKNESS*-- --THE *WOMAN!*

SEIZE *HER*-- AND WE SEIZE THE *ADVANTAGE!*

YOU ARE A *COLD* ONE, *GYPSY*-- BUT YOU ARE *RIGHT!*

MAKE ONE *MOVE*, WOMAN--AND YOU *DIE!*

WHAT--?!?

QUICKLY, *EL LOBO*-- BEFORE THE *GOLDEN-HAIR* CAN STRIKE THE *FINAL BLOW!*

ORDER THE *BATTLE* TO...

STOP, GOLDEN-HAIR-- IF YOU VALUE YOUR WOMAN'S LIFE!

WHAT--?!?

DROP YOUR HAMMER, AMIGO-- NOW!

OR I ASSURE YOU YOUR WOMAN WILL REGRET IT!

DARLING, DON'T LISTEN--!

SHE IS BRAVE, YOUR LOVER-- BUT FOOLISH!

LAY DOWN YOUR WEAPON, AS EL LOBO SAYS-- AND LET US TALK. THERE IS MUCH ABOUT US YOU DO NOT UNDERSTAND!

I KNOW ALL I HAVE NEED TO KNOW, GYPSY!

GOLDEN-HAIR, YOU KNOW NOTHING AT ALL!

THE ARMY OF THE REVOLUTION IS THE ONLY HOPE FOR OUR BELOVED COSTA VERDE!

WE WHO FIGHT THE OPPRESSOR ELMIREZ FIGHT FOR THE FREE- DOM OF THE MASSES--

--AND THOSE WHO FIGHT BESIDE US ARE BLESSED IN THE EYES OF THE GODS!

"WILL YOU FIGHT BESIDE US, GOLDEN-HAIR?"

"WILL YOU WIELD YOUR HAMMER IN THE NAME OF LIBERTY?"

DARLING, DON'T LISTEN TO HER! IT'S A TRICK!

SHE'S TRYING TO BEWITCH YOU-- JUST LIKE SHE DID FIRELORD!

YOU'RE TOO LATE, WOMAN! THE DEED IS DONE!

FROM THIS MOMENT ON, THE ONE CALLED THOR CAN HEAR ONLY ME--

--AND WITH HE AND THE FIRELORD BOTH UNDER MY CONTROL--

--THERE IS NOTHING THAT CAN STOP US NOW!

NEXT ISSUE: A RAVAGED LAND BATTLES FOR ITS LIFE AGAINST THE WORLD- SHAKING POWER OF...

"THE FLAME AND THE HAMMER!"

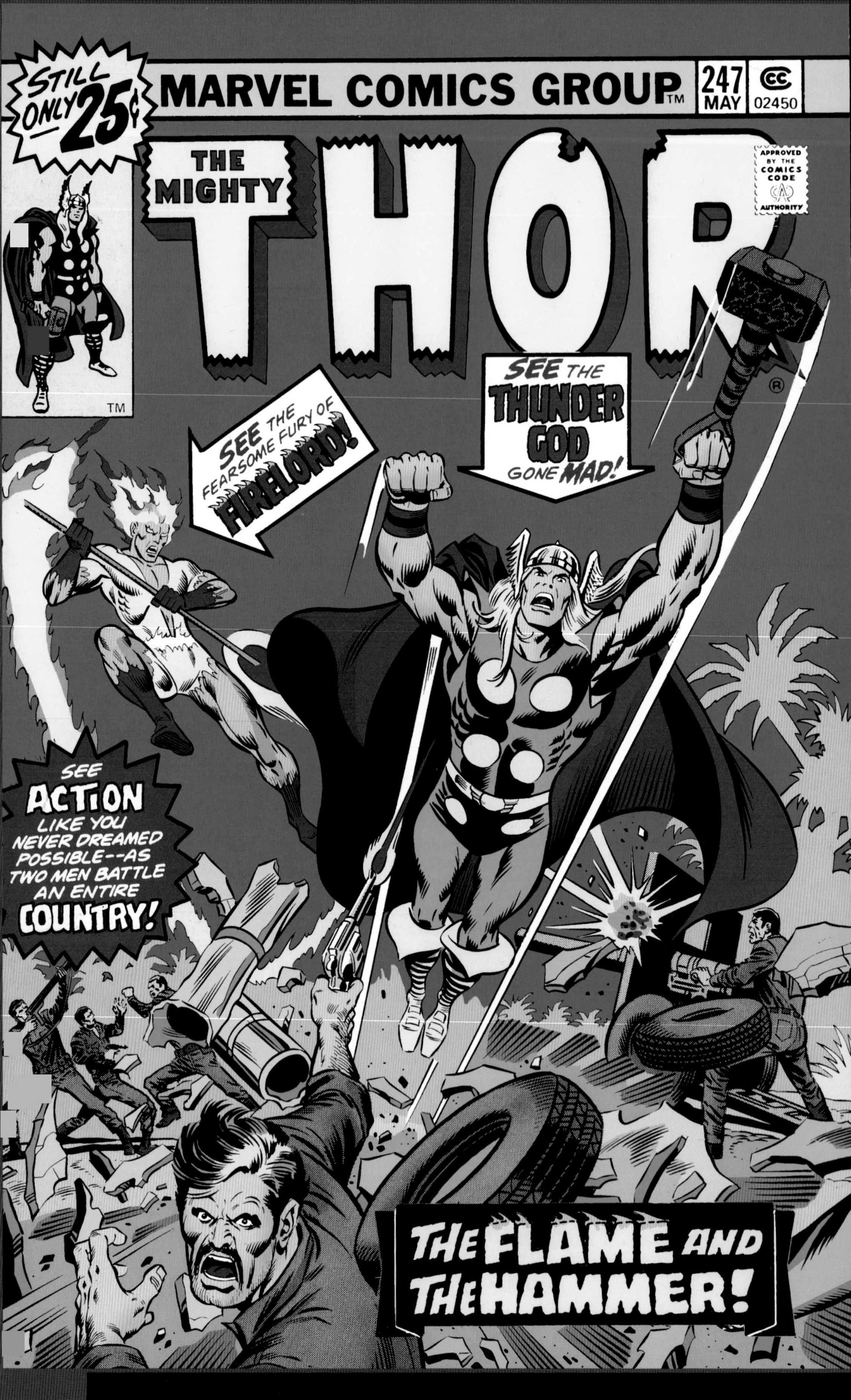
STILL ONLY 25¢
MARVEL COMICS GROUP™
247 MAY
CC 02450
APPROVED BY THE COMICS CODE AUTHORITY
THE MIGHTY THOR®
TM
SEE THE FEARSOME FURY OF FIRELORD!
SEE THE THUNDER GOD GONE MAD!
SEE ACTION LIKE YOU NEVER DREAMED POSSIBLE--AS TWO MEN BATTLE AN ENTIRE COUNTRY!
THE FLAME AND THE HAMMER!

When lame Dr. DONALD BLAKE strikes his wooden walking stick upon the ground, it becomes the mystic mallet MJOLNIR—and Blake is transformed into the Norse God of Thunder, Master of the Storm and the Lightning, Heir to the Throne of Immortal Asgard...

STAN LEE PRESENTS: THE MIGHTY THOR! ™

JV255

| LEN WEIN | JOHN BUSCEMA & JOE SINNOTT | G. WEIN | J. ROSEN | MARV WOLFMAN |
| WRITER·EDITOR | ILLUSTRATORS | COLORIST | LETTERER | TOKEN GRINGO |

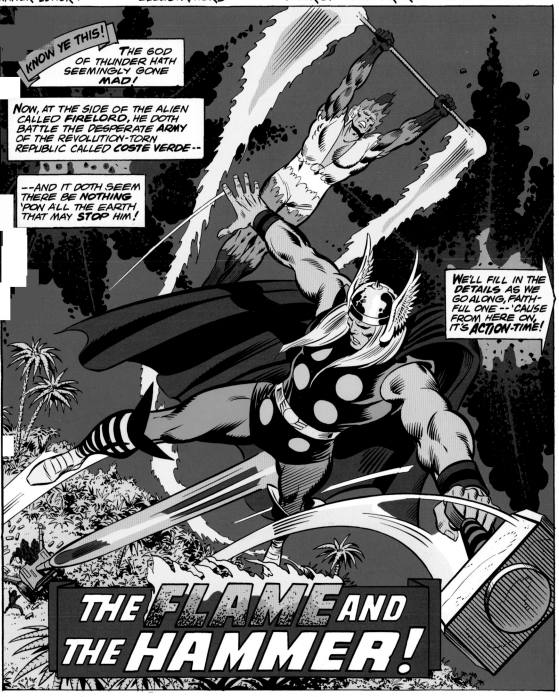

KNOW YE THIS!

THE GOD OF THUNDER HATH SEEMINGLY GONE MAD!

NOW, AT THE SIDE OF THE ALIEN CALLED FIRELORD, HE DOTH BATTLE THE DESPERATE ARMY OF THE REVOLUTION-TORN REPUBLIC CALLED COSTE VERDE--

--AND IT DOTH SEEM THERE BE NOTHING 'PON ALL THE EARTH THAT MAY STOP HIM!

WE'LL FILL IN THE DETAILS AS WE GO ALONG, FAITH-FUL ONE--'CAUSE FROM HERE ON, IT'S ACTION-TIME!

THE FLAME AND THE HAMMER!

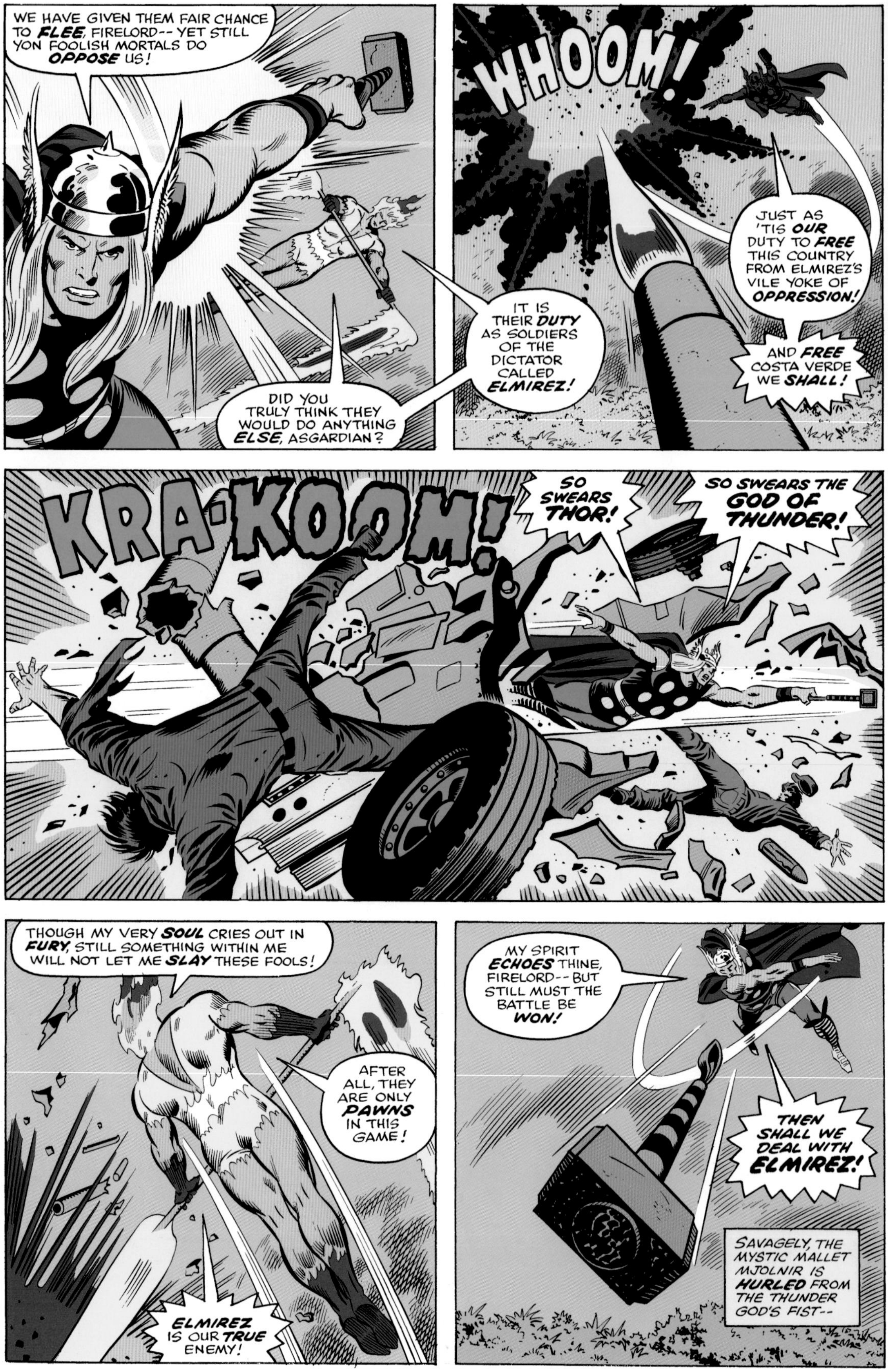

WE HAVE GIVEN THEM FAIR CHANCE TO FLEE, FIRELORD-- YET STILL YON FOOLISH MORTALS DO OPPOSE US!
DID YOU TRULY THINK THEY WOULD DO ANYTHING ELSE, ASGARDIAN?
IT IS THEIR DUTY AS SOLDIERS OF THE DICTATOR CALLED ELMIREZ!
WHOOM!
JUST AS 'TIS OUR DUTY TO FREE THIS COUNTRY FROM ELMIREZ'S VILE YOKE OF OPPRESSION!
AND FREE COSTA VERDE WE SHALL!
KRA-KOOM!
SO SWEARS THOR!
SO SWEARS THE GOD OF THUNDER!
THOUGH MY VERY SOUL CRIES OUT IN FURY, STILL SOMETHING WITHIN ME WILL NOT LET ME SLAY THESE FOOLS!
AFTER ALL, THEY ARE ONLY PAWNS IN THIS GAME!
ELMIREZ IS OUR TRUE ENEMY!
MY SPIRIT ECHOES THINE, FIRELORD-- BUT STILL MUST THE BATTLE BE WON!
THEN SHALL WE DEAL WITH ELMIREZ!
SAVAGELY, THE MYSTIC MALLET MJOLNIR IS HURLED FROM THE THUNDER GOD'S FIST--

--AND WITHOUT HIS ENCHANTED WEAPON TO SUPPORT HIS *FLIGHT*, THE EXILED PRINCE OF ASGARD SWIFTLY *PLUMMETS*--

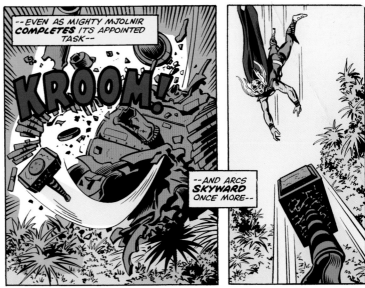

--EVEN AS MIGHTY MJOLNIR *COMPLETES* ITS APPOINTED TASK--

KROOM!

--AND ARCS *SKYWARD* ONCE MORE--

--RETURNING, AS EVER IT *MUST*, TO ITS MASTER'S *HAND!*

WITH AN ALMOST-ABNORMAL *RESOLVE*, THE THUNDER GOD CONTINUES HIS AIRBORNE *ASSAULT*--

-- EVEN AS THE FEARSOME *FIRELORD* PUTS THE FEW REMAINING COSTA VERDEAN SOLDIERS TO *ROUT!*

FLEE, AMIGOS--*FLEE!* NOTHING HUMAN CAN STAND AGAINST MONSTERS SUCH AS *THESE!*

CHOOM!

THE ARMY IS IN FULL *RETREAT*, SWEET GYPSY! YOUR WITLESS *PAWNS* HAVE SERVED US VERY *WELL* INDEED--

--EVEN *BETTER* THAN EXPECTED!

SUCH IS THE *SPELL* I HAVE WOVEN ABOUT THEM THAT THEY ACTUALLY *BELIEVE* THAT POOR, FAT, BENEVOLENT FOOL *ELMIREZ* IS THE CRUEL *DICTATOR* I'VE TOLD THEM HE IS--

--AND SO LONG AS THEY *BELIEVE* ME, THEY WILL DO WHAT- EVER I *COMMAND*, EL LOBO!

THEN SUMMON THEM *BACK*, GYPSY, THEY'VE INFLICTED *DAMAGE* ENOUGH FOR ONE DAY!

WHAT DO YOU THINK OF YOUR GOLDEN-HAIRED HERO *NOW*, WOMAN? NOT A VERY *PRETTY* SIGHT TO SEE HIM *ACT* THIS WAY, IS IT?

BUT THAT IS THE WAY HE *WILL* ACT, SO LONG AS IT SERVES OUR *PURPOSES!*

"WITH THE POWER OF BOTH *THOR* AND THE *FIRELORD* BESIDE US, WE SHALL STAND ON THE STEPS OF THE *PRESIDENTIAL PALACE* BY THIS TIME *TOMORROW!*"

THEN IF I'M GOING TO *FREE* THOR FROM THAT *GYPSY WITCH'S* *SPELL*, IT HAS TO BE-- *TONIGHT!*

AND AS THE CAPTIVE *JANE FOSTER* PLOTS HER NEXT *MOVE*--

--PLOTTING OF A WHOLLY *DIFFERENT* SORT IS COMING TO A HEAD IN THE *ROYAL THRONE ROOM* OF IMMORTAL *ASGARD!*

THOU DIDST *SUMMON* ME, SIRE?

AYE, BRAVE BALDER-- THOU HAST LEAVE TO APPROACH THE *PRESENCE!*

THY LIEGE HATH BUSINESS MOST *GRIM* TO DISCUSS WITH THEE.

I DO NOT *UNDERSTAND*, MILORD.

'TIS *SIMPLE*, BALDER, THE NOBLE *IGRON*, MY MOST TRUSTED *ADVISOR*, HATH CHARGED THEE WITH BLACK *TREASON*-- WITH PLOTTING TO *OVERTHROW* THE THRONE OF THE *REALM ETERNAL!*

HOW DOST THOU *PLEAD* TO THESE ACCUSATIONS, BALDER?

MY SWORD, MY LIFE, MY VERY *SOUL* ARE PLEDGED TO *SERVE* IMMORTAL ASGARD-- AND HE WHO IS TRULY THE THE GOLDEN REALM *INCARNATE*--

--BUT STILL DO I MOST HUMBLY FEEL THAT THOU HAST BEEN LED TERRIBLY *ASTRAY*, MOST HIGH.

THOUGH THOU DOST CALL HIM THINE *ADVISOR,* IGNOBLE IGRON DOTH SERVE *NO* CAUSE SAVE HIS *OWN!*

METHINKS-- AS DO MANY *OTHERS*-- THE SLY ONE HATH TURNED THEE *AGAINST* THINE OWN BEST JUDGMENT!

THUS IF MY WORDS HAVE BEEN IN DEFIANCE OF *ANY-ONE,* MILORD --'TIS OF *IGRON,* NOT OF *THEE!*

HELA TAKE HIM, HE KNOWS *TOO MUCH!*

WE'D BEST *IMPRISON* HIM UNTIL WE CAN FORCE HIM TO TELL US *WHO* STANDS BEHIND HIM IN *REBELLION!*

AYE, IGRON-- THOU DOST VOICE MINE *OWN* THOUGHTS *EXACTLY!*

THUS DO I FIND THE ONCE-BRAVE BALDER *GUILTY* AS CHARGED--

-- AND ORDER HIM *CHAINED* IN THE *DUNGEONS* BELOW THE PALACE ROYAL, THERE TO AWAIT MY *JUSTICE!*

I HAVE *SPOKEN!!*

MILORD, THOU HAST TRULY TAKEN LEAVE OF THY *SENSES*--

-- AND EVEN THE LOYAL *BALDER* IS NOT BOUND TO *OBEY* THE RAVINGS OF A *MADMAN!*

THOU DOST *DARE* TO CALL THE ALL-FATHER *MAD,* CHURL?

THEN THOU SHALT NOT *LIVE* TO FACE LORD ODIN'S *JUSTICE,* BALDER!

THOU SHALT *PERISH* WHERE THOU DOST *STAND!*

THEN *HAVE AT THEE,* WARRIORS OF ASGARD!

SPANG!

CHANG!

THOU SHALT FIND THE *BLOOD* OF BALDER THE BRAVE FAR TOO *PRECIOUS* FOR THE *TAKING!*

BACK, I SAY YE-- *BACK!*

THE LAST VOICE OF *SANITY* IN THE REALM ETERNAL WILL NOT BE EASILY *STILLED!*

BUT I AM GREATLY *OUT-NUMBERED* --AND IF I BE *SLAIN,* THEN *WHO* SHALL REMAIN TO TELL THE MIGHTY *THOR* OF HIS FATHER'S *AFFLICTION?*

CURSE THE FICKLE FATES!

THOUGH NE'ER BEFORE HATH BALDER TURNED AND *FLED* IN THE FACE OF *BATTLE*-- --NOW, FOR THE SAKE OF THE REALM ETERNAL-- I *MUST!*

SWIFTLY, ERE THE *ALARM* CAN BE SPREAD O'ER ALL THE GOLDEN REALM, MUST I HIE ME TO *MIDGARD*-- --THERE TO SUMMON HOME THE *THUNDER GOD* AND HIS THREE *COMPANIONS!*

BUT WHEN WE *RETURN*, I FEAR *SON* MUST BATTLE *FATHER*-- MAYHAP EVEN UNTO *DEATH!*

WHILE, ON THE *AFOREMENTIONED MIDGARD* (COMMONLY REFERRED TO AS *EARTH*)...

BY ODIN, WHAT DOTH DISTRACT THEE *NOW*, VAST VOLSTAGG?

A *PUZZLEMENT* MOST PASSING *STRANGE*, FRIEND FANDRAL.

STILL DO I SEEK TO LEARN *HOW* MERE MORTALS DO *TRAIN* THE ODDLY-GARBED CREATURES WHO *PERFORM* WITHIN YON VIEWING BOX!

COULD I BUT *DEDUCE* THEIR *SECRET*, I WOULD...

PRITHEE, VAST ONE-- *CONTAIN* THINE ALL-CONSUMING CURIOSITY! THE CITY OF NEW YORK DOTH AWAIT OUR *PLEASURE*--AND I FOR ONE WOULD BE *ON* WITH IT!

WHAT--? UNHAND ME, I SAY! THE LION OF ASGARD WILL *NOT* BE SO SHABBILY *TREATED!*

RELEASE ME SWIFTLY--OR FACE VOLSTAGG'S THUNDEROUS *WRATH!*

NEWS BULLETIN
NEWS BULLETIN

PROTESTING LOUDLY AS ONLY *HE* CAN, THE VOLUMINOUS ONE IS LED AWAY BY HIS FRIENDS, HIS STENTORIAN TONES *SMOTHERING* THE VOICE OF THE TELEVISION *NEWSCASTER*--

--WHICH IS, IN ITS WAY, QUITE A *SHAME!*

ABC

...AN UNEXPECTED *TURN* OF *EVENTS* OCCURRED TODAY IN BATTLE-RAVAGED *COSTA VERDE*...

THE HAMMER-WIELDING *THOR*, SUPPOSED INCARNATION OF THE NORSE *THUNDER GOD*, HAS JOINED THE MYSTERIOUS *FIRELORD* AT THE VANGUARD OF THE REVOLUTIONARY FORCES...

...AND IT APPEARS COSTA VERDE'S HOURS OF FREEDOM ARE *NUMBERED!*

AND THAT SEEMS AS **ARTFUL** A SEGÜE AS ANY TO RETURN US TO THE **JUNGLES** OF COSTA VERDE--

--AND THE HIDDEN ENCAMPMENT OF THE REBEL LEADER **EL LOBO!**

THE FORCES OF EL MIREZ ARE ON THE VERGE OF **DEFEAT**, MY FRIENDS!

OUR TWO-PRONGED **ATTACK** TOMORROW ON THE **CAPITAL CITY** ITSELF SHOULD CRUSH THEIR SPIRIT **COMPLETELY!**

NOW GATHER **AROUND** ME AS I EXPLAIN OUR **BATTLE PLAN**...

AND SINCE **WE** ARE NOT PERMITTED TO SIT IN ON SUCH A SECRET MEETING, WE MIGHT AS WELL TURN OUR ATTENTION TO A SMALL **TENT** ON THE VERY **EDGE** OF THE CAMP--

--WHERE A DESPERATE JANE FOSTER IS PREPARING TO INITIATE A LITTLE **MILITARY ACTION** OF HER OWN...

THAT FAT PIG **MIGUEL** IS STILL **GUARDING** MY DOOR--

--SO IF I'M GOING TO **RESCUE** MY DARLING, I'LL HAVE TO GET PAST **HIM** FIRST!

AND CONSIDERING THE WAY HE'S BEEN **EYEING** ME ALL DAY, THAT SHOULDN'T BE **DIFFICULT!**

ER--MIGUEL? C-COULD YOU COME **HERE** FOR A MINUTE?

SI, SEÑORITA,

IS THERE SOMETHING MIGUEL CAN--AH-- **DO** FOR YOU, CHIQUITA?

IT MUST BE REALLY **UNCOMFORTABLE** OUT THERE, MIGUEL.

SI, CHIQUITA-- IT **IS!**

WELL, SINCE YOU HAVE TO GUARD ME **ANYWAY,** I THOUGHT IT MIGHT BE MORE-- AH-- **PLEASANT** IF YOU GUARDED ME IN **HERE!**

KNOW WHAT I **MEAN**, HANDSOME?

SI, CHIQUITA! MIGUEL IS NO **FOOL!**

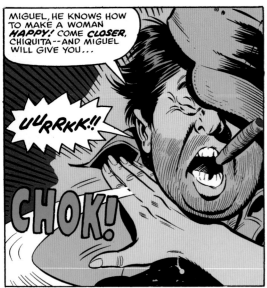

MIGUEL, HE KNOWS HOW TO MAKE A WOMAN **HAPPY**! COME **CLOSER**, CHIQUITA--AND MIGUEL WILL GIVE YOU...

UURRKK!!

CHOK!

UGLY, ALL **YOU** COULD GIVE ME IS AN **UPSET STOMACH**!

BUT IF YOU WANT TO MAKE ME **HAPPY**, YOU CAN JUST **LIE DOWN**--

--AND **STAY THERE**!

THRAK!

UUNNGH!

LARDBELLY IS **OUT** FOR THE COUNT--WHICH MEANS HE **WON'T** BE NEEDING HIS **MACHINE GUN** FOR A WHILE!

BUT **I** CAN MAKE **USE** OF IT-- **GOOD** USE!

...THEN, AFTER FIRELORD'S MEN HAVE **TAKEN** THE NORTH GATE, **THOR** WILL...

MADRE DE DIOS!

THOR ISN'T DOING **ANYTHING** FOR YOU, LOBO-- **NOT EVER AGAIN**!

WHO--?!?

BHUD-UD-UD-UD-UD-AH!

YOU GET THREE **GUESSES**, SISTER!

NOW NONE OF YOU MAKE A **MOVE**--

--OR MY **NEXT** BURST WILL BE ABOUT THREE FEET **HIGHER**!

EASY, MUCHACHO--WE WANT NO **TROUBLE** WITH YOU!

WHY DON'T YOU PUT THE **GUN** DOWN--

--AND LET US **TALK** ABOUT THIS LIKE **CIVILIZED PEOPLE**?

THE WOMAN DID NOT **SEE** ME, HIDING HERE IN THE **BUSHES**--BUT EL LOBO **DID**!

HE IS TALKING TO **DISTRACT** HER--UNTIL I CAN **ACT**!

THUS A MOMENT **LONGER**--UNTIL MY AIM IS **CERTAIN**, THEN...

AARRGGHH!!

B-DOW!

CARAMBA! THAT *WOMAN,* SHE HAS EYES LIKE A *CAT!*

I WARNED YOU ANIMALS *ONCE!*

I WON'T WARN YOU *AGAIN!*

I SWEAR TO GOD I'LL *SHOOT* THE NEXT ONE OF YOU WHO *MOVES!*

DO YOU *UNDERSTAND* ME? *DO* YOU?

SI, JANE FOSTER-- WE *UNDERSTAND.*

NOW WHAT DO YOU *WANT* FROM US?

I'D HAVE THOUGHT THE ANSWER TO *THAT* WOULD BE *OBVIOUS!*

I WANT *THOR!*

I WANT MY *DARLING* BACK-- *FREE* OF GYPSY'S *SPELL!*

AND IF GYPSY REFUSES TO *RELEASE* HIM?

WHY DON'T YOU LET HER MAKE THAT DECISION *HERSELF?*

IF I HAVE TO, I'LL *FIGHT* HER TO REGAIN THE MAN I *LOVE!*

FIGHT *YOU,* LITTLE GIRL? DON'T MAKE ME *LAUGH!*

I WOULD NOT EVEN SOIL MY *HANDS* ON YOU!

YOU HAVE BEEN *CHALLENGED,* GYPSY! IF I WERE *YOU,* I WOULD NOT *BACK DOWN!*

IT WOULD NOT DO YOU GOOD TO *LOSE FACE* IN THE EYES OF MY *MEN!*

THEN I WILL *FIGHT* HER, ACCORDING TO THE *ANCIENT RULES--*

--AND I WILL *TEAR HER APART,* AS THE *WOLF* DEVOURS THE *LAMB!*

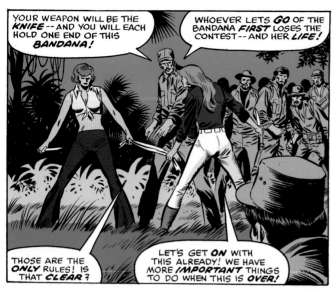

YOUR WEAPON WILL BE THE *KNIFE*-- AND YOU WILL EACH HOLD ONE END OF THIS *BANDANA!*

WHOEVER LETS *GO* OF THE BANDANA *FIRST* LOSES THE CONTEST-- AND HER *LIFE!*

THOSE ARE THE *ONLY* RULES! IS THAT *CLEAR*?

LET'S GET *ON* WITH THIS ALREADY! WE HAVE MORE *IMPORTANT* THINGS TO DO WHEN THIS IS *OVER!*

THEN SWIFTLY-- *LET THE BATTLE BEGIN!*

AND JUST AS SWIFTLY WILL IT BE *ENDED!*

WITH ANIMAL FEROCITY, THE TWO WOMEN *CLASH*, THE CLANGOR OF THEIR SLASHING BLADES DROWNED OUT BY THE BOISTEROUS *SHOUTING* OF THE REBELS WHO SURROUND THEM.

JANE FOSTER MOVES WITH AN ALMOST-*FELINE* GRACE, FAR MORE LIKE THE *WARRIOR-GODDESS* WHOSE SPIRIT GIVES HER LIFE THAN LIKE THE FRAIL, FRIGHTENED *NURSE* WHO ONCE DARED TO LOVE A *GOD*--

--WHILE THE *GOD* HIMSELF SITS SILENTLY ON THE SIDE-LINES, HIS FACE DEVOID OF *EXPRESSION*, HIS EYES BETRAYING NO HINT OF *EMOTION.*

THEN, SAVAGELY, THE RAZOR-EDGED *WEAPON* OF THE FEMALE REVOLUTIONARY SLICES AN *ARC* THROUGH THE AIR ABOVE JANE FOSTER'S HEAD--

THIS IS *IT*-- THE OPENING I'VE BEEN *WAITING* FOR--!

--AND WITH A SUDDEN-VIOLENT *SWEEP* OF JANE'S LITHELY-MUSCLED *LEG*--

--THE WOMAN CALLED **GYPSY** TOPPLES TO THE MOSS-GREEN **EARTH**--

NO-- YOU **TRIPPED** ME--!

--AND THE BATTLE IS **OVER!**

THE RULES SAID **NO HOLDS BARRED,** SISTER!

NOW EITHER YOU **SURRENDER** AND RELEASE THOR FROM YOUR **SPELL**--

--OR I WILL GLADLY **SLIT** YOUR SLIMY **THROAT!**

NO--I WILL NOT BE **HUMILIATED** LIKE THIS!

AMIGOS, ARE YOU **MEN**-- OR **DOGS?**

KILL THIS WOMAN QUICKLY-- OR THE REVOLUTION IS **LOST!**

YOUR TONE IS THAT OF A FRIGHTENED **CHILD,** GYPSY-- BUT YOUR WORDS ARE **TRUE!**

WITHOUT THOR AND THE FIRELORD BESIDE US, WE CANNOT HOPE TO **OVERTHROW** ELMIREZ--

--AND FOR THAT REASON ALONE-- **JANE FOSTER MUST DIE!**

IMPASSIVELY, THE GOD OF THUNDER WATCHES THE REBEL'S FINGER **TIGHTEN** UPON THE TRIGGER--

--THEN, SUDDENLY, HIS BROW IS **CREASED** BY THE SLIGHTEST FURROW OF **DOUBT.**

DESPITE SWEET GYPSY'S WORDS, THERE IS A **REASON** THIS WOMAN SHOULD NOT **DIE**--

--IF ONLY HE COULD **REMEMBER** WHAT IT IS.

THEN, SUDDENLY...

NAY!

NO LONGER WILL THOR SIT IDLY BY, AS ANOTHER'S MINDLESS *SLAVE!*

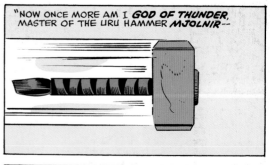

"NOW ONCE MORE AM I *GOD OF THUNDER,* MASTER OF THE URU HAMMER *MJOLNIR—*

CHOOM!

"—AND *WOE* BE UNTO ANYONE WHO DARES *THREATEN* THOR'S TRULY BELOVED!"

NO! PUT YOUR HAMMER *DOWN,* THOR!

OBEY ME, CURSE YOUR EYES— *OBEY* ME!!

MADRE DE DIOS! I-IT'S NOT *POSSIBLE—!* THE THUNDER GOD HAS *BROKEN* MY SPELL! BUT NOTHING THAT LIVES CAN *DEFY* THE POWER OF MY *MIND-JEWEL!*

SO *THAT'S* HOW YOU DO IT, HEY?

THIS LITTLE *BAUBLE* YOU'RE WEARING IS *RIGGED!*

NO—DON'T *TOUCH* IT! LEAVE IT *ALONE!*

NOT A *CHANCE,* SISTER!

I WANT TO SEE HOW YOU TWIST MEN AROUND YOUR LITTLE FINGER *WITHOUT* USING THIS FANCY *JUNK-JEWELRY* OF YOURS!

110

POR DIOS--**NO!** SINCE IT FELL FROM THE SKIES **CENTURIES** AGO, THAT GEM HAS BEEN IN MY **FAMILY!**

IT BELONGED TO MY **MOTHER**, AND **HER** MOTHER **BEFORE** HER--!

FIRELORD, YOU MUST **SAVE** IT-- BEFORE IT IS **TOO LATE!**

AS YOU **WISH**, GYPSY.

THE FLAMES OF THIS **CAMPFIRE** ARE AS **NOTHING** TO ONE WHO HAS SOARED THRU THE VERY **HEARTS** OF BLAZING **SUNS!**

THERE! YOUR PRECIOUS GEM IS **SAFE!**

THEN **GIVE** IT TO ME, YOU FOOL--**QUICKLY!**

THERE IS NO TIME TO **WASTE!**

GIVE IT TO ME, DO YOU **HEAR** ME?

GIVE IT TO ME!!

NO.

KKRRJUNNCHH!

WITHOUT THE POWER OF YOUR GEM TO **BLIND** ME, WOMAN, I HAVE JUST SEEN YOU FOR THE FIRST TIME AS YOU TRULY **ARE**--

--AND I DO NOT **LIKE** WHAT I SEE!

THEN... ALL IS **LOST!**

THE WOMAN HAS **FAILED**, MI AMIGOS! NOW IT IS ALL UP TO **US!**

SWIFTLY-- BEFORE THOR AND THE FIRELORD CAN FULLY **REGAIN** THEIR SENSES-- **ATTACK THEM!!**

KILL THEM BOTH!!

GET THEE **BEHIND** ME, MILADY! THOU HAST **DONE** THY SHARE!

NOW LET THE MIGHT OF MINE MYSTIC **MALLET** DEAL WITH YON MORTALS' FEEBLE **FIREARMS**!

SPAK AK AK AK AK

BUT IT APPEARS THEY ARE USING **MORE** THAN SIMPLE **HAND WEAPONS**, ASGARDIAN!

THEY'RE ATTACKING US WITH THE VERY **WAR MACHINES** WE HELPED THEM **CAPTURE** FROM ELMIREZ!

SLAGG!

BUT THE **JUGGERNAUT** HAS NOT BEEN BUILT THAT CAN WITHSTAND THE COSMIC FURY OF MY **FIRESTAFF**!

KEEP **FIRING**, ESTUPIDOS!

CUT THEM **DOWN** -- OR THE REVOLUTION IS **LOST**!

VOOMP!

LAY DOWN THINE **ARMS**, CHURLS, ERE I MUST...

AARRGGH!!

BWHOOM!

A TRIUMPHANT **SHOUT** RISES FROM THE REBEL RANKS WHEN THE SMOKE AT LAST **CLEARS**, TO REVEAL THE THUNDER GOD SPRAWLED **UNMOVING** IN THE DIRT--

--BUT IT IS A CHEER THAT **CATCHES** IN THEIR THROATS, WHEN THE GOLDEN-MANED HEAD **LIFTS** GRIMLY FROM THE RUBBLE--

--FIERCE **DETERMINA- TION** FAIRLY BLAZING IN SKY-BLUE **EYES**!

AGAIN, FOOLS-- BEFORE THE BLONDHAIR GETS TO HIS *FEET!*

SHOOT HIM! *SHOOT* HIM!!

WHUMP!

FOUL MORTAL, THOR DOTH SAY THEE... *NAY!*

NEVER AGAIN SHALT THOU BRING THE *THUNDER GOD* TO HIS *KNEES--*

--UNLESS THOU DOST INTEND TO BEAT HIM DOWN WITH *SCRAP!*

SKRAKKT!

DESPITE YOUR FANCY *CLOTHING,* YOUR STRANGE MANNER OF *SPEECH,* YOUR ACCURSED *HAMMER,* YOU ARE STILL ONLY *ONE* MAN AGAINST *MANY,* BLONDHAIR--

--AND, EVENTUALLY, OUR SHEER FORCE OF NUMBERS MUST *PREVAIL!*

NAY, EL LOBO-- 'TIS *THERE* THAT THOU ART *WRONG!*

FOR *THOR* IS NOT A *MAN* AT ALL--

--BUT THE IMMORTAL *GOD OF THUNDER--*

--*MASTER* OF THE ENCHANTED HAMMER *MJOLNIR--*

--*RULER* OF THE *WIND* AND THE RAGING *STORM--*

"--AND *NAUGHT* THAT LIVES MAY *DEFY* THE ODINSON'S *POWER--*

"--OR THE *WHIRLWIND* THAT IS *HIS* TO COMMAND!"

THOU WOULDST DO WELL TO **DWELL** ON THY MISTAKES, EL LOBO--

--WHEN THOU DOST FINALLY **REGAIN** THY SENSES!

OH, DARLING-- I WAS SO **WORRIED.** Y-YOU'RE **ALL RIGHT** NOW, AREN'T YOU?

WE ARE **BOTH** ALL RIGHT, JANE FOSTER--THANKS TO **YOU.** YOU ARE A MOST **EXTRAORDINARY** WOMAN.

INDEED SHE **IS,** FIRE-LORD--BUT OUR PROBLEMS ARE NOT YET **OVER.**

WHAT DO WE DO **NOW** WITH EL LOBO AND HIS **MINIONS?**

WHILE, AT COSTA VERDE'S **PRESIDENTIAL PALACE...**

THE COURTYARD IS FILLED WITH OUR MOST **ABLE** SOLDIERS, EL PRESIDENTE!

WHEN EL LOBO **ATTACKS,** WE WILL BE **READY!**

EL PRESIDENTE, ARE YOU **WELL?**

OUR PEOPLE ARE SUCH INNOCENT **LAMBS,** PEDRO. IT WILL **DESTROY** THEM IF...

EH? OH, **FORGIVE** ME, PEDRO. I WAS JUST **THINKING**--TRYING TO IMAGINE WHAT THAT FIEND EL LOBO WILL **DO** TO OUR POOR PEOPLE IF WE **LOSE** THIS FINAL BATTLE...

...LET ALONE WHAT HE WILL DO TO **ME!**

WHAT--? TH-THAT **SOUND** OUTSIDE THE WINDOW-- LIKE THE HOWLING OF A TERRIBLE **WIND!**

MADRE DE DIOS! IT IS A **TORNADO**--AND IT IS HEADING **THIS** WAY! DID WE NOT HAVE **ENOUGH** TROUBLES WITHOUT ADDING **THIS?**

WHY, POR DIOS? **WHY??**

WELL, FRANKLY, PRESIDENT ELMIREZ-- THE **ANSWER** IS ONE YOU WILL PROBABLY NOT **BELIEVE!**

BUT THE CYCLONE HAS ONLY STOPPED BY TO MAKE A **DELIVERY!**

AND, HAVING **DEPOSITED** ITS UNSAVORY CARGO SMACK IN THE **MIDDLE** OF THE PALACE COURTYARD, THE WHIRLWIND SUDDENLY **SHIMMERS**--

--AND IS **GONE**!

PUT YOUR **HANDS** OVER YOUR HEADS, ALL OF YOU-- **SWIFTLY**!

P-PLEASE-- DO NOT **SHOOT**! W-WE **SURRENDER**!

WE HAVE NOTHING LEFT TO **FIGHT** FOR, ANYWAY!

WH-WHAT IS ALL THE **COMMOTION**? IS IT...**MADRE DE MI**!

EL LOBO AND HIS **REBELS**-- DELIVERED RIGHT INTO OUR **HANDS**--!

BUT **HOW**--?!?

'TWAS THE VERY **LEAST** WE COULD DO, MORTAL.

THOR-- AND THE FLAME-HAIRED ONE CALLED **FIRELORD**--?!? **YOU** ARE RESPONSIBLE FOR THIS?

I DID **PROMISE** THEE TO DELIVER THY LAND FROM THE VILLAINOUS **EL LOBO**-- --AND THE THUNDER GOD DOTH NOT TAKE HIS VOWS **LIGHTLY**.

I--I DO NOT **UNDERSTAND** MUCH OF THIS-- BUT THAT IS NOT **UNUSUAL**.

I KNOW ONLY THAT COSTA VERDE IS DEEPLY IN YOUR **DEBT**-- --AND THAT YOU HAVE THE **BLESSINGS** OF A MOST GRATEFUL PEOPLE!

'TIS MORE THAN ENOUGH FOR **THOR**, MORTAL--

--BUT WHAT OF **THEE**, FIRELORD?

I HAVE LITTLE USE FOR **GRATITUDE**, ASGARDIAN-- --OR FOR **MANKIND** ITSELF, FOR THAT MATTER!

SO I WILL BID YOU **FAREWELL**, THUNDER GOD--

--UNTIL WE MEET **AGAIN**!

DO YOU THINK WE REALLY **WILL** SEE HIM AGAIN, DARLING?

I'VE NO **DOUBT**, JANE. SOMEHOW FIRELORD SEEMS STRANGELY **BOUND** TO THIS PALE GREEN PLANET-- --AND HE MUST KEEP **SEARCHING** UNTIL HE LEARNS THE REASON **WHY**!

NEXT: JOIN FANDRAL, HOGUN, AND VOLSTAGG IN **MARVEL SPOTLIGHT #28** FOR "**WARRIORS THREE**"

THEN BE BACK HERE NEXT MONTH FOR THE BEGINNING OF AN **EPIC**! JOIN US FOR...

"**THERE SHALL COME... REVOLUTION!**"

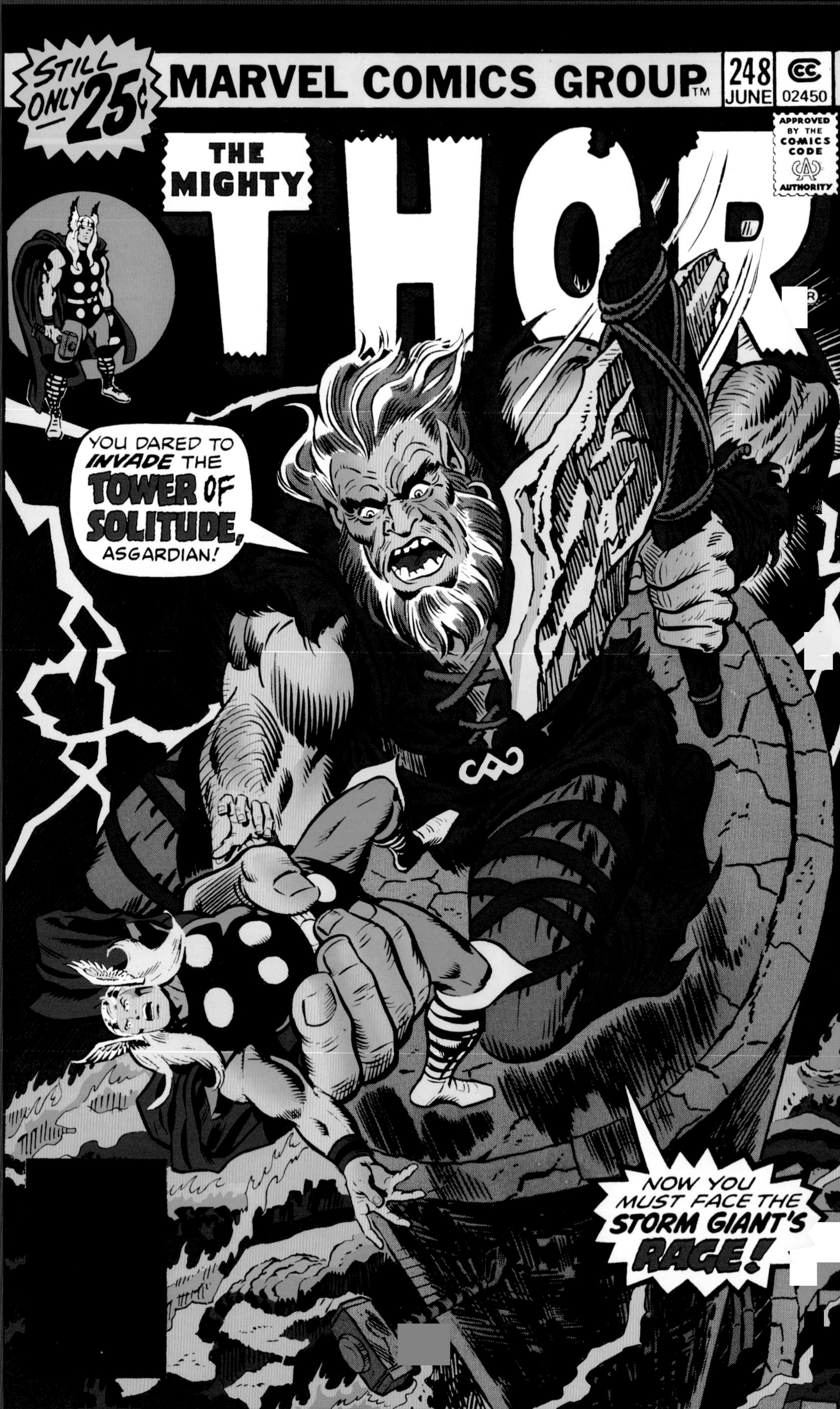
STILL ONLY 25¢
MARVEL COMICS GROUP
248 JUNE
CC 02450
APPROVED BY THE COMICS CODE AUTHORITY
THE MIGHTY THOR
YOU DARED TO INVADE THE TOWER OF SOLITUDE, ASGARDIAN!
NOW YOU MUST FACE THE STORM GIANT'S RAGE!

When lame Dr. DONALD BLAKE strikes his wooden walking stick upon the ground, it becomes the mystic mallet MJOLNIR—and Blake is transformed into the Norse God of Thunder, Master of the Storm and the Lightning, Heir to the Throne of Immortal Asgard...

STan Lee PRESENTS: THE MIGHTY THOR!™

LEN WEIN	JOHN BUSCEMA	TONY DeZUNIGA	GLYNIS WEIN	JOE ROSEN	MARV WOLFMAN
WRITER/EDITOR	ILLUSTRATOR	GUEST EMBELLISHER	COLORIST	LETTERER	GENERAL INSURGENT

THERE SHALL COME... REVOLUTION!

A MOMENT AGO, THE DAY WAS *CLEAR*; THE AFTERNOON SKY WAS A HAZY *GRAYISH-BLUE*, STREAKED WITH WISPY FINGERS OF UNCOMMITTED *CLOUDS*.

NOW, SUDDENLY, THE SKY IS *BLACK*, SCARRED BY *JAGGED DAGGERS* OF *LIGHTNING*, WASHED COLD WITH AN UNRELENTING *RAIN!*

IT IS A *STORM* TRULY WORTHY OF THE NAME THAT WELCOMES ITS GOLDEN-HAIRED MASTER *HOME*--

--BUT THE GOD OF THUNDER IS NOT AT ALL *PLEASED* AT HIS *RECEPTION!*

WE HAVE **ARRIVED**, MILADY JANE. THINE **APARTMENT** LIES JUST **BELOW** US.

A MOMENT **LONGER**-- AND THOU SHALT BE **HOME!**

THAT'S **ASSUMING**, OF COURSE, THIS ENTIRE **BUILDING** ISN'T SUDDENLY BLOWN AWAY BY THIS TERRIBLE **STORM**, THOR.

AYE, BELOVED, 'TIS INDEED A TEMPEST MOST **UNNATURAL!**

TO HAVE SPRUNG UP SO **SWIFTLY**... SO **SAVAGELY**...ONE WOULD THINK THE VERY **HEAVENS** THEMSELVES DO WRITHE IN VIOLENT **TURMOIL!**

BUT MAYHAP 'TIS MERELY...

H-H-**HELLLP!** HELP ME SOMEONE-- **PLEASE!**

THOR-- **LOOK!** ON THE SIDE OF THAT **BUILDING** ACROSS THE STREET--!

"A WINDOW-WASHER WAS **CAUGHT** IN THE SUDDEN STORM-- AND HIS SUPPORT ROPES HAVE **GIVEN WAY!**"

NOOOOOOOO

THEN STAND THEE **BACK**, JANE FOSTER-- AND GET THEE TO THY **DWELLING PLACE!**

WHAT NOW MUST NEEDS BE **DONE**, ONLY HE WHO WIELDS THE MYSTIC **MJOLNIR** CAN POSSIBLY **DO!**

WITH BUT **ONE BLOW**, MINE ENCHANTED URU HAMMER COULD **SHATTER** YON PLUMMETING STRUCTURE--

--BUT THEN THE FALLING FRAGMENTS MIGHT **ENDANGER** INNOCENT MORTALS FAR **BELOW!**

NAY, 'TIS NOT THE STRENGTH OF MINE MYSTIC **MALLET** THAT IS CALLED FOR HERE--

HOLY CROW--!

--BUT RATHER THE POWER OF MINE OWN MIGHTY *SINEWS*--

--THE *STRENGTH* THAT IS THE BIRTHRIGHT OF *THOR!*

TH-THANKS, MISTER. I *OWE* YA MY...

HEY, AIN'T YOU *THOR?* THE ONE THEY CALL THE *THUNDER GOD?*

IF YER S'POSED TA BE THE *BOSS* OF THIS FREAKY STORM, WHY DON'CHA DO SOMETHIN' TA *STOP* IT--'FORE SOMEBODY *REALLY* GETS HURT!

THY WORDS ARE RICH WITH *WISDOM,* MORTAL.

THUS LET THE RAGING TEMPEST *HEED* ITS MASTER'S *COMMAND!*

LET THE *THUNDER* GROW SILENT! LET THE *RAINS* GROW STILL! LET THE *LIGHTNING...*

AARRGGHH!!

ZZKKAAKK!!

BY *THE BEARD OF MY FATHER!* NE'ER BEFORE HAVE THE CHURNING ELEMENTS *DEFIED* THE WORD OF *THOR!*

'TIS AS IF THE VERY HEAVENS DO *REBEL* AGAINST MY WILL!

BUT EVER HATH THE MIGHTY THOR *RULED* THE STORM AND THE LIGHTNING --

--AND THUS SHALL IT EVER *REMAIN!*

COME, THOU MOST FICKLE FORCES--IF THOU DOST *DARE!*

COME YE-- AND TASTE OF THE THUNDER GOD'S MOST RIGHTEOUS *WRATH!*

THOUGH THOU DOST POSSESS THE POWER TO TEAR THIS VERY *PLANET* ASUNDER, STILL SHALL THE PRINCE OF ASGARD NEVER *FALTER!*

STILL SHALL THE SON OF ODIN NEVER *WITHDRAW!*

THOUGH THOU DOST SEEK TO SEAR THE VERY *FLESH* FROM OFF MY BONES, STILL IS THOR THY *MASTER*--

--AND STILL SHALL I *PREVAIL!!*

FOR AN INSTANT, THE SEETHING ENERGIES *CORUSCATE* UPON THE THUNDER GOD'S DEFIANT FORM--

--THEN SUDDENLY, THEY *SPUTTER*-- AND ARE *GONE!*

'TIS *OVER.* I HAVE *WON.*

THOUGH MY VERY *SOUL* CRIES OUT IN MORTAL *AGONY...*

...I...HAVE... *WON.*

AS SWIFTLY AS THEY HAD *COME,* THE STORM CLOUDS *DISPERSE*--AND THE MANHATTAN SKY IS *CLEAR* ONCE MORE.

WELL, AT LEAST AS CLEAR AS IT *EVER* IS.

BUT THE THUNDER GOD'S *THOUGHTS* ARE NOT *VERY* CLEAR AT ALL...

WHY DID THE TEMPEST *DEFY* ITS MASTER? WHY DID IT SEEK TO *DESTROY* ME?

HATH MY FATHER *STRIPPED* ME OF MY GODLY POWERS? IF *SO,* WHY HATH HE NOT *TOLD* ME?

VERILY, I SHALL FIND NO *ANSWERS* HERE. I'D BEST *RETURN* TO JANE FOSTER'S *SIDE.*

PRESENTLY...

DARLING, THANK HEAVEN YOU'RE *BACK.* SOMETHING *ELSE* HAS HAPPENED IN YOUR *ABSENCE.*

A *NEW* PROBLEM, MILADY? WHAT COULD IT POSSIBLY BE *NOW?*

TAKE A PEEK AT THE *TELEVISION*--AND SEE FOR *YOURSELF!*

THERE'S A MASSIVE *TRAFFIC TIE-UP* OVER IN CENTRAL PARK--

--AND YOU WON'T BELIEVE THE *CAUSE* OF IT!

120

BY HEIMDALL'S EYES! 'TIS *FANDRAL* THE DASHING, *HOGUN* THE GRIM, AND THE VOLUMINOUS *VOLSTAGG!*

SOOTH, THEIR TALENT FOR PLUNGING HEADLONG INTO *DISASTER* NEVER CEASES TO *AMAZE* ME!

HOW DID THEY MANAGE TO *ENTANGLE* THEMSELVES IN SUCH A SORRY SITUATION *THIS* TIME?

THEY'RE *YOUR* FRIENDS, DARLING--YOU TELL *ME.*

YOU'RE NOT GOING TO *LEAVE* THEM IN THAT MESS, ARE YOU?

MILADY, THOU KNOWEST NOT HOW SORELY I AM *TEMPTED!*

BUT, AS THOU SAYEST, THEY ARE INDEED MY *FRIENDS...* ODIN SAVE ME,

SINCE THEY DID COME TO *JOIN* ME IN MY *EXILE,* * FANDRAL, HOGUN AND VOLSTAGG HAVE STOOD EVER *STAUNCH* AT MY SIDE.

THUS, WHATE'ER THEIR DIFFICULTIES, SO MUST *THOR* STAND BESIDE *THEM...*

...NO MATTER HOW *EMBARRASSING* THE SITUATION MIGHT BECOME!

*ODIN CAST OUT GOLDILOCKS IN ISH #242.--LEN.

AND FRANKLY, THUNDER GOD, THINGS COULDN'T GET MUCH *WORSE* THAN THEY ARE *NOW...*

FIE UPON THEE, MORTAL! I SAY AGAIN-- *FIE!!*

'TIS NOT VALIANT *VOLSTAGG'S* FAULT YON MISSHAPEN VEHICLE *STRUCK* ME--

--AND I'LL NOT *LEAVE* TILL YON SLUGGARD OF A DRIVER DOTH *APOLOGIZE!*

NOW YOU LISTEN TO *ME,* YOU OVER-STUFFED TURKEY! EITHER YOU GET YOUR FAT CARCASS OUTTA HERE *NOW*--

--OR I'M GONNA RUN YOU IN SO *FAST* YOUR *SHOES* WILL HAVE TO TAKE THE NEXT *BUS!*

MILORD *THOR!* THOU HAST *RETURNED* FROM THY STRUGGLE AGAINST *FIRELORD!* *

AYE, VAST ONE.

BUT HAVE I RETURNED ONLY IN TIME TO SEE THEE *HURLED* INTO THIS FAIR CITY'S *DUNGEONS?*

*AS WITNESSED IN THE PAST TWO ISSUES, RIGHT? --LIVELY LEN.

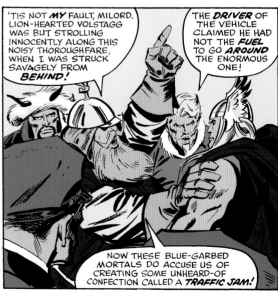

'TIS NOT *MY* FAULT, MILORD. LION-HEARTED VOLSTAGG WAS BUT STROLLING INNOCENTLY ALONG THIS NOISY THOROUGHFARE, WHEN I WAS STRUCK SAVAGELY FROM *BEHIND!*

THE *DRIVER* OF THE VEHICLE CLAIMED HE HAD NOT THE *FUEL* TO GO *AROUND* THE ENORMOUS ONE!

NOW THESE BLUE-GARBED MORTALS DO ACCUSE US OF CREATING SOME UNHEARD-OF CONFECTION CALLED A *TRAFFIC JAM!*

SURELY, IF ENSNARLING THE TRAFFIC IS ALL THOU DOST STAND *BLAMED* OF, 'TWOULD BE FAR *SIMPLER* INDEED TO CEASE POINTING THINE *ACCUSING FINGER*--

--AND INSTEAD TAKE STEPS TO *CORRECT* THE SITUATION!

HOLY BLUE HANNAH! THAT GUY'S GOT MUSCLES HE AIN'T EVEN *USED* YET!

HEY! PUT ME *DOWN,* YA LONG-HAIRED WEIRDO!

YER GONNA FOUL UP MY *METER* AN' EVERYTHIN'!

...*AS THOU* WISH, MORTAL...

...*AFTER* I HAVE POINTED THY VEHICLE IN THE *PROPER* DIRECTION!

SEVERAL MINUTES (AND SEVERAL *DOZEN* INCREDIBLE AUTO MANEUVERS) LATER, PASSING PEDESTRIANS ARE *STARTLED* BY A SPECTACLE THEY HAVE NEVER BEFORE *SEEN...*

...AND, FRANKLY, NEVER REALLY *EXPECTED* TO SEE!

WELL, IF THAT DON'T BEAT *ALL!*

I--I DON'T *BELIEVE* IT! I BEEN ON THIS BEAT FOR *FIFTEEN YEARS*--

--AND THIS IS THE *FIRST* TIME I'VE EVER SEEN TRAFFIC REALLY *MOVIN'* DURING THE *RUSH HOUR!*

TALK ABOUT *MOVING!* GRAB A LOOK AT *GOLDILOCKS* AND HIS *CHUMS!*

COME, MY BROTHERS-AT-ARMS! MILADY JANE DOTH *AWAIT* US--

--AND YE HAVE CREATED *PANDEMONIUM* ENOW FOR ONE DAY!

BUT COULD WE NOT *WALK* TO THY LADY'S ABODE, FRIEND THOR?

THOUGH WELL-FAMED VOLSTAGG DOTH TRULY POSSESS THE *HEART* OF AN EAGLE, SADLY I LACK ITS *WINGS!*

SHORTLY...

ODD, WHEN I **LEFT** HER, JANE FOSTER WAS QUITE **ALONE** IN HER DWELLING...

...YET NOW DO I HEAR **TWO** VOICES RISING FROM WITHIN!

NAY, MILORD-- 'TIS MERELY THE VIOLENT **BEATING** OF MY HEART!

AFTER OUR MAD **JOURNEY** HERE, IT FAIRLY **THUNDERS** IN MY BREAST!

HERE, **DRINK** THIS. YOU'LL FEEL MUCH...

THOR!?!

AYE, MY LOVE! BUT WHAT HAS HAPPENED IN MY ABSENCE **THIS** TIME?

WHO DOTH LIE SO **STILL** UPON YON...

BY ODIN! COULD IT **BE**...?

MILORD **THOR!** IS IT TRULY **THEE?** HAST THOU RETURNED AT **LAST?**

AYE, BRAVE BALDER... 'TIS **I**. BUT WHAT BRINGS **THEE** HERE TO EARTH?

WHY IS THY VERY GARB IN **TATTERS?**

'TIS A MOST **WOEFUL** TALE INDEED, MY PRINCE!

THE REALM ETERNAL IS IN DIRE **JEOPARDY**, MILORD! IN THE DAYS PAST, THINE OWN OMNIPOTENT FATHER HATH **EXILED** HIS GRAND VIZIER TO THE TOWER OF SOLITUDE-- AND INSTALLED THE EVIL **IGRON** IN HIS PLACE!

SINCE THEN THE ALL-FATHER HATH GROWN EVER **COLDER**, EVER MORE **CRUEL!**

HE DOTH ACT NOW WITHOUT **RHYME**, WITHOUT **REASON**-- AND HIS ACTIONS ARE CRUMBLING THE VERY **FOUNDATION** OF THE GOLDEN REALM!

VERILY, MY PRINCE-- **LORD ODIN HATH GONE MAD!!**

BUT EVEN AS ODIN **CONDEMNED** ME, EVEN AS ALL THE **GODS** DID TURN **AGAINST** ME, I SWIFTLY FLED ACROSS THE RAINBOW BRIDGE TO SEEK **THEE** OUT!

THOU MUST **RETURN** TO ASGARD **IMMEDIATELY**, LORD THOR-- FOR ONLY **THOU** COULDST HOPE TO **FACE** THY FATHER'S MADNESS-- AND **TRIUMPH!**

THEN FLY TO IMMORTAL ASGARD I **SHALL**, MY FRIEND-- AND I SHALL BATTLE ALL THE **REALM ETERNAL** IF NEEDS I MUST TILL MY FATHER'S INSANITY HATH BEEN **CURED!**

SO SWEARS THOR!

SO SWEARS THE SON OF ODIN!!

DARLING, I'M GOING **WITH** YOU!

NAY, MILADY. THOU HAST BEEN TO FABLED ASGARD ONCE **BEFORE** *--AND 'TWAS MORE THAN THY MORTAL MIND COULD **COPE** WITH!

TRUE--BUT **THEN** I DID NOT POSSESS THE LIVING **SPIRIT** OF AN ASGARDIAN **GODDESS!**

*THOR #136.-- LEN.

YOU **OWE** IT TO THE MEMORY OF THE **LADY SIF** TO BRING ME **ALONG,** THOR-- AND I'M GOING TO **HOLD** YOU TO THAT DEBT!

MAYHAP THOU ART **RIGHT,** JANE FOSTER, WE WILL **FIND OUT** SOON ENOW.

BUT, NOW, BY THE PEERLESS POWER OF THE MYSTIC MALLET **MJOLNIR...**

...LET US **BEGONE!**

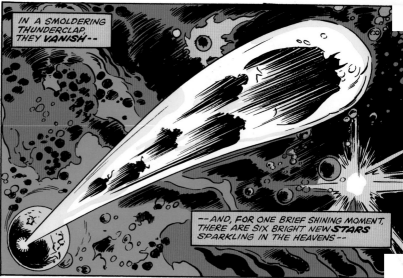

IN A SMOLDERING THUNDERCLAP, THEY **VANISH**--

--AND, FOR ONE BRIEF SHINING MOMENT, THERE ARE SIX BRIGHT NEW **STARS** SPARKLING IN THE HEAVENS--

--THEN SUDDENLY, A HANDFUL OF GRIM-VISAGED **FIGURES** STAND BOLDLY UPON THE RAINBOW BRIDGE CALLED **BIFROST...**

...FACING THE FEARSOME **HEIMDALL,** HE WHO HAS EVER BEEN **GUARDIAN** OF THE ENTRANCE TO IMMORTAL **ASGARD!**

GREETINGS, GOOD HEIMDALL. STAND THEE **ASIDE--** AND LET THY PRINCE AND HIS PARTY **PASS!**

NAY, MILORD! MUCH THOUGH I MAY **DESIRE** TO, 'TIS ODIN'S IMPERIAL DECREE THAT THOU AND THY COMPANIONS MAY NOT **ENTER** THE REALM ETERNAL!

FAITHFUL ONE, OUR LORD BE SORELY **TROUBLED!** THERE IS GRAVE **MADNESS** UPON HIS BROW-- AND ONLY **I** MAY EASE IT!

NOW, BY THE ROYAL BLOOD WHICH IS MY BIRTHRIGHT, I SAY THEE-- **STAND ASIDE!**

STAND ASIDE-- OR FEEL THE **STING** OF MY MYSTIC **HAMMER!**

THOU WOULDST RAISE THY **HAND** AGAINST THE LOYAL **HEIMDALL?**

THEN 'TIS **THY** BROW UPON WHICH **MADNESS** RESTS-- AND FOR THINE OWN **SAFETY,** YE MUST BE **SUBDUED!**

THE LOYAL HEIMDALL PURSES HIS LIPS, AND THE **TRUMPET OF VIGILANCE** SOUNDS ITS **CLARION CALL!**

THEN, THE AIR IS ABRUPTLY FILLED WITH THE THUNDEROUS **CLATTER** OF IRON-CLAD **HOOVES** POUNDING OVER COBBLESTONES OF **GOLD**--

--AND, WITH THE CRY OF **BATTLE** RISING AMONG THEM, ODIN'S OWN **ELITE GUARD** CHARGES FORTH--

--STRAIGHT TOWARDS A STEADFAST WALL OF **FLESH!**

I WILL SAY THEE **ONCE,** GOOD WARRIORS-- **LET US PASS!**

REFUSE-- AND THE BLOOD THAT IS SPILT WILL BE ON **YOUR** HANDS!

THEY HEED THEE **NOT,** FRIEND THOR!

STILL DO THEY RACE **TOWARD** US, **HATRED** GLEAMING IN THEIR EYES!

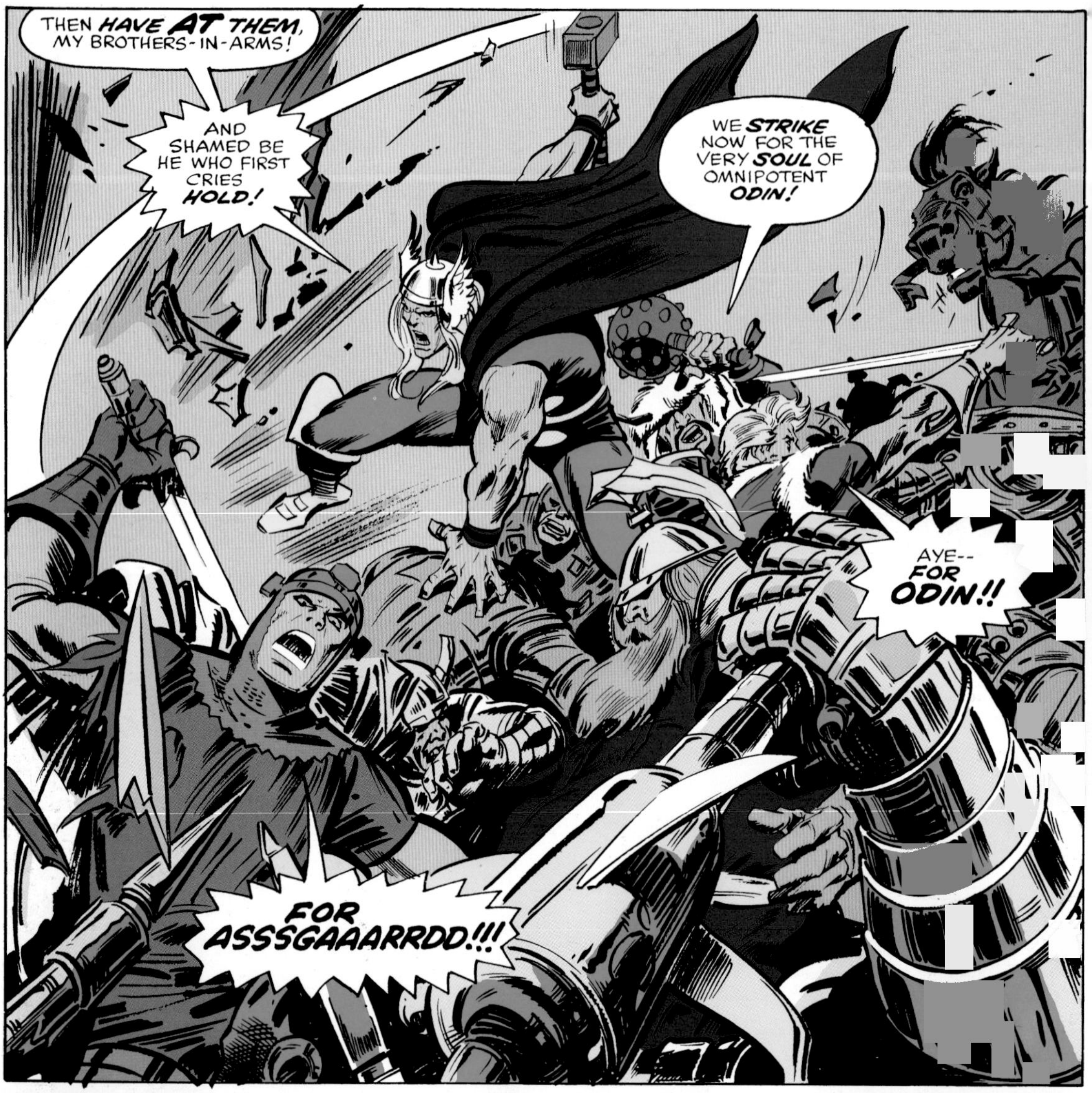
THEN HAVE AT THEM, MY BROTHERS-IN-ARMS!
AND SHAMED BE HE WHO FIRST CRIES HOLD!
WE STRIKE NOW FOR THE VERY SOUL OF OMNIPOTENT ODIN!
AYE-- FOR ODIN!!
FOR ASSSGAAARRDD!!!

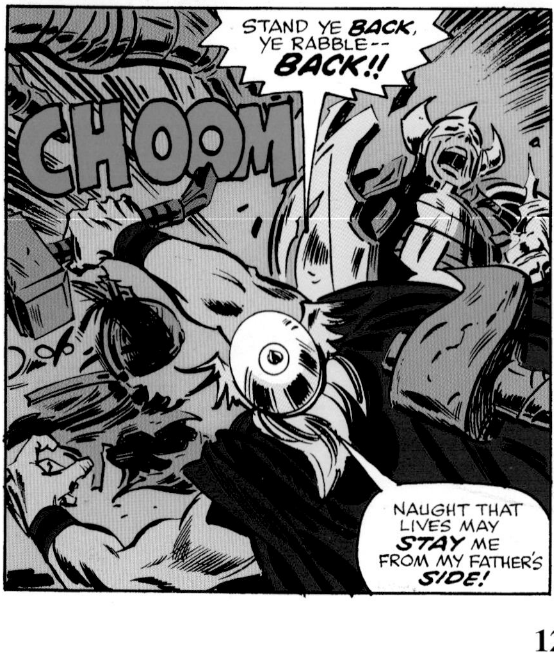
STAND YE BACK, YE RABBLE-- BACK!!
CHOOM
NAUGHT THAT LIVES MAY STAY ME FROM MY FATHER'S SIDE!

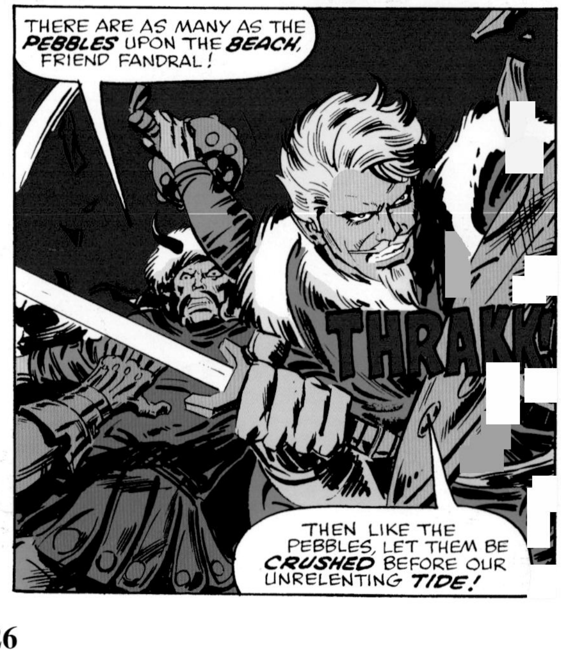
THERE ARE AS MANY AS THE PEBBLES UPON THE BEACH, FRIEND FANDRAL!
THRAKK
THEN LIKE THE PEBBLES, LET THEM BE CRUSHED BEFORE OUR UNRELENTING TIDE!

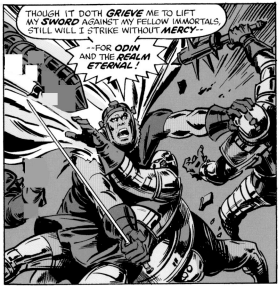

THOUGH IT DOTH **GRIEVE** ME TO LIFT MY **SWORD** AGAINST MY FELLOW IMMORTALS, STILL WILL I STRIKE WITHOUT **MERCY**--

--FOR **ODIN** AND THE **REALM ETERNAL!**

THEN STRIKE **SWIFTLY**, GOOD BALDER--

--AND MAKE THINE EVERY BLOW **COUNT!**

FOR INTERMINABLE MOMENTS, THE BATTLE **RAGES...**

...AND THEN, ALL AT ONCE--THERE IS **SILENCE!**

THE STRUGGLE BE **DONE**, MY BRETHREN.

THERE BE NONE **LEFT** TO STAND **AGAINST** US!

NAY, THUNDER GOD! **ONE** REMAINS-- AND HE SHALL **OPPOSE** THEE UNTO **DEATH!**

MILORD, LOOK **BEHIND** THEE!

IF THOU WOULDST STILL **DEFY** THY FATHER'S DECREE, MY PRINCE-- THEN BEST **SLAY** ME, AND BE **DONE** WITH IT!

FOR ONLY IN **DEATH** WILL LOYAL HEIMDALL **BETRAY** HIS POST!

NAY, VIGILANT ONE! THOU ART FAR TOO **NOBLE** TO THROW THY **LIFE** AWAY WITH SO **FUTILE** A GESTURE!

THUS DOES VOLSTAGG GRANT THEE THE GIFT OF **SLEEP**, MY GOOD AND FAITHFUL FRIEND...

CL--**CLANK**

...AND MAYEST THOU **FORGIVE** ME WHEN THOU DOST AT LAST **AWAKEN!**

H-HE LIES SO **STILL**, FRIEND THOR, HAVE I...?

NAY, VAST ONE. THOU DIDST ONLY WOUND HIS **DIGNITY**. GOOD HEIMDALL WILL **RECOVER...**

...AND THE BARDS WILL SOME DAY **SING** OF HIS **VALOR!**

NOW GATHER THE CLOAKS OF THE FALLEN *ABOUT* YE, MY FRIENDS, ERE WE *ENTER* THE CITY ROYAL.

'TWOULD NOT DO FOR US TO BE *RECOGNIZED* ERE WE *DESIRE* IT SO!

I FEAR, MILORD, 'TWILL *NOT* BE THE CITY THOU DOST *REMEMBER*!

AYE, BRAVE BALDER. IT APPEARS THOU SPEAKEST *A'RIGHT*!

VERILY, THE GOLDEN REALM DOTH SEEM SOMEHOW SORELY *TARNISHED*!

NE'ER BEFORE HAVE I SEEN SUCH *SQUALOR* IN THE STREETS...SUCH *PAIN* AND *CONFUSION* ETCHED UPON THE FACES OF THE *PEOPLE*!

MY FATHER HATH DONE ALL *THIS*?

AYE, MY PRINCE, YET STRANGELY, *DESPITE* ALL THIS, STILL DO MOST OF THE MASSES STAND *BESIDE* OUR MONARCH MOST MAD...

...OUT OF BLIND *OBEDIENCE*... OUT OF MISPLACED *LOYALTY*... OR MAYHAP, OUT OF *FEAR*!

THEN WE WILL BE SORELY *OUT-NUMBERED* IF WE ARE FORCED TO *STRIKE* AGAINST MY FATHER!

AYE, THUNDER GOD, WE WILL BE *OUT-NUMBERED* INDEED...

...BUT WE WILL NOT BE *ALONE*!

WHAT *MEANEST* THOU, BRAVE ONE?

PRAY SEE FOR *THYSELF*, MILORD.

A HANDFUL OF GOOD *WARRIORS*, HUDDLED LIKE DARK *CONSPIRATORS* ABOUT THE CANDLELIGHT!

INDEED WE ARE NOT *MANY*, LORD THOR--

--BUT OUR VERY *LIVES* ARE PLEDGED TO *SAVE* IMMORTAL ASGARD!

128

MIGHTY *HILDEGARDE*...AND THE FAIR *KRISTA!* I WOULD HAVE *THOUGHT* TO FIND YE HERE!

AND *WELL* THOU WOULDST *INDEED*, THUNDER GOD!

THERE IS *NAUGHT* WE WOULD NOT VENTURE TO FREE THE *MIND* OF ALMIGHTY *ODIN!*

SO SPEAKS *BRODAG THE BLACK* AS WELL, MILORD!

AND *HOLVAR OF THE SINGLE EYE* ECHOES HIS WORDS!

COSAK THE CRIMSON-HAIRED WOULD KNOW WHEN WE *BEGIN* OUR CAMPAIGN!

SKOVAL THE SHAGGY ONE WOULD BE *ON* WITH IT, MILORD!

THY LOYALTY DOES ME GREAT *HONOR*, WARRIORS -- BUT BEFORE WE MAY MOVE TO *FREE* NOBLE ODIN, WE MUST...

WE MUST FIRST HAVE A VIABLE *BATTLE PLAN*, THOR!

IF YOU WISH TO *CURE* YOUR FATHER'S *INSANITY*, YOU MUST FIRST *KNOW* WHAT'S GOING ON IN HIS *MIND*...

...AND NO ONE KNOWS THE MIND OF THE ALL-FATHER *BETTER* THAN HIS FAITHFUL FRIEND AND ADVISOR...

...THE WISE AND GENTLE *GRAND VIZIER!*

IF YOU WOULD *FREE* THE MIND OF *ODIN*, THUNDER GOD, FIRST GO TO THE *TOWER OF SOLITUDE* --

-- AND *FREE* THE GRAND VIZIER!

TEMPER, MILADY. SUCH *FURY* SOUNDS NOT AT ALL *LIKE* THEE.

BUT STILL JANE FOSTER SPEAKS *TRULY*, MY FRIENDS, IF WE ARE TO *AID* MY FATHER, WE MUST *ASSAULT* THE TOWER OF SOLITUDE --

-- AND WE MUST DO SO *TONIGHT!*

WHILE, IN THE *THRONE ROOM* OF THE PALACE ROYAL...

THINGS ARE *NOT* GOING VERY *WELL* AT ALL, LORD ODIN!

I HAVE RECEIVED WORD FROM *HEIMDALL* -- AND MY WORST *FEARS* HAVE BEEN *REALIZED!*

THOR AND HIS ACCURSED COMPANIONS HAVE *RETURNED* TO ASGARD AT LAST!

AND WHAT DOST THOU PROPOSE I **DO** ABOUT THAT FACT, FRIEND IGRON?

'TIS FOR **THEE** TO SAY, ALMIGHTY ONE. THINE IS THE **POWER** --

--AND THE THUNDER GOD IS **NOTHING** IF NOT THE ALL-FATHER'S **SON!**

AYE, SLY ONE. THOR IS INDEED ODIN'S **OFFSPRING.**

BUT IF HE DOTH **DARE** TO LIFT HIS HAND AGAINST THE ONE WHO NOW SITS UPON THIS **THRONE** --

--I DO **SWEAR** TO THEE, BY THE **FIRE** THAT DOTH RAGE WITHIN MY BREAST--

--**THOR** SHALL BE ONLY A **CORPSE!**

AND THE FALL OF **NIGHT** ONLY MIRRORS THE **DARKNESS** IN THE THUNDER GOD'S OWN **SOUL...**

WHAT HATH DRIVEN MY MOST NOBLE FATHER **INSANE?** IS IT MERELY THE INFLUENCE OF THE EVIL **IGRON,** AS BALDER DOTH SAY...

...OR IS IT SOMETHING **MORE?**

HAS MY OWN REBELLIOUS NATURE AT LAST BECOME **MORE** THAN MY FATHER CAN **BEAR?**

ONCE HE DID ORDER ME NEVER AGAIN TO KEEP COMPANY WITH THE MORTAL **JANE FOSTER...** AND NOW SHE WALKS THE VERY STREETS OF **ASGARD** AT MY SIDE,

CAN **THIS** BE THE CAUSE OF LORD ODIN'S **MADNESS?** AND, IF SO, WHAT AM I TO **DO?** IF I MUST **CHOOSE** BETWEEN THEM, DO I CHOOSE MINE OWN **FATHER...**

...OR THE WOMAN I **LOVE?**

WHICHEVER, 'TIS A CHOICE THAT MUST **WAIT!**

THERE IT STANDS **BEFORE** US, MY FRIENDS-- THE **TOWER OF SOLITUDE!**

'TIS **THERE,** LORD THOR, THAT THY FATHER DID **EXILE** THE GRAND VIZIER--

--SO THE LEARNED ONE MIGHT BETTER STUDY THE **ANCIENT SCROLLS,** SAID ODIN...

"...BUT BALDER WONDERS WHAT NEED A **SCHOLAR** HAS FOR SO FEARSOME A **GUARD?**"

"'TWILL NOT BE **EASY** TO ENTER YON TOWER, MIGHTY THOR!"

THEN TAKE THY **WEAPONS** IN HAND, MY FRIENDS--

--AND LET RING THE CRY OF **BATTLE!**

FOR **ASGARD!**

FOR **JUSTICE!**

FOR THE **FREEDOM OF THE REALM ETERNAL!**

PRESS **ON,** MY FRIENDS! **ASK** NOT FOR **QUARTER**-- AND **GIVE** NONE!

NEVER HAVE I SEEN THE THUNDER GOD MORE **FURIOUS,** MORE **RELENTLESS!**

'TIS ALMOST AS IF HE DOTH BLAME **HIMSELF** FOR HIS FATHER'S **AFFLICTION!**

STAND YE **ASIDE,** CHURLS--

--OR FACE THE **AWESOME** MIGHT OF **VOLSTAGG!**

'TIS THINE **AWESOME** **WEIGHT** I FEAR, VAST ONE!

THE BATTLE IS EVENLY **MATCHED,** MY FORCES HOLD THEIR **OWN!**

THERE IS NO **NEED** HERE FOR THE **HAMMER OF THOR!**

THUS SHALL I SEEK INSTEAD THE **HEIGHTS** OF THE TOWER OF SOLITUDE--

--FOR 'TIS **THERE** I SHALL FIND THE **GRAND VIZIER!**

BUT AS THE THUNDER GOD **ROUNDS** THE WINDING STAIRS...

COME **CLOSER**, LITTLE ONE! ONE STEP **MORE**--AND I SHALL **CRUSH** YOU IN MY ALL-ENVELOPING **FIST**!

BY THE RAINBOW **SPAN**! 'TIS A **STORM GIANT**!

ODIN HAS SET ONE OF ASGARD'S GREATEST **FOES** TO GUARD THE AGED **VIZIER**!

AND, BY ODIN'S **COMMAND**, ALL WHO SEEK TO **FREE** THE OLD ONE MUST BE **DESTROYED**...

SKRRAKK!

...LIKE **THIS**!!

THY BATTLE-AXE BE SWIFT AND **STRONG**, GIANT ONE!

BUT AFTER ALL THE MILLENNIA OUR TWO RACES HAVE BEEN AT **WAR**, THOU SHOULDST **KNOW**--

GROOM!

--NOTHING CAN MATCH THE POWER OF THE MYSTIC MALLET **MJOLNIR**!

THOU WOULDST DO WELL TO **DWELL** ON THAT, OGRE, WHEN THOU DOST **AWAKEN**...

...IF THOU DOST **AWAKEN**!

AND AS THE MIGHTY ASGARDIAN'S LEATHER-CLAD FEET SLAP SOFTLY ALONG THE GRIM TOWER'S TWISTING **CORRIDORS**...

MY FATHER'S MADNESS MUST BE **GREAT** INDEED, THAT HE WOULD IMPRISON HIS CLOSEST **COMRADE** THUS.

BUT MAYHAP THE WISE ONE CAN SHED SOME **LIGHT** ON THIS DARK MYSTERY...

...WHEN I **FIND** HIM!

MILORD **THOR**! PRITHEE-- OVER **HERE**!

ZOUNDS! 'TIS THE GRAND VIZIER'S OWN GNARLED **HAND**--!

STAND **AWAY** FROM THE **DOOR,** LEARNED ONE--

--AND LET THE GOD OF THUNDER **FREE** THEE FROM THINE UNJUST *IMPRISONMENT!*

KKRRUUUMMP!!

MY PRINCE, THANK THE FATES THOU HAST **FOUND** ME! THE REALM ETERNAL HATH SUFFERED **GREATLY** IN THINE ABSENCE!

SO I HAVE ALREADY **LEARNED,** MOST WISE VIZIER!

THEN IF THOU DOST **KNOW** OF THINE HOMELAND'S **PLIGHT,** MILORD--THOU KNOWEST **TOO** WHAT MUST BE **DONE!**

THOU MUST FACE THINE OWN MOST NOBLE **FATHER,** AND **FREE** HIM FROM HIS **MADNESS**--

--BEFORE LORD ODIN DOTH **DESTROY** US ALL!!

INDEED...

MY LIEGE, THOR AND HIS COMPANIONS HAVE **STRUCK** AT THE TOWER OF SOLITUDE, AS I FEARED --

--AND **FREED** THE GRAND VIZIER!

AS THOU SAYEST, FRIEND IGRON... 'TWAS TO BE **EXPECTED!**

THE MOMENT I HAVE LONG BEEN **WAITING** FOR WILL SOON BE **UPON** US, SLY ONE --

--THE MOMENT WHEN THE MIGHTY THOR MUST **DIE!**

NEXT ISSUE: BECAUSE YOU **DEMANDED** IT, THE RETURN OF **KARNILLA THE NORN QUEEN**...AND THE RETURN OF THE STUNNING **SIF!** PLUS, THE MOST STARTLING **SHOCK** ENDING OF ALL! BE HERE FOR...

THE THRONE AND THE FURY!

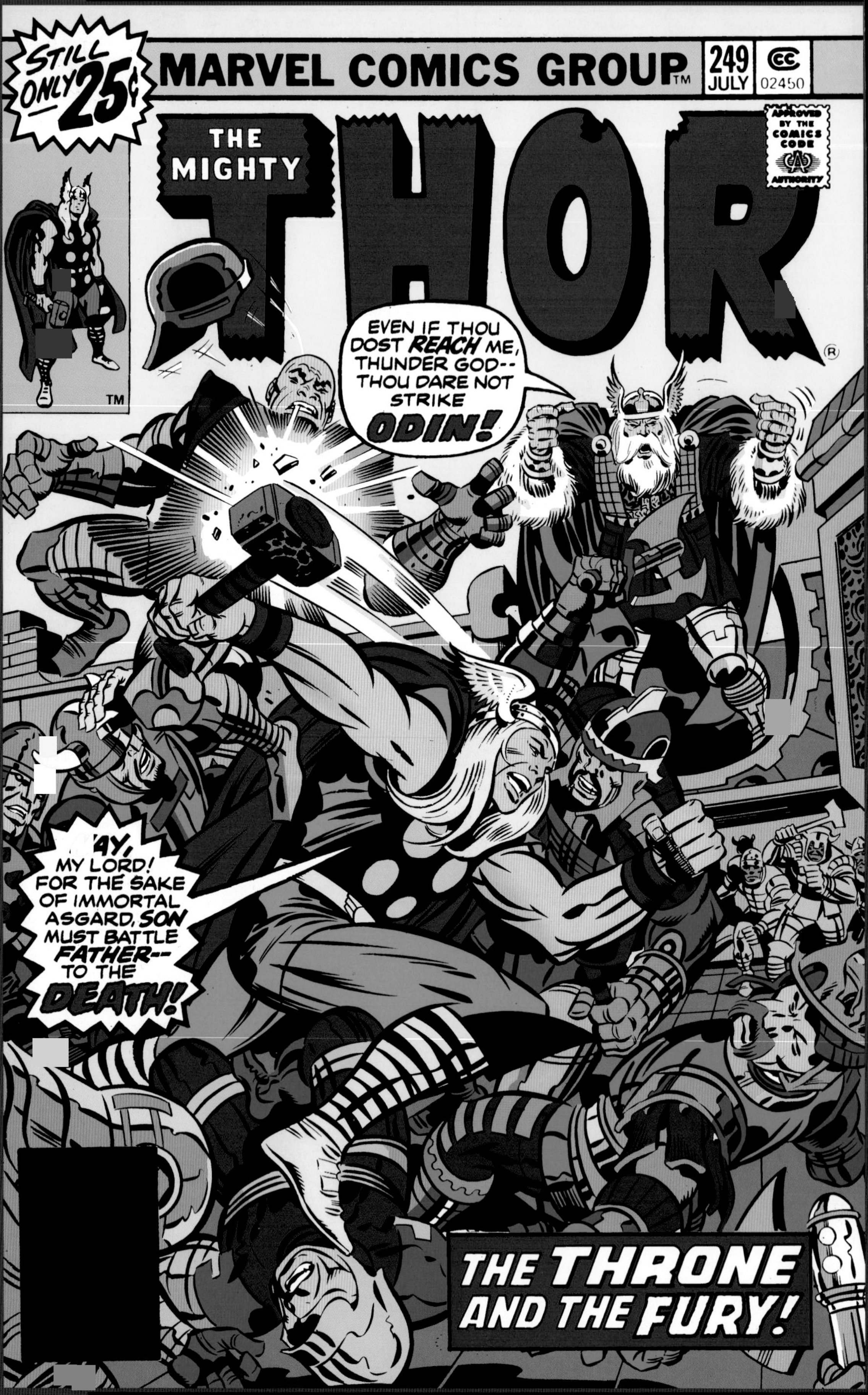
STILL ONLY 25¢
MARVEL COMICS GROUP™
249 JULY
CC 02450
APPROVED BY THE COMICS CODE AUTHORITY
THE MIGHTY THOR®
EVEN IF THOU DOST REACH ME, THUNDER GOD-- THOU DARE NOT STRIKE ODIN!
AY, MY LORD! FOR THE SAKE OF IMMORTAL ASGARD, SON MUST BATTLE FATHER-- TO THE DEATH!
THE THRONE AND THE FURY!

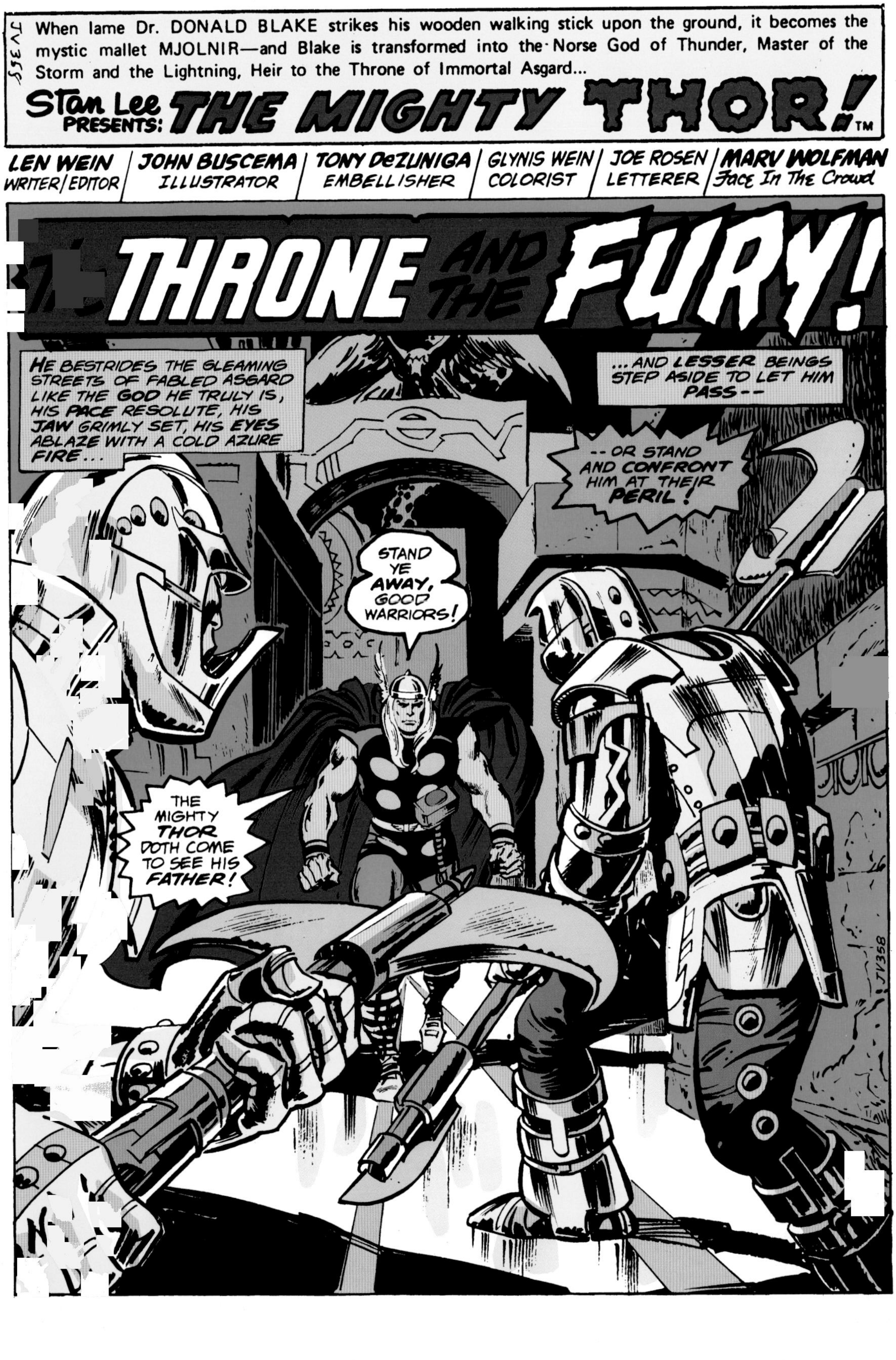
When lame Dr. DONALD BLAKE strikes his wooden walking stick upon the ground, it becomes the mystic mallet MJOLNIR—and Blake is transformed into the Norse God of Thunder, Master of the Storm and the Lightning, Heir to the Throne of Immortal Asgard...
Stan Lee PRESENTS: THE MIGHTY THOR!™
LEN WEIN WRITER/EDITOR
JOHN BUSCEMA ILLUSTRATOR
TONY DeZUNIGA EMBELLISHER
GLYNIS WEIN COLORIST
JOE ROSEN LETTERER
MARV WOLFMAN Face In The Crowd
THRONE AND THE FURY!
HE BESTRIDES THE GLEAMING STREETS OF FABLED ASGARD LIKE THE GOD HE TRULY IS, HIS PACE RESOLUTE, HIS JAW GRIMLY SET, HIS EYES ABLAZE WITH A COLD AZURE FIRE...
...AND LESSER BEINGS STEP ASIDE TO LET HIM PASS--
--OR STAND AND CONFRONT HIM AT THEIR PERIL!
STAND YE AWAY, GOOD WARRIORS!
THE MIGHTY THOR DOTH COME TO SEE HIS FATHER!

NAY, THUNDER GOD-- THOU MAYEST NOT **PASS!**

ALMIGHTY **ODIN** HATH DECREED HE DOTH NOT WISH TO **SEE** THEE!

IF **SO,** 'TIS FOR **HIM** TO TELL ME, WARRIOR--

--NOT FOR SUCH AS **THEE!**

NE'ER **BEFORE** HAVE THE GATES OF THE PALACE ROYAL BEEN **BARRED** TO ME--

--AND NEITHER WILL IT BE SO **NOW**--!

ZOUNDS!!

SOME UNSEEN BARRIER **IMPEDES** MY PROGRESS!

I CAN DRAW NO **CLOSER** TO THE ALL-FATHER'S **DOMICILE!**

NOR **SHALT** THOU, MOST OFFENSIVE OFFSPRING!

FOR THY MANY **SINS** AGAINST THE **THRONE** OF THE REALM ETERNAL--

--THOU ART NOT **WELCOME** IN THY **FATHER'S** HOUSE!

MY LIEGE, DOTH MY LOVE FOR THE MORTAL JANE FOSTER SO **OFFEND** THEE THAT THOU WOULDST CAST OUT THINE OWN **SON** FROM THY HEART--

--AND TURN **AGAINST** THE VERY SUBJECTS WHO DO **WORSHIP** THEE?

VERILY, MILORD, THOU ART SUFFERING A GREAT **SICKNESS** OF THE SOUL!

I PRAY THEE, LET ME **IN** THAT I MIGHT HUMBLY **SPEAK** WITH THEE!

NAY, THUNDER GOD-- THERE BE NOT WORDS ENOW IN ALL THE LANGUAGES OF MEN TO MEND THE **RIFT** THAT HATH GROWN BETWEEN US!

THINE AUDIENCE IS **DENIED,** REBELLIOUS ONE!

BEGONE!!

ALTHOUGH I WANTED NOT TO *BELIEVE* IT, 'TIS AS BALDER AND THE OTHERS HAVE *SAID*--

--MY FATHER BE *NOT* IN HIS RIGHT *MIND!*

YET WHETHER ODIN'S MADNESS BE *MY* DOING OR THE WORK OF THE EVIL *IGRON,* STILL MUST I...

EH? THAT SOUND *BEHIND* ME--!?!

"'TIS ODIN'S OWN *PALACE GUARD*--AND THEIR *VISAGE* DOTH SEEM MOST *GRIM* INDEED!"

LAY DOWN THY *HAMMER,* THUNDER GOD-- AND *SURRENDER!*

THOU ART NOW OUR *PRISONER!*

GOOD WARRIORS, I SHALL SAY THEE THIS BUT *ONCE!* THOUGH THY COURAGE IS *COMMENDABLE,* THE GOD OF THUNDER SUBMITS TO *NO MAN!*

STAND YE ASIDE AND LET ME *PASS,* OR BY THE SPIRES OF THE GOLDEN REALM--

--I SHALL GO RIGHT *THRU* YE!

EVEN IF WE *WANTED* TO SET THEE FREE, ODINSON-- WE *CANNOT!*

WE HAVE BEEN CHARGED WITH THY *CAPTURE,* AND WE MUST DO AS SO *ORDERED*--

--OR *PERISH* IN THE ATTEMPT!

THEN, THOUGH I GAIN NO GREAT *SATISFACTION* IN RAISING MINE ENCHANTED MALLET *AGAINST* YE--

SO BE IT!

SKRAKKTT!

THE BATTLE IS *FIERCE*, AND TERRIBLY *ONE-SIDED*--

--BUT ONE-SIDED IN THE THUNDER GOD'S *FAVOR*, IT WOULD SEEM--

--UNTIL A DISTANT *MURMUR* GROWS TO A NEAR-AT-HAND *ROAR*, AND THE GOLDEN-MANED ASGARDIAN *WHIRLS* TO FIND...

REINFORCEMENTS-- RACING *THIS* WAY--!

HAD I NO *CHOICE*, I WOULD STAND AND FACE THEM *ALL*--

--BUT 'TWOULD SEEM *DISCRETION* MAY SERVE FAR *BETTER* HERE THAN UNNECESSARY *VALOR!*

THOUGH MY VERY SOUL DOTH ACHE FOR *COMBAT*, THERE BE MORE *IMPORTANT* MATTERS TO CONCERN ME NOW--

--SO 'TIS TIME I MADE MY *EXIT*--

--AS ONLY HE WHO WIELDS THE MYSTIC MALLET MJOLNIR *CAN*--

CHOOM!

"--AN EXIT THAT WILL SWIFTLY *SEAL* ITSELF BEHIND ME!"

THE THUNDER GOD HATH *FLED*-- BUT HE HATH LEFT BEHIND HIS *MARK!*

'TWILL TAKE TIME TO FREE THOSE TRAP-PED BY THIS *RUBBLE*, BUT WHEN WE ARE *DONE*--

--WE WILL SEEK OUT THE ONCE-NOBLE *THOR*-- AND *SLAY* HIM!

VERILY, IT SEEMS MY FATHER'S *MADNESS* DOTH NOW AFFECT ALL THE *REALM ETERNAL!*

THERE IS BUT ONE POCKET OF *SANITY* LEFT IN ALL THIS TROUBLED LAND-- AND 'TIS *THERE* I MUST HIE ME TO *NOW!*

"TO THE HIDDEN *HEADQUARTERS* OF THE LOYAL INSURRECTIONISTS LED BY *BALDER THE BRAVE!*"

WELCOME *BACK*, MY PRINCE! FROM THE DOWNCAST EXPRESSION 'PON THY FACE, THINE AUDIENCE WITH THY FATHER WENT NOT *WELL!*

IN TRUTH, FRIEND BALDER, IT WENT MOST *TERRIBLE!* I HAD TO *FIGHT* MY WAY TO *FREEDOM!*

AND, WORSE YET, AN UNSEEN *BARRIER* NOW SURROUNDS THE PALACE ROYAL-- A BARRIER EVEN MINE ENCHANTED *MALLET* CANNOT PENETRATE!

FORGIVE ME, MY FRIENDS, BUT I KNOW NOT WHAT NEXT TO *DO!*

IF ALL THY BEST EFFORTS HAVE *FAILED* THEE, MILORD, 'TIS NO *SHAME* TO ASK FOR *ASSISTANCE*

COME WITH ME TO THE DARK CAVERN OF *KARNILLA THE NORN QUEEN!* LET US TRY TO *CONVINCE* THAT ALL-POWERFUL SORCERESS TO *JOIN* OUR MOST WORTHY CAUSE!

OUR COMRADES WILL GO OUT ACROSS THE LAND-- AND TRY TO *RALLY* THE PEOPLE TO OUR SIDE!

AS EVER, VIZIER, THOU DOST SPEAK *WISELY*-- BUT I WOULD HAVE THE NOBLE BALDER *ACCOMPANY* US ON OUR QUEST!

MAYHAP HER DEEP *AFFECTION* FOR THE BRAVE ONE WILL HELP TO *SWAY* THE NORN QUEEN'S HEART!

WHATEVER THOU DOST *WISH*, MY PRINCE... ALTHOUGH I WOULD HAVE IT *OTHERWISE!*

AND WHAT ABOUT *ME*, DARLING?

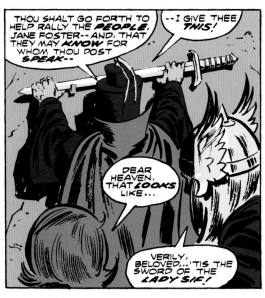

THOU SHALT GO FORTH TO HELP RALLY THE *PEOPLE*, JANE FOSTER-- AND, THAT THEY MAY *KNOW* FOR WHOM THOU DOST *SPEAK*--

--I GIVE THEE *THIS!*

DEAR HEAVEN, THAT *LOOKS* LIKE...

VERILY, BELOVED...'TIS THE SWORD OF THE *LADY SIF!*

AYE, AND SINCE THE *SPIRIT* OF THE GODDESS SIF NOW GIVES THEE LIFE, JANE FOSTER--!

--BY RIGHTS, THIS GLEAMING WEAPON BELONGS TO *THEE!*

I-IT'S SO *HOT* TO THE TOUCH...A-AS IF IT WERE SEETHING WITH *POWER!*

SHEER *AGONY* TO HOLD IT...BUT I CAN'T *LET GO*...

I...CAN'T...

TOOM!

WRITHING IN SUDDEN TORMENT, JANE FOSTER FLAILS SAVAGELY ABOUT, ACCIDENTALLY SLAMMING THE SHINING *WEAPON* SHE HOLDS AGAINST A NEARBY GRANITE *WALL* --

--AND INSTANTLY, THE TERRIFIED WOMAN IS BATHED IN AN UNNATURAL *LIGHT*--

WH--WHAT'S *HAPPENING* TO ME?

--A LIGHT THAT SLOWLY *FADES* TO REVEAL, NOT THE FRAIL FORM OF A FRIGHTENED *MORTAL,* BUT RATHER --

--A MIRACLE!

BY BIFROST'S *RAINBOW SPAN!* IT CANNOT *BE*--!

BUT IT *IS,* MILORD-- IT *IS!* JANE FOSTER HATH *VANISHED* --

"--AND IN HER PLACE, THERE STANDS -- *THE LADY SIF!*"

THOR?

BELOVED?

OH, PRAISE *ODIN* -- I HAVE *RETURNED* TO THEE AT LAST!

BUT, HOW, MILADY-- *NOW*--?

MAYHAP *I* CAN ANSWER THAT, THOR!

WHEN JANE FOSTER DID LAY *DYING* ON EARTH, SIF *SACRIFICED* HER CORPOREAL FORM THAT HER *SPIRIT* MIGHT GIVE THE MORTAL WOMAN *LIFE!*

I BELIEVE THAT SOMEHOW *BOTH* SPIRITS NOW DWELL WITHIN A *SINGLE* FORM-- AND THAT, HERE IN THE *REALM ETERNAL,* 'TIS THE SPIRIT OF THE LADY SIF WHICH *DOMINATES!*

THEN WERE WE TO *RETURN* TO EARTH, WOULD SIF BECOME *JANE FOSTER* ONCE MORE?

IN TRUTH, MILORD, I DO NOT *KNOW!* THAT IS FOR THE *FUTURE* TO DECIDE!

AND I FEAR WE MAY NOT *HAVE* A FUTURE, UNLESS WE CARRY OUT OUR *APPOINTED TASKS* --

--AND *SWIFTLY!*

140

WHILE, IN THE FIERCELY-FORTIFIED *PALACE ROYAL...*

TREAD WITH UTMOST *CARE*, GOOD WARRIORS!

IF EVER THE *ODINSWORD* SHOULD *SLIP* FROM ITS SCABBARD, THE *UNIVERSE* ITSELF IS *FORFEIT!*

MILORD, THINKEST THOU DOST THE PROPER THING? NE'ER BEFORE HATH THE ODINSWORD BEEN *MOVED* FROM ITS MOST SACRED *CHAMBER!*

EVEN THY MOST LOYAL *SUPPORTERS* HAVE NOW BEGUN TO WONDER ABOUT THY VERY *SANITY!*

THEN *LET* THEM WONDER, IGRON!

I AM THE *WISDOM*, THE *WILL*, AND THE *WAY*--AND I DO WHAT I MUST TO *PROTECT* MY THRONE!

BESIDES, SLY ONE, ONCE THE ODINSWORD HATH BEEN *INSTALLED* WHERE I COMMAND IT, THERE WILL BE *NONE* IN ALL ASGARD WHO WILL DARE TO *OPPOSE* ME--

--LEST THEY WISH TO BRING ABOUT THE FLAMING *END* OF ALL THAT IS!

GENTLY, DOLTS-- LAY THE SWORD DOWN *GENTLY!*

NOW, ASGARDIANS, BRING THE GOLDEN *THRONE* ITSELF HERE TO ME--AND SET IT DOWN SOFTLY *ATOP* THE MIGHTY ODINSWORD!

DO IT *SWIFTLY*-- LEST YE DESIRE TO FEEL MY *WRATH!*

SO! NOW I SEE THY *PLAN*, MILORD-- BUT DOST EVEN *THOU* DARE SUCH A *RISK?*

TO ACHIEVE MY *PURPOSE*, FRIEND IGRON-- I WILL DARE *ANYTHING!*

I WILL *RULE* IMMORTAL ASGARD-- AND I *ALONE*--OR I SWEAR BY ALL THE POWERS OF *DARKNESS*--

--I WILL *DESTROY* IT!

BUT WHILE THE REALM ETERNAL STILL *ENDURES*, WHY DON'T WE NOW TURN OUR ATTENTION TO THE DESOLATE *WASTELANDS* BEYOND THE BOUNDARIES OF THE ROYAL CITY--

THOU HAST HARDLY *SPOKEN* SINCE OUR JOURNEY BEGAN, MILORD! ARE THY THOUGHTS SO SORELY *TROUBLED?*

'TIS NOT MY *THOUGHTS* THAT TROUBLE ME, VIZIER-- 'TIS MY *HEART!* I'D BELIEVED I HAD *LOST* IT FOREVER TO THE MORTAL *JANE FOSTER*--

--BUT SEEING THE LADY *SIF* ONCE MORE, FEELING HER TENDER *HAND* UPON MY *CHEEK*... I SIMPLY DO NOT *KNOW!*

--AND BRACE OURSELVES FOR *ACTION!*

THE HEART CAN BE MOST *FICKLE* INDEED, FRIEND THOR! METHINKS THAT IS WHY I'D RATHER NOT HAVE *ACCOMPANIED* THEE HERE!

IN TRUTH, TO LOOK UPON KARNILLA'S TIMELESS *BEAUTY* AGAIN MAY BE MORE THAN I CAN *BEAR!*

'TIS A PROBLEM THOU SHALT NOT *LIVE* LONG ENOUGH TO *WORRY* ABOUT, LITTLE FLEA!

BY *ODIN!* 'TIS A GIANT *BARBARIC*--A WARRIOR GUARDIAN OF THE NORN QUEEN'S *DOMAIN!*

THE DENIZENS OF ACCURSED ASGARD ARE NOT *WELCOME* HERE, INSECTS!

'TIS NOT THY *WELCOME* I *SEEK*, BARBARIC--

--'TIS THE *AID* OF THY SORCERESS *MISTRESS!*

YOU MAY SEEK KARNILLA, GODLING -- --BUT YOU HAVE FOUND ONLY *DEATH!*

SKROOM

WE CAME TO THY LAND IN *PEACE*, ENORMOUS ONES-- BUT STILL DIDST THOU *ATTACK* US WITHOUT *CAUSE*, WITHOUT *MERCY!*

VERY WELL THEN! IF 'TIS *BATTLE* THOU DOST *SEEK*--

--THEN BATTLE SHALT THOU *HAVE!*

THOU HAST MADE THY *CHOICE*, BARBARICS!

NOW FEEL THE MATCHLESS *MIGHT* OF THE MYSTIC MALLET *MJOLNIR*--

--AND KNOW THOU WOULDST HAVE CHOSEN FAR MORE *WISELY* TO HAVE SOUGHT *SHELTER* RATHER THAN *COMBAT*--

THRAMM!

--FOR THOUGH THE GOD OF THUNDER IS *RENOWNED* FOR HIS *MERCY*--

--SO TOO IS HE *LEGENDARY* FOR HIS MOST *RIGHTEOUS WRATH!*

THUS *COME*, YE HOWLING WINDS AND LIGHTNING!

COME YE *FORTH* AT THY MASTER'S *COMMAND*--

--TO *SMITE DOWN* THOSE WHO WOULD STAND BEFORE ME IN UNWARRANTED *ANGER!*

THE BARBARICS *FLEE* IN BLIND *PANIC*, FRIEND THOR!

'TWAS *THEIR* DECISION TO MAKE, BRAVE *BALDER!*

WE HAD NO WISH TO FIGHT EVEN SUCH *PRIMITIVE* CREATURES AS *THEY*--

--BUT THE VERY *FATE* OF THE GOLDEN REALM IS AT STAKE HERE--

--AND NAUGHT THAT DWELLS BETWIXT HEAVEN AND HELL WILL *STAY* US FROM ATTAINING OUR *GOAL!*

143

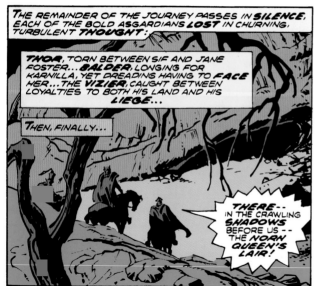

THE REMAINDER OF THE JOURNEY PASSES IN *SILENCE*, EACH OF THE BOLD ASGARDIANS *LOST* IN CHURNING, TURBULENT *THOUGHT*:

THOR, TORN BETWEEN SIF AND JANE FOSTER... *BALDER*, LONGING FOR KARNILLA, YET DREADING HAVING TO *FACE* HER... THE *VIZIER*, CAUGHT BETWEEN LOYALTIES TO BOTH HIS LAND AND HIS *LIEGE*...

THEN, FINALLY...

THERE-- IN THE CRAWLING *SHADOWS* BEFORE US -- THE *NORN QUEEN'S LAIR!*

HOBBLING THEIR FRIGHTENED HORSES, THE THREE GRIM IMMORTALS STRIDE CAUTIOUSLY INTO THE DARKENED CAVERN'S HUNGRY *MAW*.

DOWN TWISTING PASSAGEWAYS THEY WANDER, DRAWN EVER *ONWARD* BY AN ALMOST- ETHEREAL *SINGING*, LIKE SOME LORELEI'S IRRESISTIBLE *SIREN CALL*.

THEN, ABRUPTLY, THE QUESTING ASGARDIANS STEP *OUT* OF THE DARKNESS-- AND INTO THE *LIGHT!*

NORN QUEEN, THE GOD OF THUNDER DOTH GIVE THEE *GREETINGS!*

ENTER, THOR-- AND THY *COMPANIONS* AS WELL! KARNILLA HATH BEEN *EXPECTING* THEE!

'TIS THY FATHER'S SUPPOSED *MADNESS* THAT BRINGS THEE HERE, IS IT NOT?

IF THOU KNOWEST *THAT*, WITCH WOMAN-- THEN THOU MUST KNOW AS WELL THAT WE HAVE COME HERE TO ASK THINE *AID!*

ONLY *THEE*, OF ALL WHO DWELL WITHIN THE REALM ETERNAL, POSSES *POWER* ENOW TO SUNDER THE ENCHANTED *BARRIER* THAT PREVENTS ME FROM *ENTERING* MY FATHER'S PALACE!

WILT THOU *ALLY* THYSELF WITH US, KARNILLA?

I HAVE *AWAITED* THIS DAY FOR AGES, THUNDER GOD -- THE DAY WHEN THOU WOULDST *PROSTRATE* THYSELF BEFORE ME THUS!

THY PLEA IS MOST *TOUCHING* INDEED, BUT STILL I SAY THEE...

NAY!

DOST THOU **KNOW** WHAT THOU DOST **SAY**, NORN QUEEN? IF ODIN'S MADNESS DOTH CONTINUE **UNCHECKED**, 'TWILL SWIFTLY ENVELOPE THINE **OWN** DOMAIN AS WELL!

THINE ONLY **HOPE** IS TO UNITE THY POWERS WITH **OURS** ERE THE ALL-FATHER PASSES BEYOND **REDEMPTION**!

UNITE MYSELF WITH **THEE**? WHY **SHOULD** I?

WHAT HAVE ASGARDIANS EVER SHOWN THE NORN QUEEN SAVE **HATRED**... **LOATHING**... **FEAR**...

...AND **WORST** OF ALL... **SCORN**!

PRITHEE, KARNILLA -- LET NOT THINE ANIMOSITY TOWARDS **ME** TURN THEE AGAINST ALL THE **REALM ETERNAL**!

'TWAS NOT **THEY** WHO DID SPURN THE **LOVE** THOU DIDST SO SELFLESSLY OFFER, 'TWAS **I**!

IF THOU DOST SEEK **VENGEANCE**, KARNILLA -- PRAY SUFFER IT UPON **BALDER** ALONE!

THOU DOST PRESUME **TOO MUCH**, ASGARDIAN --

-- TO EVEN **THINK** THE OMNIPOTENT NORN QUEEN WOULD EVER **DEIGN** TO FEEL AFFECTION FOR SUCH AS **THEE**!

SLAP!

KARNILLA, NOW THAT BALDER'S **HUMILIATION** IS COMPLETE, I PRAY THEE -- **LISTEN** TO US!

THOU ART FAR TOO **WISE** TO THROW AWAY THY KINGDOM FOR THE HOLLOW TASTE OF **VENGEANCE**!

CONSIDER WHAT IS AT **STAKE** HERE, WITCH WOMAN -- **CONSIDER**!

I... HAVE ALREADY DONE PRECISELY **THAT**, OLD ONE!

THEN THOU MUST **KNOW** WHAT WILL SURELY OCCUR SHOULDST THOU **REFUSE** US THINE AID!

WILT THOU HAVE THE SCRIBES PORTRAY THEE AS HISTORY'S **BLACKEST BETRAYER**?

I...

I CARE NOT **HOW** HISTORY DOTH **PAINT** ME, VIZIER --

-- BUT STILL, THINE ARGUMENTS HATH *MERIT!*

AYE, AGED ONE ...FOR HER OWN REASONS, KARNILLA WILL *AID* THEE!

THEN LET US BE ON OUR *WAY,* NORN QUEEN !

TIME GROWS MORE *PRECIOUS* WITH EVERY PASSING *MOMENT!*

THE JOURNEY *BACK* TO THE ROYAL CITY PASSES FAR MORE *SWIFTLY* THAN THE JOURNEY *OUT!*

THE GLEAMING *SPIRES* STILL RISE LIKE QUESTING *FINGERS* TOWARD THE STARS, BUT NOW THEY SEEM SOMEHOW SADLY *TARNISHED* --

-- AS IF THEY WERE FINGERS REACHING BLINDLY OUT FOR *HELP!*

AND *SOON,* WITHIN THE DEPTHS OF THE *CITY* ITSELF...

HOLD, MY FRIENDS! IT SEEMS A *WELCOMING COMMITTEE* DOTH AWAIT US!

BUT THE POWER OF MINE *MYSTIC MALLET* SHALL SWIFTLY CLEAR A PATH FOR US TO...

THUNDER GOD -- *WAIT!*

IF I AM TRULY TO BE A *PART* OF THY REBELLIOUS BAND --

-- THEN 'TIS TIME THE NORN QUEEN DID STRIKE HER FIRST *BLOW!*

AND 'TIS A BLOW VERY *WELL* STRUCK INDEED!

THOU ART TRULY *ONE* OF US *NOW,* KARNILLA!

BUT I FEAR THE *NEXT* BARRIER BEFORE US WILL NOT BE SO EASILY *REMOVED!*

THERE! DOST THOU *SEE*, KARNILLA? EVEN ENCHANTED *MJOLNIR* CANNOT PENETRATE THIS UNSEEN *SHIELD* THAT SURROUNDS THE PALACE ROYAL!

THEN STAND THEE *BACK*, ODINSON--

--AND LET US SEE IF THE *SORCERY* OF THE NORNS CAN *SURPASS* THINE URU HAMMER'S SHEER *BRUTE FORCE!*

MINE IS THE POWER TO SUNDER *MOUNTAINS*, TO PART THE *SEAS*, TO BEND THE VERY *HEAVENS* TO MY WILL--

--BUT ALAS, IT IS *NOT* POWER ENOW TO *PIERCE* THE MYSTIC BARRICADE BEFORE US!

THOU DIDST THY *BEST*, NORN QUEEN! ONE COULD ASK FOR NOTHING *MORE!*

KARNILLA, ART THOU *INJURED?*

IF SO, 'TIS NOT *THINE* AFFAIR, BALDER! I WILL DEAL WITH MY PROBLEMS *ALONE!*

NAY, WITCH WOMAN! *ALONE* EACH OF US HATH ACCOMPLISHED *NAUGHT!*

BUT MAYHAP 'WERE WE TO *JOIN FORCES* AGAINST THIS ACCURSED *OBSTRUCTION--*

"-- OUR POWERS *COMBINED* WOULD PROVE *STRONG* ENOUGH TO *BREACH* THE VEIL AT LAST!"

MORE **POWER**, NORN QUEEN-- **MORE!**

THE BARRIER DOTH BEGIN TO **TREMBLE!** IT BEGINS TO **GIVE WAY--!**

BY **ASGARD'S GOLDEN GATES!!**

A GAPING **APERTURE** HATH APPEARED IN THE VERY **AIR** BEFORE US!

FOLLOW ME **THRU** IT, FRIENDS-- AND **SWIFTLY!**

WE **TRY**, MILORD-- BUT WE **CANNOT!**

WITHOUT THE ADDED POWER OF THY **MYSTIC MALLET** TO HOLD IT **OPEN**, THE BARRIER HATH SEALED ITSELF **ANEW!**

'TIS UP TO THEE ALONE TO DEAL WITH THY FATHER'S **MADNESS**, THOR!

GOOD **LUCK**, MY PRINCE! THE PRAYERS OF ALL THY PEOPLE GO **WITH** THEE!

VERILY, BRAVE BALDER-- I HOPE I WILL NOT **NEED** THEM!

SO, THUNDER GOD--

--AGAINST THY FATHER'S **IMPERIAL COMMAND**, THOU HAST **RETURNED!**

I COULD DO LITTLE **ELSE**, MY LIEGE!

A GOOD SON'S PLACE IS **BESIDE** HIS FATHER IN TIME OF SICKNESS AND **NEED!**

THEN COME AHEAD IF THOU DOST **INSIST**, MY **INSOLENT** SON--

--AND SEE FOR YOURSELF WHAT **LITTLE** NEED THY SIRE **HATH** OF THEE!

SOLEMNLY, THE GOD OF THUNDER *FOLLOWS* THE ANGRY IMAGE ALONG THE CASTLE'S WINDING *CORRIDORS*, UNTIL HE FINALLY REACHES...

THE ROYAL *THRONE-ROOM!*

WHAT HAST THOU *DONE* TO IT?

SOMETHING DOTH *TROUBLE* THEE, THUNDER GOD?

MAYHAP THOU DOST NOT *LIKE* THE NEW *DECOR?*

A *PITY*...BUT CONSIDERING THE TENOR OF THE PEOPLE THESE DAYS, WE THOUGHT IT A NECESSARY *ADDITION!*

IN TRUTH, ODINSON, WE HAVE BEEN *EXPECTING* THEE HERE FOR QUITE SOME TIME!

WE ARE TRULY *AMAZED* IT HATH TAKEN THEE SO *LONG* TO FINALLY *ARRIVE!*

BUT NOW THAT HE IS *HERE*, IGRON, THE QUESTION DOTH *PRESENT* ITSELF--

--WHAT ARE WE TO *DO* WITH HIM?

MY LIEGE, I...I DO NOT *UNDERSTAND!*

I RETURNED TO THE REALM ETERNAL BECAUSE I WAS TOLD A TERRIBLE *MADNESS* DID PLAGUE THEE--

--A MADNESS FOSTERED BY *THE DEVIOUS IGRON*, HE WHO THOU HAST TAKEN AS THINE *ADVISOR* IN PLACE OF THE WISE *VIZIER!*

AND IN A MANNER OF *SPEAKING*, ODINSON--THEY TOLD THEE *TRUE!*

I AM NOW INDEED THE GOOD *RIGHT HAND* OF HE WHO DOTH SIT UPON THE *THRONE!*

AYE, I AM *THAT*...AND *MORE!*

BUT *WHY*, MY LIEGE? WHY HAST THOU TURNED THY *BACK* UPON ALL THOU HAST SO LONG *BELIEVED* IN?

TO TAKE A CRAVEN JACKAL SUCH AS *IGRON* INTO THY CONFIDENCE... MY FATHER, 'TIS SO *UNLIKE* THEE!

'TIS *THERE* WHERE THOU ART SADLY *MISTAKEN* THUNDER GOD!

TO DO WHAT I HAVE DONE IS VERY *MUCH* LIKE ME, GODLING!

VERY *MUCH* LIKE ME *INDEED*!!

HA HA HA HA

LOOK AT THE STARK *BEWILDERMENT* ETCHED UPON THE GOD OF THUNDER'S *FACE*, ALMIGHTY ONE!

THE TRUSTING FOOL STILL HATH NOT *REALIZED* THE SIMPLE *TRUTH*!

WHAT TRUTH, LORD ODIN? OF WHAT DOTH THE EVIL IGRON *SPEAK*?

I PRAY THEE, MY LIEGE-- PLEASE *ANSWER* ME! I CAN ENDURE THIS *CONFUSION* NO LONGER!

"THEN GAZE UPON HIM THOU DIDST THINK TO BE THY *FATHER*, THUNDER GOD--

"--AND THE TRUTH SHALL BE *REVEALED* TO THEE AT LAST!"

BY VOLSTAGG'S BEARD! ODIN'S VERY *FORM* HATH BEGUN TO SHIMMER--TO *CHANGE*--!

150

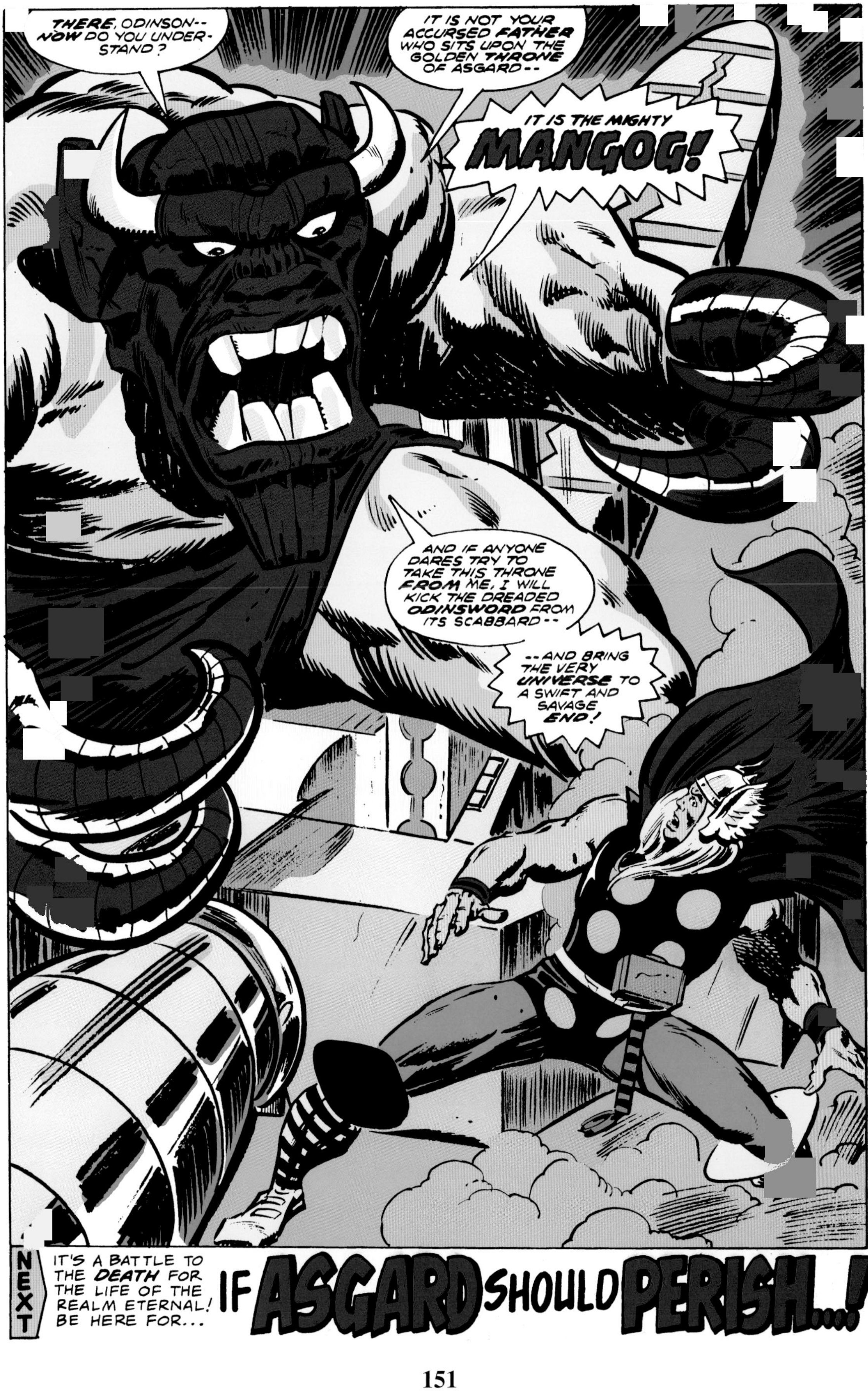
THERE, ODINSON-- NOW DO YOU UNDERSTAND?
IT IS NOT YOUR ACCURSED FATHER WHO SITS UPON THE GOLDEN THRONE OF ASGARD--
IT IS THE MIGHTY MANGOG!
AND IF ANYONE DARES TRY TO TAKE THIS THRONE FROM ME, I WILL KICK THE DREADED ODINSWORD FROM ITS SCABBARD--
--AND BRING THE VERY UNIVERSE TO A SWIFT AND SAVAGE END!
NEXT
IT'S A BATTLE TO THE DEATH FOR THE LIFE OF THE REALM ETERNAL! BE HERE FOR...
IF ASGARD SHOULD PERISH...!

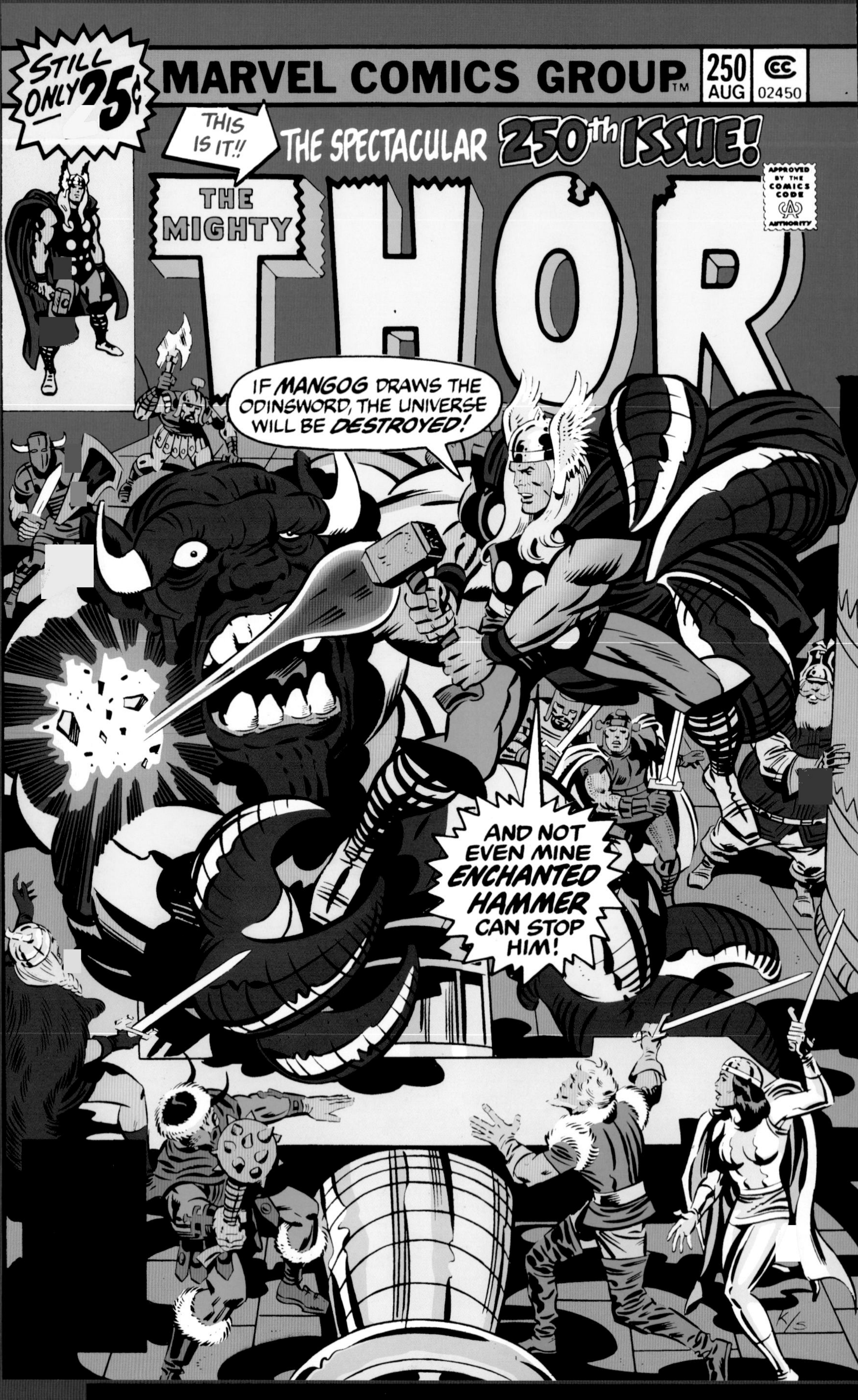
STILL ONLY 25¢
MARVEL COMICS GROUP™
250 AUG
CC 02450
THIS IS IT!!
THE SPECTACULAR 250th ISSUE!
APPROVED BY THE COMICS CODE AUTHORITY
THE MIGHTY THOR
IF MANGOG DRAWS THE ODINSWORD, THE UNIVERSE WILL BE DESTROYED!
AND NOT EVEN MINE ENCHANTED HAMMER CAN STOP HIM!

When lame Dr. DONALD BLAKE strikes his wooden walking stick upon the ground, it becomes the mystic mallet MJOLNIR—and Blake is transformed into the Norse God of Thunder, Master of the Storm and the Lightning, Heir to the Throne of Immortal Asgard...

Stan Lee PRESENTS: THE MIGHTY THOR!™

IF ASGARD SHOULD PERISH...!

AYE, THUNDER GOD--'TIS THE MIGHTY MANGOG WHO NOW RULES IMMORTAL ASGARD!

AND IF ANYONE DARES TRY TO STEAL THE GOLDEN THRONE FROM ME, I WILL PULL THE DREADED ODINSWORD FROM ITS SCABBARD--

--AND BRING THE VERY UNIVERSE TO A SWIFT AND FIERY END!!

AND ON THAT GRIM NOTE, PREPARE THYSELF FOR WONDERMENT SUCH AS THOU HAST NE'ER BEFORE KNOWN--STARTING NOW!

JOURNEY BEYOND THE IMAGINATION WITH... LEN WEIN WRITER/EDITOR * JOHN BUSCEMA ILLUSTRATOR * TONY DeZUNIGA EMBELLISHER * JOHN COSTANZA letterer * GLYNIS WEIN colorist WE PROMISE YOU WON'T REGRET IT!

153

AT LAST IT DOTH ALL BECOME *CLEAR!* MY NOBLE FATHER DID NOT GO *MAD!* RATHER *THOU* DIDST *USURP* HIS RIGHTFUL PLACE UPON THE THRONE!

BUT *HOW?* WHERE DID SUCH AS THEE GAIN *POWER* ENOW TO OVERCOME ALMIGHTY *ODIN?*

THERE BE TIMES, THUNDER GOD, WHEN THE FICKLE *FATES* CAN BE MOST *KIND.*

...AND THOSE WHO WOULD BE *MORE* THAN KINGS!

'TWAS NOT TO BE IGRON'S LOT TO DWELL IN DARK *DISGRACE* FOREVER, BUT RATHER TO SIT AT THE SIDE OF *KINGS...*

THOU DOST SPEAK IN *RIDDLES,* SLY ONE. MAKE THY MEANING *PLAIN!*

EVEN NOW, HIS ARROGANCE KNOWS NO *BOUNDS,* IGRON!

NAY, MANGOG. 'TIS ONLY RIGHT THE THUNDER GOD SHOULD KNOW THE *TRUTH* BEFORE HE DIES--

LET US JUST *SLAY* THE ODINSON-- AND BE *DONE* WITH HIM!

--FOR 'TWILL MAKE HIS PASSING INTO *VALHALLA* ALL THE MORE *BITTER!*

"IRONICALLY, 'TWAS ODIN'S OWN DOING THAT DID LEAD TO HIS ULTIMATE *DOWN-FALL,* FOR 'TWAS ODIN WHO DID CON-SIGN ME TO THE DANK *DUNGEONS* BENEATH THE PALACE ROYAL, WHEN MY SCHEME TO GAIN *CONTROL* OF THE REALM ETERNAL MET WITH FINAL *DEFEAT!* *

"I DID MARK MY TIME THERE *WELL,* PLOTTING, PLANNING--FOR I KNEW THE DAY WOULD DAWN WHEN I WOULD HAVE MY *REVENGE!*

* AS DRAMATICALLY DISPLAYED IN *THOR #217.* --LEARNED LEN.

"BUT WHEN THAT DAY OF RETRIBUTION FINALLY *ARRIVED,* I ALMOST DID NOT *KNOW* IT FOR WHAT IT WAS--

"--FOR THE CLARION CALL OF VENGEANCE CAME AS A SOFT *SKITTERING* IN THE CORNER OF MY CELL!"

OD'S BLOOD! MUST I NOW SHARE MY FOUL IMPRISONMENT WITH FILTHY *RODENTS?*

I WOULD SOONER *CRUSH* THE CURSED THING BENEATH MY *HEEL!*

"I RAISED MY BOOT TO *STRIKE,* BUT SOMETHING ABOUT THE SMALL, SCURRYING FORM SEEMED *UNNATURAL,* AND I PLUCKED IT FROM THE FLOOR TO DISCOVER..."

'TIS NO *RODENT--* BUT THE MONSTER MEN CALL *MANGOG!*

PUT ME *DOWN,* ASGARDIAN-- OR FEEL MY AWESOME *WRATH!*

ODIN DOTH NEED *EXPLAIN* HIMSELF TO *NO ONE,* GUARD!

I AM THE *WISDOM,* THE *WILL,* AND THE *WAY*--AND THOU WOULDST DO WELL TO *REMEMBER* THAT!

F-FORGIVE ME, MILORD, I--I MEANT THEE NO *OFFENSE.*

"THEN I WATCHED IN *SATISFACTION* AS MANGOG STRODE OFF TO TAKE HIS PLACE UPON THE GOLDEN THRONE..."

VERILY THE CROWN OF COMMAND DOTH SIT *WELL* UPON THE MONSTROUS ONE'S *BROW.*

MAYHAP SOMEDAY SOON 'TWILL SIT AS WELL UPON *MINE!*

AND IN THE DAYS SINCE *PAST,* MANGOG AND I HAVE *RESHAPED* THE REALM ETERNAL TO OUR *LIKING*--

--FOR NONE WILL DARE STAND *AGAINST* US!

NAY, INSIDIOUS ONE--*I* DARE!

I SHALL *TELL* THE PEOPLE OF THY DEVILISH *DECEPTION*-- AND WE SHALL DRAG THEE *SCREAMING* FROM THE THRONE!

THUNDER GOD, THY *NAIVETE* DOTH TRULY *ASTOUND* ME!

TELL YOUR SIMPLE-MINDED PEOPLE WHATEVER YOU *WILL,* GODLING--BUT THEY'RE *NOT* GOING TO BELIEVE YOU!

AFTER ALL, MY PRINCE-- WHAT *PROOF* HAST THOU OF ANY OF THIS?

WHAT *EVIDENCE* IS THERE TO SHOW THAT REGAL ODIN IS *NOT* ALL HE DOTH *APPEAR* TO BE?

THY FOUL MASQUERADE CANNOT ENDURE *FOREVER,* CHURLS! SOONER OR LATER, THOU SHALT MAKE A *MISTAKE,* AND THEN...

ZOUNDS!!

AYE, THUNDER GOD, 'TIS *THOU* WHO DIDST *ERR*--

--IN THINKING THOU WOULDST EVER BE ALLOWED TO *LEAVE* THE PALACE ROYAL!

MALEVOLENT ONE, THOU ART TRULY MAD IF THOU THINKEST ME SO EASILY DEFEATED!

SKROOO

I AM PLEDGED TO *WARN* THE CITIZENS OF ASGARD OF THY BASE AND HEINOUS *TREACHERY*--

CHONK

--AND THERE BE NOT *POWER* ENOW IN ALL THE REALM ETERNAL TO *STAY* ME FROM MY GIVEN *DUTY!*

WHAMM!

BUT, UNFORTUNATELY, THE POWER OF THE REALM ETERNAL FAIRLY PALES BEFORE THE POWER OF HE WHO IS ITS MONARCH--

--AND EVEN THE *GOD OF THUNDER* MUST FALL BEFORE THE FULL UNLEASHED FURY OF *ODIN*--

--OR THE FURY OF HE WHO WEARS THE ALL-FATHER'S *FACE!* GUARDS, *REMOVE* THIS VERMIN FROM MY *SIGHT*--

--AND CARRY HIM OUT BEFORE THE CITY *GATES!*

THE GOD OF THUNDER HATH CONSPIRED TO *OVERTHROW* THY JUST AND RIGHTFUL *RULER!*

NOW LET HIM SERVE AS A BITTER *EXAMPLE,* THAT NO ONE *ELSE* WILL DARE COMMIT SO VILE AN ACT *AGAIN!*

BUT EVEN *NOW,* THOSE WHO *SHARE* THE THUNDER GOD'S CAUSE ARE SPREAD ACROSS THE *COUNTRY-SIDE*--

--EACH *STRIVING* IN HIS OR HER OWN WAY TO *RALLY* THE ASGARDIAN PEOPLE TO THEIR SIDE.

OF COURSE, SOME ARE MORE *SUBTLE* IN THEIR URGING THAN OTHERS.

BUT, AT LAST, DESPITE MUCH FRIGHTENED **PROTEST**, EACH OF THOR'S COMRADES **RETURNS** FROM THE OUTLANDS WITH AN ANGRY **ENTOURAGE** IN TOW...

ONWARD, GOOD WARRIORS!

VALOROUS **VOLSTAGG** DOTH LEAD YE ON TO **TRIUMPH!**

ACROSS THE REALM ETERNAL, THE SCENE IS **REPEATED** OVER AND OVER...

HO, GRIM HOGUN-- I SEE THOU HAST DONE **WELL!**

NO BETTER THAN **THEE**, DASHING **FANDRAL**-- OR OUR **BRETHREN!**

THEN WHAT ARE WE **WAITING** FOR, MY FRIENDS?

ON TO THE **PALACE ROYAL!**

TO THE **PALACE ROYAL**-- AND **VICTORY!!**

THE CRY OF **BATTLE** HOT UPON THEIR LIPS, THE GRIM-VISAGED **WARRIORS** POUR THRU THE GLEAMING **GATES** OF THE GOLDEN CITY--

--**WEAPONS** IN HAND, READY FOR **ANYTHING**--

--ANYTHING, THAT IS, SAVE THAT WHICH THEY ACTUALLY **FIND!**

BY **VOLSTAGG'S BILLOWING BEARD!**

'TIS NOT **POSSIBLE**--!

BRAVE BALDER, PRAY TELL ME 'TIS BUT A **DREAM!**

WOULD THAT I **COULD**, MILADY **SIF**--BUT I **CANNOT!**

"'TIS INDEED THE NOBLE *GOD OF THUNDER*-- SHACKLED AND BOUND WITH HIS ENCHANTED *HAMMER* ALMOST TANTALIZINGLY OUT OF REACH--AND *HUNG* BEFORE THE GATES OF THE CITY LIKE SOME GREAT UNGAINLY *SCARECROW!*

"BY THE GOLDEN SPIRES, HOW CAN THIS *BE?*"

WHAT MATTERS THE *REASON,* BALDER, WHEN MY BELOVED DOTH *SUFFER* SO?

I PRAY THEE, HELP ME *RELEASE* HIM ERE...

TAKE NOT ANOTHER *STEP,* LADY SIF!

LIFT THINE HAND TO *COMFORT* THE TREASON-OUS THUNDER GOD-- AND THOU SHALT FEEL MY RIGHTEOUS *WRATH!!*

IN ODIN'S NAME, *WHO*--?

A MOST **WELL-CHOSEN** EXPLETIVE, MY **DEAR**--FOR 'TWAS INDEED IN **ODIN'S** NAME THAT THOU WERT COMMANDED TO **HALT!**

'TWAS **I** WHO DID ORDER THE THUNDER GOD THUS **HUNG** THERE--

--AND 'TIS THERE HE SHALL **REMAIN** UNTIL I DEEM **OTHERWISE!**

BUT MY LIEGE, DOST THOU NOT THINK THE PUNISHMENT UNSEEMINGLY **HARSH?**

THE GOD OF THUNDER IS THINE OWN **SON** AFTER ALL--AND JUSTICE HATH NO **MEANING** LEST IT BE TEMPERED WITH **MERCY.**

DOST THOU ONCE MORE PRESUME TO **CONTRADICT** THY LORD AND MASTER, **VIZIER?**

NAY, MY LIEGE-- NEVER WOULD I ARGUE THY **WISDOM.** I MERELY SUGGEST MOST **HUMBLY** THAT THOU HAST...

HOLD THY **TONGUE,** VIZIER! I HAVE HEARD ENOUGH **DISSENSION** OF LATE TO LAST ME AN **ETERNITY!**

I AM **ODIN,** MONARCH MOST HIGH OF IMMORTAL **ASGARD**--

--AND I WILL BE **OBEYED!!**

LIES.

HE DOTH...SPEAK **LIES** MOST... FIERCELY **FOUL.**

'TIS NOT THY...RIGHTFUL **LIEGE...** WHO STANDS BEFORE YE..., BUT RATHER...THE MALEVOLENT,...

AARRGGHH!!

SILENCE, PERFIDIOUS ONE!

THOU SHALT SPREAD THY **SEDITION** NO FURTHER!

WELL **DONE,** ALMIGHTY SIRE.

162

MY LIEGE, WHY DIDST THOU *STRIKE*?

THOU WERT WARNED TO HOLD THY *TONGUE*, WIZENED ONE!

HHUUNNHH!!

NOW *ODIN* SHALL HOLD IT *FOR* THEE!

WE SAY THEE-- *ENOUGH!* THY *MADNESS* CANNOT BE ALLOWED TO *CONTINUE!*

THE THUNDER GOD IS ALREADY THY *PRISONER!* THERE WAS NO *NEED* TO....

THEN IT HATH *COME* AT LAST-- THE MOMENT I HAVE SO LONG BEEN *EXPECTING!*

FINALLY, THOU HAST ALL TURNED *AGAINST* ME LIKE RABID *DOGS* SNAPPING AT MY *HEELS!*

THEN IF AS A *DOG* THOU DOST *ACT*, BLACK-HANDED BALDER--

--A DOG SHALT THOU *BE!!*

OD'S BLOOD!

WITH BUT A *GESTURE*, THE ALL-FATHER HATH *TRANSFORMED* BRAVE BALDER INTO-- A *CUR!*

BUT SHALL THAT *DETER* US FROM OUR *DUTY*, MY BROTHERS-IN-ARMS?

NAY, FRIEND HOGUN! FOR ONCE, *MY* SOUL BE AS GRIM AS THINE *OWN*!

THEN WE MUST *FIGHT ON*, MY FRIENDS--AYE, EVEN UNTO...

BUT THE **REST** *OF DASHING FANDRAL'S SOLEMN PLEDGE IS* **LOST** *AMIDST A SUDDEN FLURRY OF* **BRAYING**, **GRUNTING**, *AND* **HOWLING--**

--AS THE THREE BOLD ASGARDIANS **JOIN** *THE BARKING BALDER IN* **DEFEAT!**

A DEFEAT NOT **EVERYONE** *IS YET READY TO* **ADMIT!**

MILADY SIF-- *COME THEE BACK!*

NAY, LOYAL HILDE-GARDE-- I *CANNOT!*

MY BELOVED THOR MUST BE *FREED* FROM HIS UNJUST *IMPRISON-MENT!*

I *BEG* THEE, LORD ODIN-- THOU MUST COME TO THY *SENSES* ERE... *NO!*

SO THOU WOULDST RISK ALL TO *RESCUE* THY PRECIOUS *THUNDER GOD*, AY?

THEN 'TIS *ALL* THAT THOU SHALT *LOSE*, MY DEAR LADY SIF!

LET US SEE IF THE OH-SO-NOBLE THOR CAN FEEL *ANYTHING* FOR THEE NOW...SAVE *REVULSION!*

IN ASGARD, THERE IS AN ANCIENT *PROVERB* ABOUT THE *PEBBLES* THAT BROKE THE TROLL KING'S *BACK.*

TO HIS *DISMAY,* THE MIGHTY THOR NOW *UNDER-STANDS* THAT PROVERB'S MEANING ALL TOO *WELL!*

I SAY THEE-- *ENOUGH!*

NO LONGER CAN I STAND IDLY BY WHILST THOU DOST COMMIT SUCH TER-RIBLE *ATROCITIES* AGAINST MY CLOSEST *COMPANIONS*--

--AND THE RAVEN-TRESSED *GODDESS* THAT I *LOVE!*

NAY, DESPITE MINE OVERWHELMING *EXHAUSTION,* DESPITE THE UNIMAGINABLE *STRAIN*--

--I SHALL BE FREE OF THE CURSED *SHACKLES* WHICH DOTH BIND ME--

--OR *PERISH* IN THE ATTEM--

PROPHETIC *WORDS,* THUNDER GOD-- ALL TOO SADLY *PROPHETIC* INDEED!

DOST THOU *SEE?* THERE IS NOT A BEING IN ALL ASGARD WHO CAN STAND BEFORE MY *POWER!*

EVEN THE GOD OF THUNDER HATH BEEN *CRUSHED* LIKE SOME INSIGNIFICANT *INSECT!*

I PRAY THEE, ALMIGHTY ONE-- *CONTROL* THYSELF!

THERE DOTH BE NO *NEED* FOR THEE TO *CONFIRM* THE VAGUE SUSPICIONS ALREADY GROWING AMONGST THY *PEOPLE!*

THOU WOULDST HAVE ME *DENY* MY LONG-SOUGHT *VICTORY* FOR THE SAKE OF THAT *MINDLESS RABBLE?*

LOOK UPON THEM, SLY ONE-- THEY ARE BUT *SHEEP,* READY TO BE LED TO PASTURE OR TO *SLAUGHTER* AS THEIR MASTER SEES *FIT!*

AND MAKE NO *MISTAKE,* IGRON-- I *AM* THEIR *MASTER!*

I--AND I *ALONE!*

BUT WHAT ABOUT *ME,* MY LIEGE.

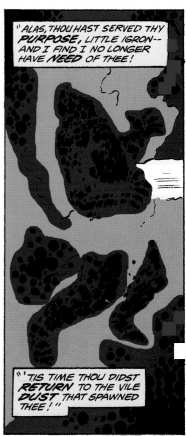

"*ALAS,* THOU HAST SERVED THY *PURPOSE,* LITTLE IGRON-- AND I FIND I NO LONGER HAVE *NEED* OF THEE!"

"*'TIS* TIME THOU DIDST *RETURN* TO THE VILE *DUST* THAT SPAWNED THEE!'"

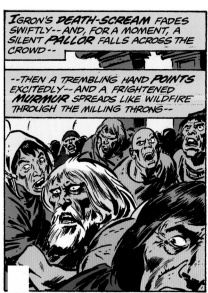

IGRON'S **DEATH-SCREAM** FADES SWIFTLY--AND, FOR A MOMENT, A SILENT **PALLOR** FALLS ACROSS THE CROWD--

--THEN A TREMBLING HAND **POINTS** EXCITEDLY--AND A FRIGHTENED **MURMUR** SPREADS LIKE WILDFIRE THROUGH THE MILLING THRONG--

--A MURMUR THAT FINDS ITS **VOICE** IN THE DEFIANT FIGURE OF **HILDEGARDE!**

VARLET, THOU ART NOT OUR GOOD AND NOBLE LORD **ODIN**--

AYE, WOMAN--AND THERE IS LITTLE YOU CAN DO TO **STOP** ME!

--BUT THE MALEVOLENT **MENACE** WHO HATH EVER BEEN CALLED **MANGOG!**

THOUGH MY STOLEN VISAGE HAS **FADED** WITH IGRON'S **DEATH**, STILL NO GOD LIVES IN ALL OF ASGARD WITH THE POWER TO **DEFY** ME!

NAY, MONSTER--

EH?

--**THOR** DOTH DEFY THEE--

--UNTO **DEATH**-- AYE, AND **BEYOND!**

THOU HAST **TWISTED** THE POWER OF THE REALM ETERNAL TO THY FOUL **WILL!**

THOU HAST SOUGHT TO **SULLY** THE ALL-FATHER'S PROUD AND NOBLE **NAME!**

"AND FOR THOSE **CRIMES** AND MYRIAD **OTHERS** YET UNCOUNTED, SHALT THOU NOW FEEL THE MIGHT OF MINE ENCHANTED **URU** HAMMER--

"--AND THOU SHALT KNOW IT STRIKES FOR **JUSTICE**--AND FOR **VENGEANCE!**"

WITLESS GODLING, YOUR WEAPON WILL **NOT** STRIKE AT ALL!

MANGOG IS STILL **POWER INCARNATE**--

WAK!

--AND ALTHOUGH IT IS NO LONGER THE POWER OF AN **ENTIRE RACE**, IT IS STILL POWER SUPPLIED ME BY THE **WORSHIP** OF YOUR SIMPLE-MINDED **SUBJECTS**--

--AND THAT IS POWER **ENOUGH** FOR THE **TASK** WHICH LIES BEFORE ME!

NAY, MONSTROUS ONE, THOU CANST NOT **MEAN**...

THUNDER GOD, I **WARNED** YOU THAT IF I COULD NOT **RULE** ASGARD, I WOULD **DESTROY** IT--

--AND MANGOG ALWAYS KEEPS HIS **WORD**!

KRUMMM!

THOR'S WORD DOTH BE **HIS** BOND AS WELL, FOUL DEMON--

--AND I HAVE SWORN TO PUT AN **END** TO THEE!

IMPUDENT **FLEA**!

ODIN'S EYES! I HAD **FORGOTTEN** MANGOG'S FLASHING **TAIL**!

YOU ARE ALMOST NOT WORTH THE **BOTHER** IT WILL TAKE TO **SLAY** YOU!

AND 'TIS A LAPSE OF MEMORY THAT MAY COST THE VERY **UNIVERSE**!

FOR MANGOG DOTH SEEK TO REACH THE ENCHANTED **ODIN-SWORD**--

WRUUNCH!

--AND IF ANY SAVE THE **ALL-FATHER** HIMSELF DOTH DRAW THAT DREADED WEAPON FROM ITS **SCABBARD**, 'TWILL SIGNAL THE DAWN OF **RAGNAROK**--

--THE DAY WHEN ALL THAT MAN AND GOD HATH WROUGHT MUST **PERISH**!

I MUST **HALT** THE MONSTROUS ONE ERE... NAY, 'TIS **TOO LATE**--!

"THE GLOATING MANGOG HATH BREACHED THE VERY **RAMPARTS** OF THE PALACE IMPERIAL--

"--AND THERE BE **NAUGHT** TO STAND BETWIXT **HIM** AND HIS MOST TERRIBLE **GOAL**!"

ONE MOMENT *LONGER*-- AND I SHALL *REPAY* ACCURSED ODIN FOR HIS *CRIME* AGAINST MY *RACE!*

ONE MOMENT *MORE*-- AND I SHALL HAVE MY LONG-SOUGHT *REVENGE!*

THEN THAT MOMENT MUST NEVER COME TO *PASS*, THOU HEINOUS BEAST!

AYE, MANGOG-- NEVER SHALT THOU LAY THY FILTHY *CLAW* UPON THE ODIN-SWORD WHILST THE GOD OF THUNDER DOTH *LIVE!*

THOR?!?

THEN YOU SHALL LIVE *NO LONGER*, LITTLE GNAT!

MANGOG EXISTS SOLELY TO *KILL*-- AND *YOU* SHALL BE MY GREATEST *VICTIM!*

THINE ONLY VICTIM SHALL BE *THYSELF*, MONSTER!

FOR THE *HATRED* THAT FILLS THY SOUL SHALL SOON *CONSUME* THEE LIKE A RAGING *FLAME*--

--LEAVING NAUGHT BUT BITTER *ASHES* TO MARK THAT THOU HADST EVER *BEEN!*

YOU *FELLED* ME, THUNDER GOD! NONE BUT *ODIN* HAS EVER DONE THAT *BEFORE!*

VERILY, MANGOG-- I AM NOBLE ODIN'S *SON!*

'TIS *HIS* BLOOD THAT FLOWS WITHIN ME-- AND 'TIS IN *HIS* GLORIOUS NAME THAT I *DEFEND* THE REALM ETERNAL!

THEN IN *HIS* NAME SHALL YOU BE TORN *LIMB* FROM WRITHING *LIMB*, IF NEED BE--

-- SO THAT I MAY *REACH* THE WAITING *ODINSWORD* AT LAST!!

BACK, I SAY THEE, FOUL DEMON-- **BACK!** THOU SHALT NOT **PASS!**

THERE IS NO WAY YOU CAN **STOP** ME, GODLING!

I HAVE **AWAITED** THIS DAY FOR TIME BEYOND RECKONING, AND NOTHING WILL **STAY** ME FROM...

WH-WHAT IS **HAPPENING** TO ME? I BEGIN TO GROW **WEAK**, AS IF...

NO! I--I'M FADING AWAY! YOU'VE **TRICKED** ME, THUNDER GOD--

--BUT I'LL NOT BE **CHEATED** OF MY **VENGEANCE!**

I MUST REACH THE **ODINSWORD!!**

I MUSSSSSSSS...

MANGOG'S FINAL SOUND IS MOST **APPROPRIATE** INDEED: THE ANGRY **HISS** OF THE **SERPENT** FLEEING PARADISE.

FOR A TIME, THE THUNDER GOD STANDS **ALONE**, LOST IN THOUGHT AND SILENT **PRAYER**, UNTIL...

BELOVED, ART THOU...?

AYE, MILADY... I AM **WELL.**

THE REALM ETERNAL STILL **STANDS.**

IT DOTH SEEM MANGOG'S **SORCERY** HATH FADED WITH HIS **PASSING** --BUT WHAT WROUGHT THE MONSTROUS ONE'S **END?**

WITHOUT THE **WORSHIP** OF OUR PEOPLE TO **SUSTAIN** HIM, METHINKS MANGOG LITERALLY... **USED HIMSELF UP!**

HE DID THINK HE COULD **DESTROY** THE GOLDEN REALM... BUT HE WAS **WRONG.**

FOR SO LONG AS MEN OF GOOD WILL DOTH **LIVE**-- --THERE SHALL **ALWAYS BE AN ASGARD!!**

NEXT ISSUE: JOIN THE GOD OF THUNDER ON A GRIM JOURNEY TO **VALHALLA**, AS THE QUEST FOR THE MISSING **ODIN** BEGINS WITH A **BLAST!** BE HERE FOR...

TO HELA... AND BACK!

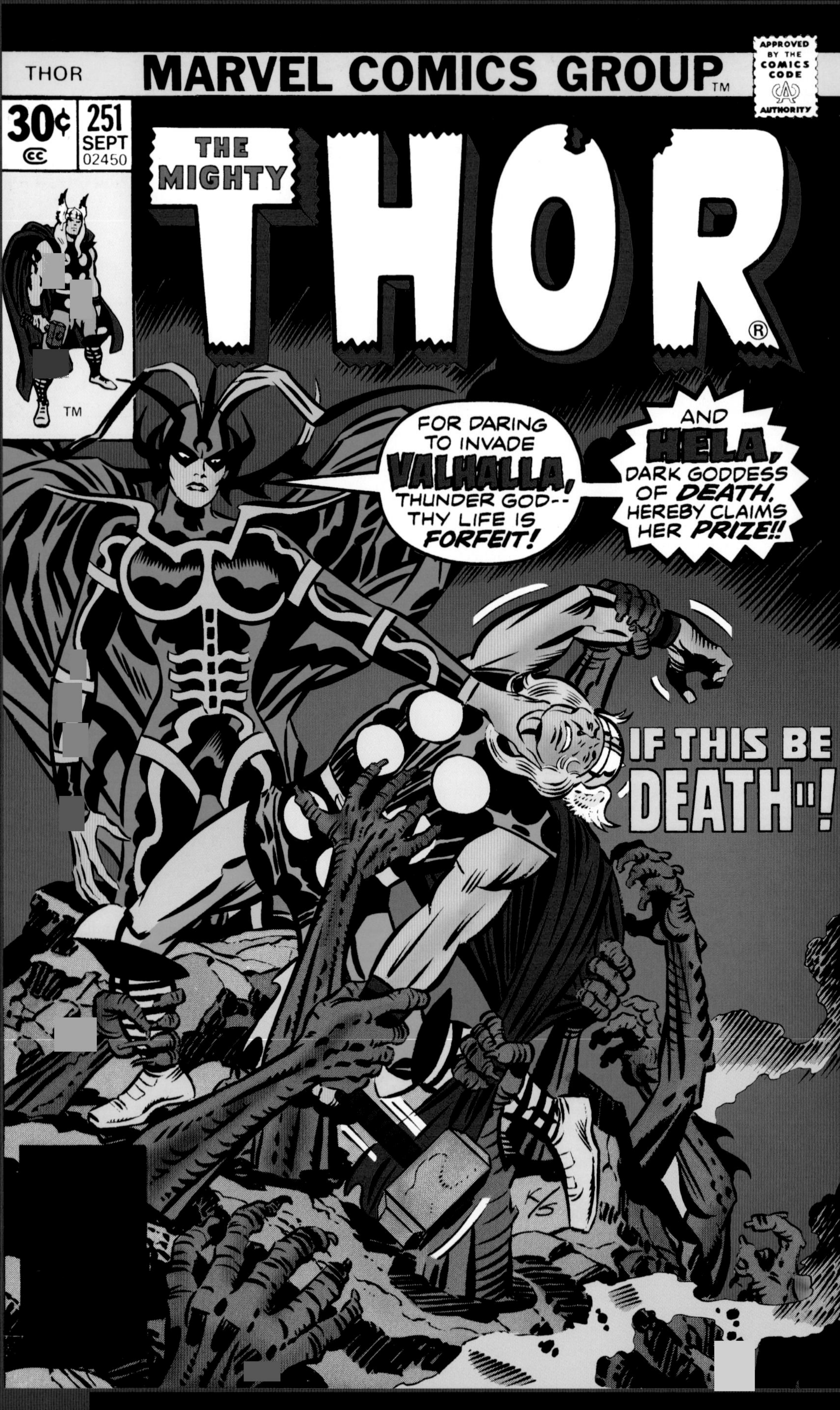

THOR
MARVEL COMICS GROUP
APPROVED BY THE COMICS CODE AUTHORITY
30¢
251 SEPT 02450
THE MIGHTY
THOR
FOR DARING TO INVADE VALHALLA, THUNDER GOD-- THY LIFE IS FORFEIT!
AND HELA, DARK GODDESS OF DEATH, HEREBY CLAIMS HER PRIZE!!
IF THIS BE DEATH"!

When lame Dr. DONALD BLAKE strikes his wooden walking stick upon the ground, it becomes the mystic mallet MJOLNIR—and Blake is transformed into the Norse God of Thunder, Master of the Storm and the Lightning, Heir to the Throne of Immortal Asgard...

Stan Lee PRESENTS: THE MIGHTY THOR!™

LEN WEIN WRITER / EDITOR | **JOHN BUSCEMA & TONY DeZUNIGA** ILLUSTRATORS | **GLYNIS WEIN** COLORIST | **CONDOY** LETTERER

TO HELA AND BACK

THERE IS A **STORM** BREWING.

AYE, EVEN THOUGH HE WHO IS ITS RIGHTFUL **LORD** AND **MASTER** SITS BROODING IN SOLEMN SOLITUDE, THERE IS A RAGING **TEMPEST** BREWING THAT MAY SOON THREATEN TO SWEEP **WORLDS** AWAY BEFORE IT--

--FOR IT IS A **TEMPEST** BREWING BEHIND THE THUNDER GOD'S OWN ANGRY AZURE **EYES!**

MILORD **THOR?**

MAY I **SPEAK** WITH THEE, BELOVED?

EH? OH. FAIR *SIF*, PRAY *FORGIVE* ME, MILADY.

NAY, MY LOVE. I'VE ONLY NOW *ARRIVED*-- TO SADLY FIND THEE SITTING IN REPOSE MOST *GRIM* INDEED!

HAST THOU BEEN STANDING THERE *LONG*?

ARE THY *THOUGHTS* AS TROUBLED AS THY *VISAGE*, MILORD?

AYE, MILADY.

DOST THOU STILL *MOURN* THE LOSS OF THE MORTAL WOMAN *JANE FOSTER*? I KNOW, IN THY HEART, 'TIS *SHE* THOU DOST TRULY *LOVE*--

--BUT IS THE ETERNALLY-FAITHFUL *SIF* SUCH A SORRY *SUBSTITUTE*?

NAY, GENTLE ONE-- NOT *ALL*!

THOU ART *FAIRER* THAN FAIR HAS ANY *RIGHT* TO BE, GOOD SIF. THROUGH THY NOBLE *SACRIFICE*, THY SPIRIT AND JANE FOSTER'S ARE AS *ONE**--

--AND I WOULD *LOVE* THAT SHINING *SPIRIT*-- THAT SELFLESS *HEART*-- IF THY FORM WERE CARVED OF *STONE*!

* SINCE *THOR* #236.
--LEN.

'TIS THE *DISAPPEARANCE* OF MY MOST NOBLE *FATHER* THAT DISTURBS ME, BELOVED. FOR IF ODIN HATH *PERISHED*, MUST THE *REALM ETERNAL* ITSELF NOT FOLLOW SOON *AFTER*?

BUT ALL IS NOT YET *LOST*, MY PRINCE. EVEN NOW, THE WISE *VIZIER* DOTH SEEK THY SIRE'S *WHERE-ABOUTS*!

THEN LET US *HIE* TO THE AGED ONE'S *CHAMBERS*, MY LADY, THAT WE MIGHT LEARN WHAT HE HATH *FOUND*--

--IF, IN TRUTH, THERE IS ANYTHING TO *BE* FOUND!

MILORD THOR! KARNILLA AND I HAVE BEEN *AWAITING* THEE. HAST THOU FINISHED THY *MEDITATION*?

AYE, BRAVE *BALDER*-- BUT MY MIND RESTS NOT *EASIER* FOR IT!

HAST THOU *LOCATED* THE ALL-FATHER YET, VIZIER?

FOR DAYS NOW, THUNDER GOD, I HAVE STUDIED THE *STARS*, AND SOUGHT IN DARK *SHADOWS* FOR THE ANSWER THOU DOST DESPER-ATELY *SEEK*--!

AND....?

AND I FEAR I HAVE DISCOVERED *NAUGHT*, MILORD UPON ALL THE MANY SPHERES AND PLANETS *KNOWN* TO THOSE OF IMMORTAL *ASGARD*--

--NO *TRACE* CAN THERE BE FOUND OF ALMIGHTY *ODIN!*

NOT A *TRACE?* THEN DOST THOU *THINK*--? COULD IT *BE*--?

IS THE NOBLE ODIN TRULY... *DEAD?*

THOUGH MY VERY *SOUL* DOTH SHRIVEL WITHIN ME AT THE THOUGHT, MY PRINCE...AYE, 'TIS *POSSIBLE!*

BUT WHO MAY SAY FOR *CERTAIN*, WHEN EVEN MINE OWN ARCANE POWERS CANNOT PIERCE THE VEIL THAT HIDES *VALHALLA*--

--THE *DREADED* DIMENSION OF *DEATH!*

THEN, VERILY, I HAVE NO CHOICE BUT TO *GO* TO THAT DARK DOMAIN--

--AND LEARN THE *ANSWER* FOR MYSELF!

NAY, MY LOVE-- THOU SPEAKEST *MADNESS!*

'TIS *TRUE*, THOR. OFTEN HATH THE DEATH-GODDESS *HELA* SOUGHT TO *CLAIM* THEE! WHY *OFFER* THYSELF TO HER *NOW?*

IF THE ALL-FATHER TRULY BE *SLAIN*, MILORD-- THY PEOPLE SHALL HAVE ALL THE MORE *NEED* OF THEE!

NOT TO MENTION THY LOVING LADY *SIF!*

I HAVE NO *CHOICE*, MY FRIENDS! THOR IS NAUGHT IF NOT HIS *FATHER'S SON*...

...AND A *PRINCE* MAY NOT *SHIRK* HIS APPOINTED *DUTY!*

IT IS A SAD-EYED *ASSEMBLAGE* THAT GATHERS TO BID THE THUNDER GOD *FAREWELL*...

MERELY SAY THE *WORD*, FRIEND THOR-- AND THE MIGHTY SWORD OF *VOLSTAGG* IS THINE TO *COMMAND!*

SO SAY WE *ALL*, MIGHTY ONE!

THE LIVES OF DASHING *FANDRAL* AND GRIM *HOGUN* ARE DEVOTED TO THY *SERVICE!*

AS EVER, THY **LOYALTY** TOUCHES MY HEART, FRIEND FANDRAL--BUT THIS BE A TASK FOR MYSELF **ALONE!**

THE REALM ETERNAL SHALL REQUIRE MEN OF THY **DEVOTION** SHOULD I FAIL TO **RETURN** FROM MY QUEST!

THEN GO IN **GLORY,** THUNDER GOD--

--AND KNOW THAT THE FIGHTING HEARTS OF THY **FRIENDS** GO WITH THEE!

AS DOTH THE BROKEN HEART OF **SIF,** MILORD.

IF THERE DOTH BE ANY **JUSTICE**-- ANY **MERCY**-- IN THIS COLD UNIVERSE, THOU SHALT **RETURN** TO ME!

THOU **MUST** RETURN TO ME!

I SHALL **TRY,** MILADY!

BY ALL THE **GODS**-- I SHALL **TRY!**

I CHARGE THEE, MY FRIENDS-- **PROTECT** THE REALM ETERNAL WHILE I AM **GONE!**

NE'ER BEFORE IN ALL ITS GOLDEN YEARS HATH IT BEEN SO **VULNERABLE** AS NOW!

THY WISH IS OUR **COMMAND,** NOBLE ONE!

THEN ONLY ONE BOON **MORE** DO I ASK OF THEE IN MY ABSENCE...

...I BID YE **PRAY** FOR ME!

THEN, WITH A SOLEMN **PLEDGE** UPON HIS LIPS, THE GOD OF THUNDER RIDES **OUT** OF THE GOLDEN CITY--AND INTO THE MOUNTAIN **MISTS!**

VERILY, THE JOURNEY TO VALHALLA BE A **TREACHEROUS** ONE--

--BUT 'TIS A JOURNEY THAT **MUST** BE TAKEN IF OMNIPOTENT **ODIN** IS TO BE **FOUND!**

INDEED, I WOULD RIDE WILLINGLY INTO THE FIERY JAWS OF **FAFNIR THE DRAGON** IF IT WOULD LEAD ME TO THE ONE I **SEEK!**

FOR 'TIS A FORCE FAR STRONGER THAN **DUTY** THAT DOTH URGE ME EVER ONWARD--

--'TIS THE ALL-ABIDING **LOVE** OF A FAITHFUL **SON** FOR HIS NOBLE **FATHER!**

174

BEHOLD, BRAVE STEED-- THE *MISTS OF MIDNIGHT* NOW DOTH SWIRL ABOUT US!

THIS THEN SHALL BE THE *TEST* OF THE THUNDER GOD'S COURAGE! FOR ONCE I PASS *THRU* THESE RAVAGING *WINDS*, THERE IS NAUGHT THAT WILL *STAY* ME FROM VALHALLA--

--AND FROM A CONFRONTATION WITH *DEATH* ITSELF!

FEAR NOT THE FEARSOME *HOWLING*, GOOD HORSE. THOR SHALL LEAD THEE *SAFELY* THRU THIS SOUND AND FURY.

NNEEIGH

I PRAY THEE-- *MOVE ON!* TOGETHER WE WILL GO WHERE NO *LIVING* MAN OR GOD HATH EVER *DARED* TO TREAD *BEFORE!*

THERE CAN BE NO *TURNING BACK* NOW, STEED!

BEFORE US STANDS THE *GOLDEN BRIDGE* WHICH SPANS THE WORLDS OF THE LIVING AND THE DEAD, LINED WITH THE *SHIELDS* OF THOSE BRAVE WARRIORS FALLEN IN BATTLE, *GLEAMING* WITH A BRILLIANCE BEYOND MORTAL KEN--!

I EXPECTED ONE DAY TO *WALK* THIS GLITTERING PATH, NOBLE STEED-- BUT NEVER DID I DREAM 'TWOULD BE SO *SOON!*

LOOK *THERE*, BRAVE HORSE! THE TOWERING HILLS OF *VALHALLA* AT LAST LOOM BEFORE US--

--WHERE THE MOST *DARING* AND MOST *GALLANT* WARRIORS OF ALL ARE SAID TO BE MAJESTICALLY MARSHALLED IN ENDLESS ARRAY!

'TIS *THERE* WE MUST TRAVEL, HORSE-- IF WE ARE TO *FIND* THE NOBLE...

NNEIGH

EH? MY STEED *TOPPLES*--AS IF STRUCK A MORTAL *BLOW*--!

175

VERILY, IT DOTH SEEM THE ALL-CONSUMING *FEAR* WAS *TOO* MUCH FOR THIS VALIANT BEAST'S STOUT HEART TO *ENDURE!*

REST THEE *WELL,* THOU GOOD AND FAITHFUL STEED. THOU HAST NAUGHT BUT VERDANT *PASTURES* BEFORE THEE... NOW...

...AND THOU SHALT BE *REMEMBERED!*

IT REMAINS FOR THOR *ALONE* NOW TO CONTINUE THE QUEST FOR *ODIN--*

--AND TRULY DO I SWEAR THAT NOT EVEN *DEATH* SHALL *STOP* ME!

STILL THE SAME SOUR-HUMORED *THUNDER GOD,* AY? ONE WOULD THINK THE JOURNEY TO VALHALLA SHOULD HAVE *RELEASED* THEE FROM ALL THY WORLDLY *WOES!*

OD'S BLOOD! THOU ART...

I AM *HAROKIN THE BARBARIAN,* THY ONCE-AND-FORMER *FOE** --

--AND GLADLY DO I *WELCOME* THEE TO THIS BOLD *COMPANY,* ASGARDIAN!

SOOTH, BUT WE SHALL FIGHT *BATTLES* BOTH WILD AND WONDERFUL NOW THAT *THOU* HAST JOINED US!

THOU ART SADLY *MISTAKEN,* HAROKIN! THOR HATH *NOT* COME HENCE TO *JOUST* WITH THEE!

THEN FOR WHAT *OTHER* PURPOSE DOTH A WARRIOR ENTER THE *DIMENSION OF DEATH*--IF NOT TO JOIN THE *BROTHERHOOD OF BATTLE?*

*AS WITNESSED BACK IN *THOR* #129-133.--LEN.

176

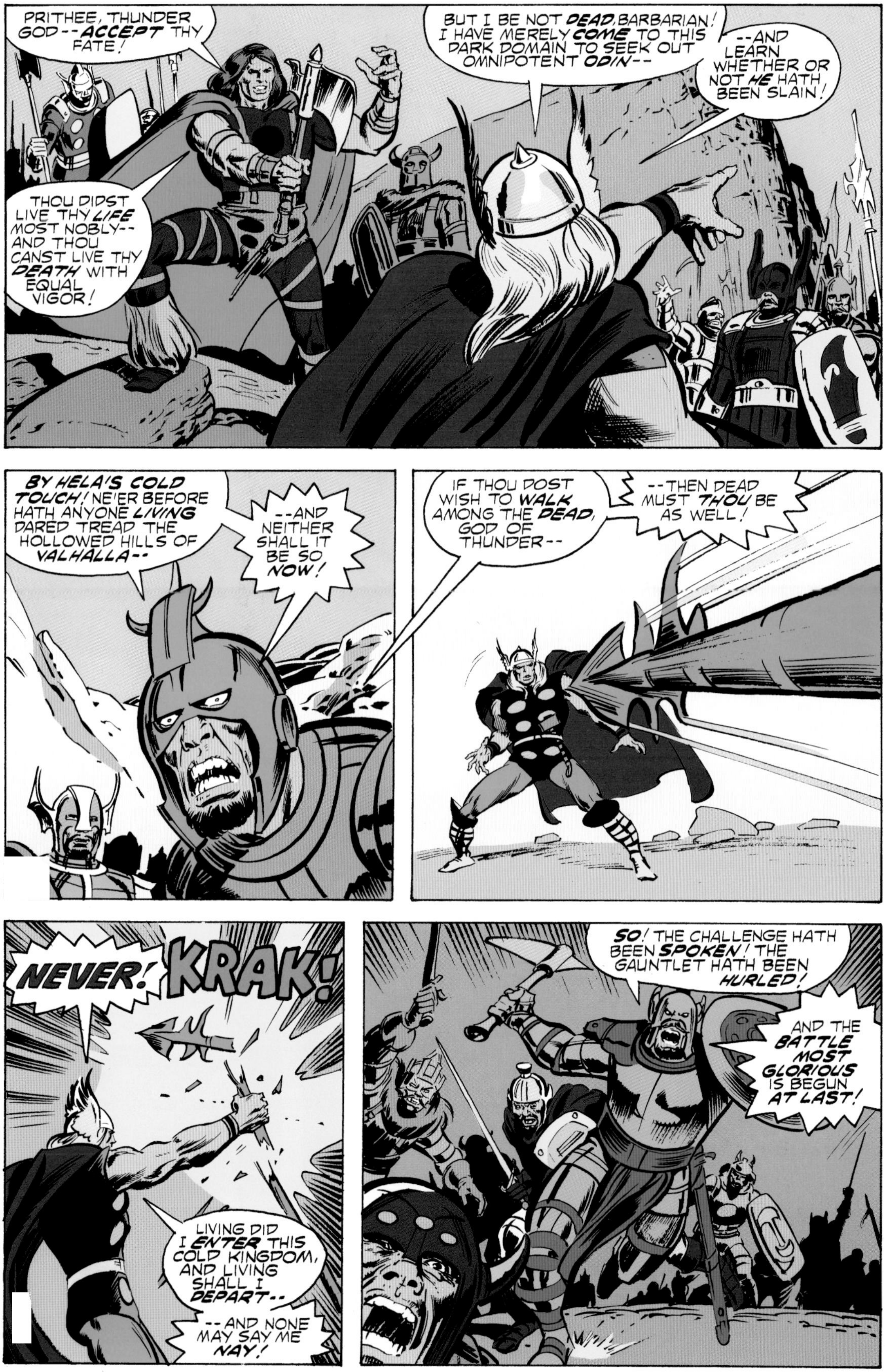

PRITHEE, THUNDER GOD--ACCEPT THY FATE!
THOU DIDST LIVE THY LIFE MOST NOBLY--AND THOU CANST LIVE THY DEATH WITH EQUAL VIGOR!
BUT I BE NOT DEAD, BARBARIAN! I HAVE MERELY COME TO THIS DARK DOMAIN TO SEEK OUT OMNIPOTENT ODIN--
--AND LEARN WHETHER OR NOT HE HATH BEEN SLAIN!
BY HELA'S COLD TOUCH! NE'ER BEFORE HATH ANYONE LIVING DARED TREAD THE HOLLOWED HILLS OF VALHALLA--
--AND NEITHER SHALL IT BE SO NOW!
IF THOU DOST WISH TO WALK AMONG THE DEAD, GOD OF THUNDER--
--THEN DEAD MUST THOU BE AS WELL!
NEVER!
KRAK!
LIVING DID I ENTER THIS COLD KINGDOM, AND LIVING SHALL I DEPART--
--AND NONE MAY SAY ME NAY!
SO! THE CHALLENGE HATH BEEN SPOKEN! THE GAUNTLET HATH BEEN HURLED!
AND THE BATTLE MOST GLORIOUS IS BEGUN AT LAST!

DESPITE MY *WARNING,* THOU DOST STILL DARE TO *ATTACK* ME, WITHOUT *QUALM,* WITHOUT *MERCY?*

THEN, BY THE BRISTLING BEARD OF ODIN-- *SO BE IT!!*

CHOOM!

IF 'TIS UNRELENTING *COMBAT* YE DO *SEEK,* MAD WARRIORS--

--YE SHALL *FIND* FAR MORE THAN THOU HADST *BARGAINED* FOR!

AYE, THAT'S THE *SPIRIT,* THUNDER GOD! FORGET THINE *INHIBITIONS!* LET THE BATTLE-FRENZY *TAKE* THEE!

WIELD THY WEAPON *PROUDLY*--FOR NOW TRULY ART THOU *ONE* OF US!

NAY, HAROKIN-- NOT SO LONG AS MY *LIEGE* AND MY *LAND* FACE MORTAL *PERIL!*

FOR THINE *OWN* SAKE, HAROKIN--ORDER THY WARRIORS TO LAY DOWN THEIR *ARMS,* ERE THE MYSTIC MALLET *MJOLNIR* BE FORCED TO WREAK FURTHER *HAVOC* IN THEIR RANKS!

178

SURRENDER, THUNDER GOD? I THINK *NOT!*

RATHER WE SHALL BATTLE ALL THE MORE *FIERCELY*--

FOOL!

--UNTIL THOU DOST FINALLY DEIGN TO *JOIN* US!

WHILE WE CONTINUE THIS SENSELESS *COMBAT*, THE REALM ETERNAL DOTH TOTTER ON THE VERY BRINK OF *DESPAIR*--

--FOR WANT OF ITS RIGHTFUL *LORD AND MASTER!*

BUT THOR HATH SWORN TO *FIND* THE MISSING *ALL-FATHER*--

--AND *NOTHING* SHALL MAKE ME *BREAK* MY SOLEMN *VOW!*

I WARN THEE, WARRIORS --REMAIN WHERE THOU HAST *FALLEN* LEST... *EH?*

BY THE GOLDEN *SPIRES!* IT CANNOT *BE*--!

"*THERE*--ATOP THAT ROCKY *KNOLL*--A SHADOWY *FIGURE* DOTH SURVEY THE FIELD OF BATTLE--

"--A FIGURE MY POOR TORTURED HEART DOTH *RECOGNIZE*--!"

ALMIGHTY *ODIN!*

BY ALL THE GODS-- CAN IT TRULY BE *THEE?*

BUT ERE THE GOD OF THUNDER CAN LEARN THE *ANSWER* TO THAT ALL-IMPORTANT QUESTION, WE MUST *RETURN* FOR A MOMENT TO THE PALACE IMPERIAL OF GOLDEN *ASGARD*--

--WHERE *OTHER* QUESTIONS ARE CRYING TO BE *ASKED*...

DOST THOU THINK THERE BE ANY *HOPE* FOR THE VALIANT THOR'S *SURVIVAL*, KARNILLA?

WHERE THERE BE *LIFE*, BALDER-- THERE WILL ALWAYS BE ROOM FOR *HOPE*!

WE'VE NO RECOURSE BUT TO WAIT AND *SEE*!

YET *WAITING* CAN OFTIMES BE THE MOST *TERRIBLE* TASK OF ALL, NORN QUEEN.

THIS DO I *KNOW*, BRAVE BALDER... ALL TOO *WELL*.

VERILY, THE REALM ETERNAL OWE THEE *THANKS*, FOR AIDING US IN BATTLE 'GAINST THE MONSTROUS *MANGOG*--BUT THY WORK HERE IS *DONE*, KARNILLA!

WHY DOST THOU *REMAIN*?

*THESE THREE ISSUES *PAST*.--LEN.

THE QUEEN OF THE NORNS NEEDS EXPLAIN HERSELF TO *NO ONE*, ASGARDIAN! THOU WOULDST DO WELL TO *REMEMBER* THAT!

IN TRUTH, WITCH-WOMAN, I SAY THEE...

STILL, ART THOU TRULY THAT *ANXIOUS* FOR KARNILLA TO TAKE HER *LEAVE*?

...NAY!

WHILE, BACK IN *VALHALLA*...

WHY DOST THOU STAND THUS *MOTIONLESS*, MY LIEGE? DOST THOU NOT *RECOGNIZE* ME?

'TIS *THOR*, THY MOST DEVOTED *SON*! I HAVE COME TO TAKE THEE *AWAY* FROM THIS CRUEL AND CURSED LAND!

I HAVE COME TO TAKE THEE... *HOME*!

NAY, THUNDER GOD!

THOU SHALT DO NOTHING OF THE *KIND*--

-- NOT SO LONG AS MIGHTY *HAROKIN* DOTH STAND TO *OPPOSE* THEE!

ERE THOU CANST HOPE TO *LEAVE* VALHALLA, THOU MUST EARN THE *RIGHT*--

--IN *SAVAGE COMBAT*!

THRAK!

AND IN THE HEAT OF *BATTLE*, THERE BE NONE MORE SAVAGE THAN *HAROKIN*!

ONCE DID HAROKIN BESEECH THEE TO *LEAD* THE AWESOME HOSTS OF VALHALLA*-- BUT NEVER *AGAIN*!

*IN *THOR* #154 --KNOW--IT-- ALL LEN.

NOW, IT DOTH SEEM, THOU ART FIT ONLY TO *SERVE* ME!

THE SON OF ODIN SERVES *NO MAN*, BARBARIAN-- SAVE HIS OWN OMNIPOTENT *FATHER*!

THOU HAST TAKEN *CONCERN* FOR MY SUFFERING LIEGE AS A SIGN OF *WEAKNESS*, HAROKIN --

--AND THAT IS AN *ERROR* THOU CANST ILL AFFORD TO *MAKE*!

THE THUNDER GOD HATH *FELLED* THE ANGRY HAROKIN!

THEN *QUICKLY*, COMRADES-- UNLEASH THE BATTERING *BLUDGEON-BOW*, THAT GRIM WEAPON CONSTRUCTED BY THE FEARSOME *TROLLS* THEMSELVES!

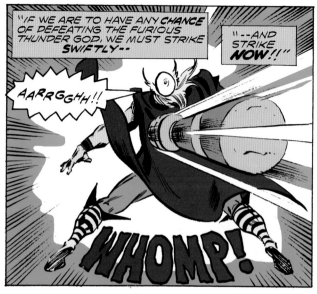

"IF WE ARE TO HAVE ANY *CHANCE* OF DEFEATING THE FURIOUS THUNDER GOD, WE MUST STRIKE *SWIFTLY*--

"--AND STRIKE *NOW*!!"

AARRGGHH!!

AT LAST, THE THUNDER BE *SILENT*, MY BRETHREN! THE MIGHTY THOR HATH *FALLEN*--

--AND PERCHANCE HE SHALL NEVER *RISE* AGAIN!

THE WARRIOR'S TAUNTING WORDS ARE OMINOUSLY *COLD*--

--AND ITS *ECHOES* SEND CHILL RIPPLES UP THE SUPINE SPINE OF THE LADY SIF, WHO WAITS IN FEAR AND FRUSTRATION A *LIFETIME* AWAY...

ANY. *WORD,* VIZIER?

NONE, MILADY-- BUT AT TIMES SUCH AS THIS, BETTER *NO* NEWS THAN *GRIM* NEWS!

STILL I AM SORELY *FRIGHTENED,* WISE ONE!

THERE BE NO *NEED,* FAIR SIF-- FOR OF ALL THE MANY *GODS* OF THE REALM ETERNAL, THERE BE NONE MORE *POWERFUL* THAN THE GOD OF *THUNDER!*

MANY TIMES HATH DARK *HELA* COVETED THE LIFE OF *THOR*-- AND ALWAYS HATH SHE FAILED TO *SECURE* IT!

THUS I SAY THEE, YOUNG GODDESS-- *BE OF BRAVE HEART!*

MERE WORDS CANNOT *COMFORT* ME NOW, OLD ONE!

TOO OFTEN BEFORE HAVE I *LOST* MY BELOVED--TO THE MORTAL *JANE FOSTER*--TO THE CLARION CALL OF *BATTLE*--BUT EVER HATH HE *RETURNED* TO ME!

IF I LOSE HIM NOW TO *DEATH,* VIZIER-- THEN I LOSE MY LOVE *FOREVER!*

BUT THE BATTLE BE NOT *LOST,* MILADY, UNTIL THE FINAL *FIST* HATH BEEN RAISED, UNTIL THE FINAL *BANNER* HATH FALLEN!

THE THUNDER GOD SHALL *RETURN* TO THEE, GOOD SIF-- AND HE SHALL BRING HIS *FATHER* WITH HIM!

I PRAY THOU SPEAKEST A'*RIGHT,* VIZIER--FOR IF *THOR* SHALL PERISH, SO TOO SHALT THE SOUL OF *SIF!*

AND PERHAPS IT IS THAT SORROWFUL PLEDGE THAT *JARS* THE FALLEN THUNDER GOD FROM HIS *STUPOR...*

WH...WHERE....?

I HEAR BOISTEROUS *VOICES.* I AM FALLEN ON THE FIELD OF *BATTLE* THEN! BUT HAVE I JOINED THE *DEAD* OR--?

NAY... MY HEART STILL *POUNDS* WITHIN MY BREAST! THEN I MUST BIDE MY *TIME...* WHILST I REGAIN MY *STRENGTH...*

HATH THE ODINSON RECOVERED *CONSCIOUSNESS* YET?

NAY, MIGHTY HAROKIN! IT DOTH SEEM THE BLUDGEON- BOW HATH PUT AN *END* TO THE THUNDER GOD'S *QUEST!*

TRULY ART THOU *MAD* IF THOU *THINKEST* THERE BE *ANYTHING* THAT WILL STAY ME FROM *FREEING* MY NOBLE FATHER FROM THY DARK DOMAIN!

NE'ER BEFORE HATH ANYONE *RECOVERED* SO SWIFTLY FROM SO *SAVAGE* AN ASSAULT!

BUT HE HATH NOT RECOVERED *FULLY*, WARRIOR!

VALHALLA'S GATES! THE THUNDER GOD DOTH RISE TO HIS *FEET* ONCE MORE!

SEE HOW HIS SINEWS *TREMBLE*! HE IS STILL *WEAK* OF LIMB --!

AND THAT *WEAKNESS* SHALL BE HIS ULTIMATE *UNDOING*, MY BROTHERS-IN-ARMS!

VERILY, THE THUNDER GOD SHALL BECOME *ONE* WITH OUR BOLD BROTHERHOOD *AT LAST*!

BEFORE I WOULD BECOME ONE WITH SUCH AS *THEE*, KNAVE --

-- I WOULD TOIL ENDLESS-LY IN THE BLAZING *FURNACES* OF THE CURSED *TROLLS*!

WHOOM!

THE VERY *FATE* OF THE REALM ETERNAL HANGS IN DIRE *JEOPARDY* -- AND ALL THAT *CONCERNS* YE IS THE UNENDING *COMBAT* THOU THINKEST GIVES YE *PURPOSE*!

WELL, THE PRINCE OF ASGARD HATH HIS *OWN* PURPOSE HERE -- HIS OWN MOST PRECIOUS *GOAL* --!

AND THAT GOAL DOTH *AWAIT* ME AT THE CREST OF YONDER *HILL!*

HAVE *FAITH*, MY FATHER! SOON SHALL THE BATTLE BE *OVER*--

--AND THY FAITHFUL *SON* SHALL ONCE MORE STAND STAUNCH AT THY *SIDE!*

THE BATTLE IS OVER *NOW*, GODLING! LAY DOWN THINE ENCHANTED *HAMMER*...OR THOU SHALT MOST CERTAINLY *PERISH!*

BY ODIN! WHO DARES SPEAK THUS TO...*NAY!* NOT *THEE!*

BOW THY *HEADS*, MY BRETHREN ...'TIS *SHE!*

AYE, WARRIOR--*HELA* HATH AT LAST *RETURNED* TO HER DOMAIN...

...AND SHE IS SORELY *DISPLEASED* AT WHAT SHE *FINDS* HERE!

THUNDER GOD, WHAT DOST THOU *WANT* HERE THAT THOU WOULDST *DARE* INVADE THE VERY *SANCTITY* OF THE DEATH-QUEEN'S TIMELESS *REALM?*

I BUT SEEK MY NOBLE *FATHER*, UNFEELING ONE-- AND METHINKS I HAVE *FOUND* HIM!

184

THOU ART SADLY *MISTAKEN*, ASGARDIAN!

THE REGAL *ODIN* DOTH NOT DWELL AMONG THE *LEGIONS OF THE LOST!*

DARK GODDESS, THOR DOTH CALL THEE-- *LIAR!*

WITH MINE OWN *EYES* HAVE I SEEN THE *ALL-FATHER* STANDING SOLEMN AND STILL ATOP YON LOFTY SPIRE!

THOU HAST SEEN NAUGHT BUT THAT WHICH THOU DIDST *WISH* TO SEE, THUNDER GOD-- *PHANTASMS* -- MERE *ILLUSIONS* --

--BUT I SUPPOSE THAT BE SOMETHING THOU MUST LEARN FOR *THYSELF!*

AYE, GRIM ONE --

--AND NOT EVEN THY COLD AND FINAL *TOUCH* COULD NOW *STAY* ME FROM THE ONE I SEEK!

'TWILL BE A DAY OF GREAT *REJOICING* WHEN THE *LORD MOST HIGH* OF ETERNAL *ASGARD* DOTH RETURN TO HIS WAITING *THRONE!*

A DAY FOR *LAUGHTER* AND *CHEERING* AND FREE-FLOWING *ALE*--! VERILY, A DAY FOR...

NAY! IT-- IT CANNOT-- IT *MUST* NOT-- BE --!

WHAT *IS* IT, MY SON? WHY DOST THOU LOOK SO *PALE?*

SURELY THE SORRY VISAGE OF GRAY-HAIRED *GROMBAR* DOTH NOT CAUSE THEE SUCH *DESPAIR!*

185

MAYHAP 'TIS MERELY THAT THE LOFTY CLIMB HATH *TIRED* THEE! IF SO, I PRAY THEE-- TAKE *COMFORT* FROM THIS OLD MAN'S *HAND!*

NAUGHT... 'TWAS ALL FOR NAUGHT...

NAY, YOUNG ONE--'TIS NOT *SO!* NO MAN'S LIFE HATH EVER GONE FOR *NAUGHT!*

SURELY, THOU DIDST LIVE MOST *NOBLY* IF GRIM HELA HATH CHOSEN TO NUMBER THEE AMONGST THIS PROUD *COMPANY!*

I SAY THEE, YOUNG WARRIOR--MAKE THE *BEST* OF MATTERS HERE! VERILY, TO DWELL IN DARK *VALHALLA* BE NOT AS *TRAGIC* AS THOU DOST THINK!

AFTER A TIME, THOU SHALT COME TO *ACCEPT* THINGS FOR WHAT THEY *ARE!* MAYHAP THOU SHALT COME TO *ENJOY* THEM!

ACCEPT THIS MADNESS, OLD ONE?

ENJOY IT?

THOR DOTH SAY THEE-- *NAY!*

NAY!!

A THOUSAND TIMES DO I SAY THEE-- *NAY!*

THE THUNDER GOD'S FRUSTATED *RAGE* AND *RESENTMENT* FLOWS UNFETTERED THEN, AND THE CLOUD-SWEPT SKIES OF THE KINGDOM CALLED *VALHALLA* ROIL AND CHURN IN RESPONSE TO THEIR MASTER'S *MOOD.*

FOR A TIME BEYOND *TIME,* THIS DIMENSION OF THE DEAD KNOWS A SAVAGE *STORM* UNLIKE ANY IT HAS EVER KNOWN *BEFORE...*

THEN AT LAST, HIS FURY **EXHAUSTED**, THE GOD OF THUNDER COMES **DOWN** FROM THE MOUNTAIN--

--HIS NOBLE HEAD **BOWED** BENEATH A BURDEN ALMOST TOO GREAT FOR EVEN A **GOD** TO BEAR.

ART THOU FINALLY **SATISFIED**, ASGARDIAN?

THY **PARDON**, DEATH-QUEEN! I SHALL **TROUBLE** THEE NO LONGER!

THEN FARE THEE **WELL**, ODINSON... UNTIL WE MEET **AGAIN**!

THOU DOST PERMIT THE THUNDER GOD TO **LEAVE**, MISTRESS-- WHEN, WITH BUT A **TOUCH** OF THY COLD HAND, HE WOULD BE THINE **FOREVER**?

AYE, HAROKIN-- HE IS FREE TO CONTINUE HIS **QUEST** FOR HIS MISSING **FATHER**!

WHEN THE GODDESS OF DEATH DOTH COME AT LAST TO **CLAIM** THE MIGHTY THOR, 'TWILL BE ON **HER** TERMS--

--AND IN HER OWN GOOD **TIME**!

THOU ART BEING UNSEEMLY **MERCIFUL**, GRIM ONE.

MERCIFUL, BARBARIAN? NAY, I THINK **NOT**. 'TWOULD BE FAR MORE **COMPASSIONATE** FOR ME TO SLAY THE ASGARDIAN **NOW**--

--RATHER THAN LET HIM GO FORTH TO FACE THE UNIMAGINABLE **TORMENTS** THAT AWAIT HIM WHEN HE RETURNS TO THE WORLD OF THE **LIVING**!

NEXT ISSUE • *THE QUEST FOR ODIN MOVES INTO HIGH GEAR, AS THE MIGHTY THOR BATTLES **ULIK**, THE **TERROR OF THE TROLLS**! BE HERE FOR...* **"A DRAGON AT THE GATES!"**

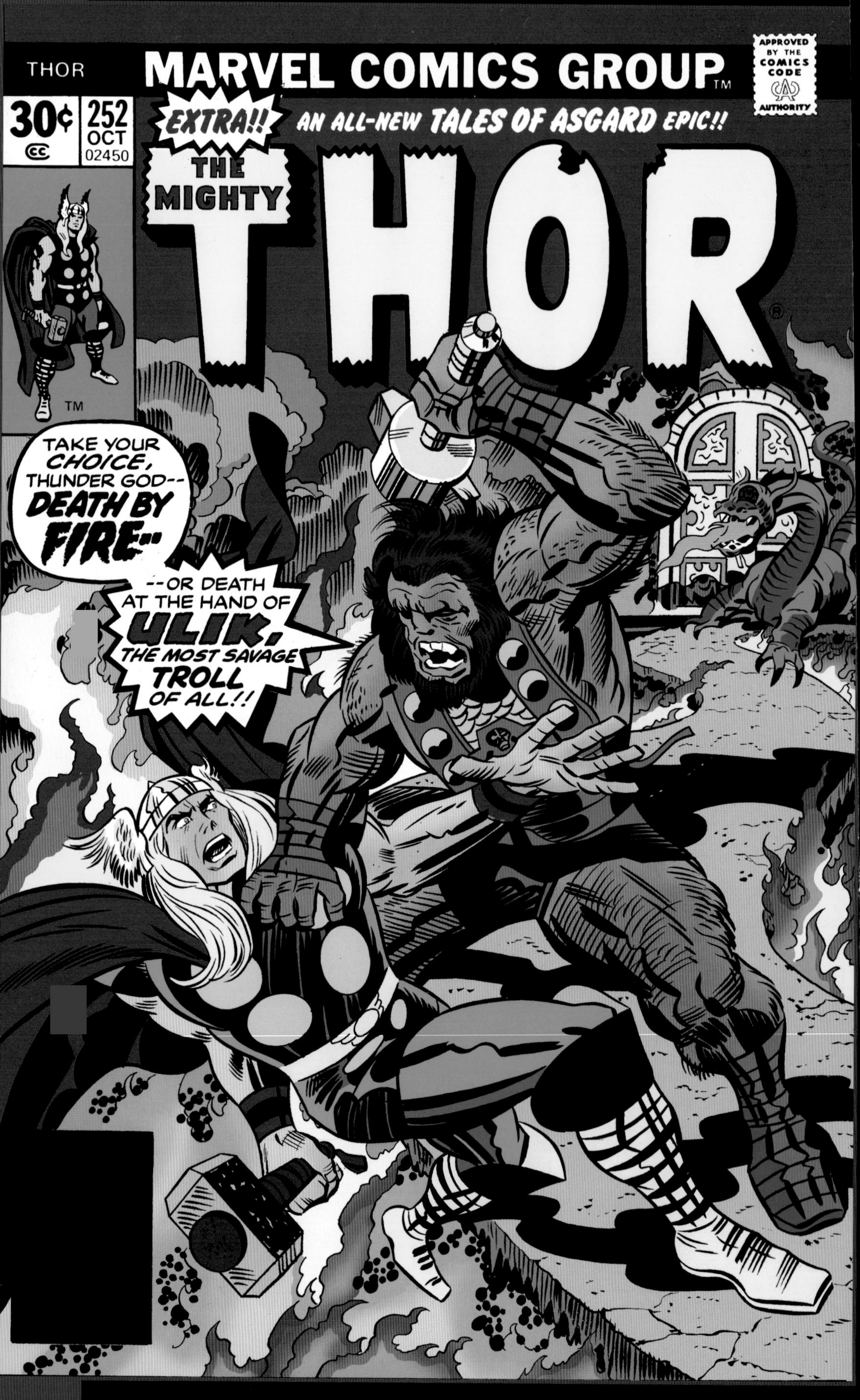
THOR
MARVEL COMICS GROUP
30¢
252 OCT
02450
APPROVED BY THE COMICS CODE AUTHORITY
EXTRA!!
AN ALL-NEW TALES OF ASGARD EPIC!!
THE MIGHTY
THOR
TAKE YOUR CHOICE, THUNDER GOD-- DEATH BY FIRE--
--OR DEATH AT THE HAND OF ULIK, THE MOST SAVAGE TROLL OF ALL!!

When lame Dr. DONALD BLAKE strikes his wooden walking stick upon the ground, it becomes the mystic mallet MJOLNIR—and Blake is transformed into the Norse God of Thunder, Master of the Storm and the Lightning, Heir to the Throne of Immortal Asgard...

STAN LEE PRESENTS: THE MIGHTY THOR! ™

LEN WEIN WRITER/EDITOR ✷ JOHN BUSCEMA & TONY DeZUNIGA ILLUSTRATORS ✷ GLYNIS WEIN COLORIST

A DRAGON AT THE GATES!

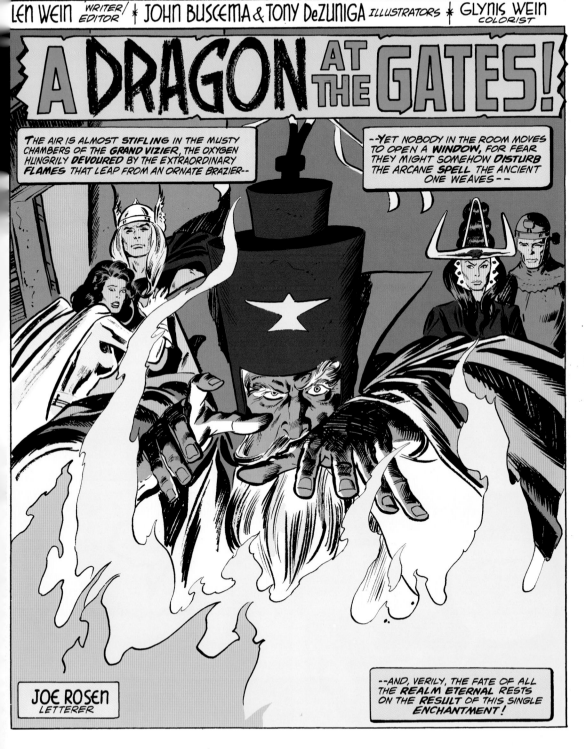

THE AIR IS ALMOST **STIFLING** IN THE MUSTY CHAMBERS OF THE **GRAND VIZIER**, THE OXYGEN HUNGRILY **DEVOURED** BY THE EXTRAORDINARY **FLAMES** THAT LEAP FROM AN ORNATE BRAZIER--

--YET NOBODY IN THE ROOM MOVES TO OPEN A **WINDOW**, FOR FEAR THEY MIGHT SOMEHOW **DISTURB** THE ARCANE **SPELL** THE ANCIENT ONE WEAVES--

JOE ROSEN LETTERER

--AND, VERILY, THE FATE OF ALL THE **REALM ETERNAL** RESTS ON THE **RESULT** OF THIS SINGLE **ENCHANTMENT!**

I PRAY THEE, MILORD THOR-- BE THERE NO *OTHER* WAY TO LEARN THY FATHER'S *WHEREABOUTS?*

NAY, FAIR SIF. TO DARK *VALHALLA* ITSELF HAVE I GONE, IN SEARCH OF THE NOBLE *ODIN* *--

-- BUT NARY A *TRACE* HAVE I FOUND OF HIM!

*LAST ISH, RIGHT?--LEN.

VERILY, IF WE MUST NOW DELVE INTO *REALMS UNKNOWN* FOR SOME SIGN OF OUR ALMIGHTY *LIEGE*--

--THEN *SO BE IT!*

BELOVED, *PLEASE*--!

THOU WOULDST DO WELL TO *HEED* THY LADY, THUNDER GOD.

KARNILLA SPEAKS *TRUE*, MY PRINCE. PRAY HAVE A *CARE*-- LEST THOU SOMEHOW *OFFEND* FORCES BEYOND OUR KEN.

THY WORDS OF CAUTION ARE *NOTED*, BRAVE BALDER. BUT, FOR THE SAKE OF ALL *ASGARD*, STILL DO I SAY-- *CARRY ON, VIZIER!*

ART THOU *CERTAIN*, ODINSON?

AYE, WISE ONE. WHATEVER THE *OUTCOME*, I SHALL HAVE NO *REGRETS.*

THEN, AT THY *COMMAND*, MILORD-- I NOW DO *SUMMON* HE WHO ALONE MIGHT GRANT THEE THE *KNOWLEDGE* THOU DOST SO DESPERATELY *SEEK!*

ONCE AGAIN, THE AGED VIZIER TAKES UP THE ARCANE *CHANT*. HIS WORDS ARE SPOKEN IN LANGUAGES EVEN *GODS* HAVE LONG SINCE *FORGOTTEN*--

--BUT THEY ARE *EFFECTIVE* WORDS NONETHELESS!

WHO HATH SUMMONED FORTH THE GRIM *GUARDIAN* OF THE DARK WELL OF WISDOM?

WHO HATH SUMMONED *MIMIR?*

190

'TIS **THOR**, GOD OF THUNDER, PRINCE OF ASGARD, WHO HATH **CALLED** THEE HERE, ALL-WISE ONE--

--FOR REGAL **ODIN**, MONARCH MOST HIGH OF THE REALM ETERNAL, HATH SOMEHOW **VANISHED** FROM OUR MIDST--

--AND WE PRAY THAT THOU CANST **TELL** US WHERE TO **FIND** HIM!

WHAT? AGAIN??

ONCE BEFORE DIDST THOU CALL ON MIMIR TO SEEK THY MISSING **FATHER**, AND THEN DID MIMIR **AID** THEE *--

--FOR SUCH WAS MY **DUTY** TO THY SIRE.

* BACK IN **THOR** #240. -- LEN.

BUT **NO ONE** MAY SEEK THE SAME KNOWLEDGE **TWICE** IN MIMIR'S NAME!

ERE I WOULD **TELL** THEE WHAT THOU DOST WISH TO **KNOW**, THUNDER GOD-- I WOULD HAVE **TRIBUTE** PAID ME, AS **BEFITS** THE FOUNT OF KNOWLEDGE!

MERELY **ASK** IT, MIMIR-- AND IT SHALL BE **THINE**!

THEN LOOK THEE INTO MY **FLAMES**, ODINSON-- AND BEHOLD THE MIGHTY **DRAGON** THAT GUARDS THE GOLDEN GATES TO THE **REALM BELOW**!

FOR 'TIS ITS CYCLOPEAN **RUBY EYE** WHICH I DO **DEMAND** OF THEE!

NAY, WISE MIMIR! 'TIS NOT THOR'S **WAY** TO STEAL THAT WHICH DOTH NOT **BELONG** TO HIM, BUT...

...BUT...

...BUT FOR THE SAKE OF ODIN AND IMMORTAL **ASGARD**...

...THOR SHALL **DO**...WHATE'ER HE **MUST**.

INDEED THOU **SHALT**, THUNDER GOD.

AND THUS, I TRUST I SHALL NOT **HEAR** FROM THEE **AGAIN**!

HA HA HA HA HA

BUT ALMOST BEFORE THE ECHOES OF MIMIR'S BONE-CHILLING LAUGH HAVE *FADED*, THE GOD OF THUNDER AND HIS COMPANIONS STAND UPON THE VERY *THRESHHOLD* OF THE MYSTERIOUS *REALM BELOW...*

ART THOU CERTAIN THOU SHOULDST *RISK* THIS MAD ENDEAVOR, FRIEND THOR?

IN TRUTH, THE THUNDER GOD DOTH HAVE NO *CHOICE*, BALDER.

INDEED, NORN QUEEN, AS MY FATHER'S *SON*, I DO WHAT *MUST* BE DONE--THOUGH MY *SOUL* SHALL KNOW NO *SATISFACTION* FROM THE DEED!

VERILY, THIS CRATER DOTH YAWN DOWN INTO A DARKNESS THAT SEEMS TO *SWALLOW* ALL LIGHT... AND ALL *HOPE*.

KEEP THYSELF *WELL*, MILADY SIF. I SWEAR I SHALL *RETURN* TO THEE ERE LONG.

AND SIF SHALL BE *WAITING*, MY LOVE... AS *ALWAYS*.

FEAR *NOT*, MY PRINCE. WE SHALL GUARD THE REALM ETERNAL *WELL* IN THINE ABSENCE.

AND I COULD LEAVE GOLDEN ASGARD IN NO *SAFER* HANDS THAN *THINE*, BRAVE BALDER.

SO IT HATH COME TO *THIS* THEN--

--THAT A *PRINCE OF THE REALM* SHOULD DESCEND INTO THIS SMOLDERING EMBODIMENT OF DESPAIR AS NOTHING MORE THAN A COMMON *THIEF!*

THERE BE LITTLE ENOUGH OF *VALUE* IN THIS DESOLATE DOMAIN ALREADY.

WOULD THAT I WERE NOT FORCED TO *STEAL* THE SINGLE SOURCE OF *LIGHT* THAT REMAINS HERE.

VERILY, THE FICKLE *FATES* DOTH WEAVE A TAPESTRY OF MOST *DEVIOUS* DESIGN.

FIRST, ALMIGHTY ODIN DOTH GIVE HIMSELF *AMNESIA*, THAT HE MIGHT WALK AMONG MORTALS AS *ONE* OF THEM--

--THEN EVIL *IGRON* AND THE MONSTROUS *MANGOG* SEIZE THE GOLDEN THRONE IN THE ALL-FATHER'S *ABSENCE*--

--AND FINALLY, OUR LORDLY LIEGE IS *STOLEN AWAY* EVEN AS HE SEEKS TO *RETURN* TO THE REALM ETERNAL!*

*ALL DISPLAYED IN DETAIL OVER THESE MANY MONTHS PAST. --LEN.

AYE, IT HATH BEEN A TIME MOST PASSING *STRANGE* FOR IMMORTAL *ASGARD*--

--AND I FEAR THE *MADNESS* BE NOT YET *OVER!*

BUT I MUST NOT LET MY *MUSINGS* LULL ME FROM THE TASK AT HAND!

COUNTLESS *TUNNELS* DOTH LOOM NOW BEFORE ME--

--AND I MUST CONSIDER MOST CAREFULLY *WHICH* OF THEM TO *PURSUE!*

FOR A PATH *WRONGLY* TAKEN HERE--

--COULD LEAD ME STRAIGHT TO THE TERRIBLE KINGDOM OF THE INSANELY-SAVAGE *TROLLS*--

--AND I CAN ALLOW *NAUGHT* TO STAY ME FROM MY MOST SACRED *QUEST!*

AND, AT THE TUNNEL'S OTHER *END*...

SO! I FIND NOT KING GEIRRODUR'S BLAZING *FURNACES* AFTER ALL--

--BUT ONLY A ROUGH-HEWN *BRIDGE* THAT APPEARS TO SPAN AN ENDLESS *OCEAN OF FLAME!*

'TIS INDEED A SIGHT TO MAKE *MOST* MEN TURN ON THEIR HEEL AND *FORSAKE* THEIR CHOSEN PATH--

--AND THUS I PRESS EVER *ONWARD!*

--BUT THE GOD OF THUNDER DOTH KNOW WHAT LIES AT THE *END* OF THIS CRUMBLING SPAN--

THE UNIMAGINABLE **HEAT** FROM THE FLAMING SEA FAIRLY **BLISTERS** THE THUNDER GOD'S **FLESH**, BUT STILL HE MOVES ON, UNMINDFUL OF THE **PAIN**...

...UNTIL, AT LAST...

BY ODIN! 'TIS JUST AS MIMIR **DESCRIBED** IT! BEFORE ME STAND THE GLEAMING **GATES** OF THE REALM BELOW--

--AND GUARDING THEM, **THE DRAGON OF THE RUBY EYE!**

PRAISE BE! MY QUEST IS **OVER!**

WITH YON BEHEMOTH'S GLITTERING **ORB** IN HAND, MIMIR SHALL AT LAST GRANT ME THE PRECIOUS **KNOWLEDGE** I DO SEEK!

ONLY A MOMENT **LONGER**, AND THEN...

STAND **ASIDE**, ASGARDIAN! THAT SHIMMERING JEWEL IS **NOT** YOURS TO CLAIM!

WHAT--? WHO **DARES--??**

I DARE, THUNDER GOD! I, BEFORE WHOM THE VERY **MOUNTAINS** TREMBLE!

OR HAVE YOU SO SOON **FORGOTTEN** HE WHOM LEGENDS HAVE EVER CALLED-- **ULIK THE INVINCIBLE!**

ULIK-- MIGHTIEST OF ALL THE TROLLS!!

NAY, TROLL! THOR HATH NOT **FORGOTTEN** THEE!

THEN NEITHER HAVE YOU FORGOTTEN ULIK'S **POWER**-- OR THE BOUNDLESS FURY OF ULIK'S **RAGE!**

STEP ASIDE-- OR **DIE!!**

AGAIN I COMMAND YOU, GODLING-- STEP ASIDE, AND LET ULIK CLAIM HIS PRIZE!

ULIK, THOR DOTH SAY THEE-- NAY!

THE GOD OF THUNDER DOTH STAND ASIDE FOR NO *MAN* OR *GOD*-- LET ALONE FOR A LOWLY *TROLL!*

THEN GO AHEAD AND *HOLD* YOUR GROUND, ASGARDIAN --

--AND LET *THIS* BE THE PLACE THEY *BURY* YOU!

THBOOM!

I DID NOT COME HERE TO DO *BATTLE* WITH YOU, THUNDER GOD--

--BUT THE VERY *SURVIVAL* OF THE MIGHTY TROLL EMPIRE DEPENDS ON ULIK SECURING THE *RUBY EYE*--

--AND I WILL DO WHAT I *MUST* TO SAVE MY *PEOPLE!*

NOW LIE *STILL*, THOR-- AND I WILL MAKE YOUR *DEATH-BLOW* MERCIFULLY *SWIFT!*

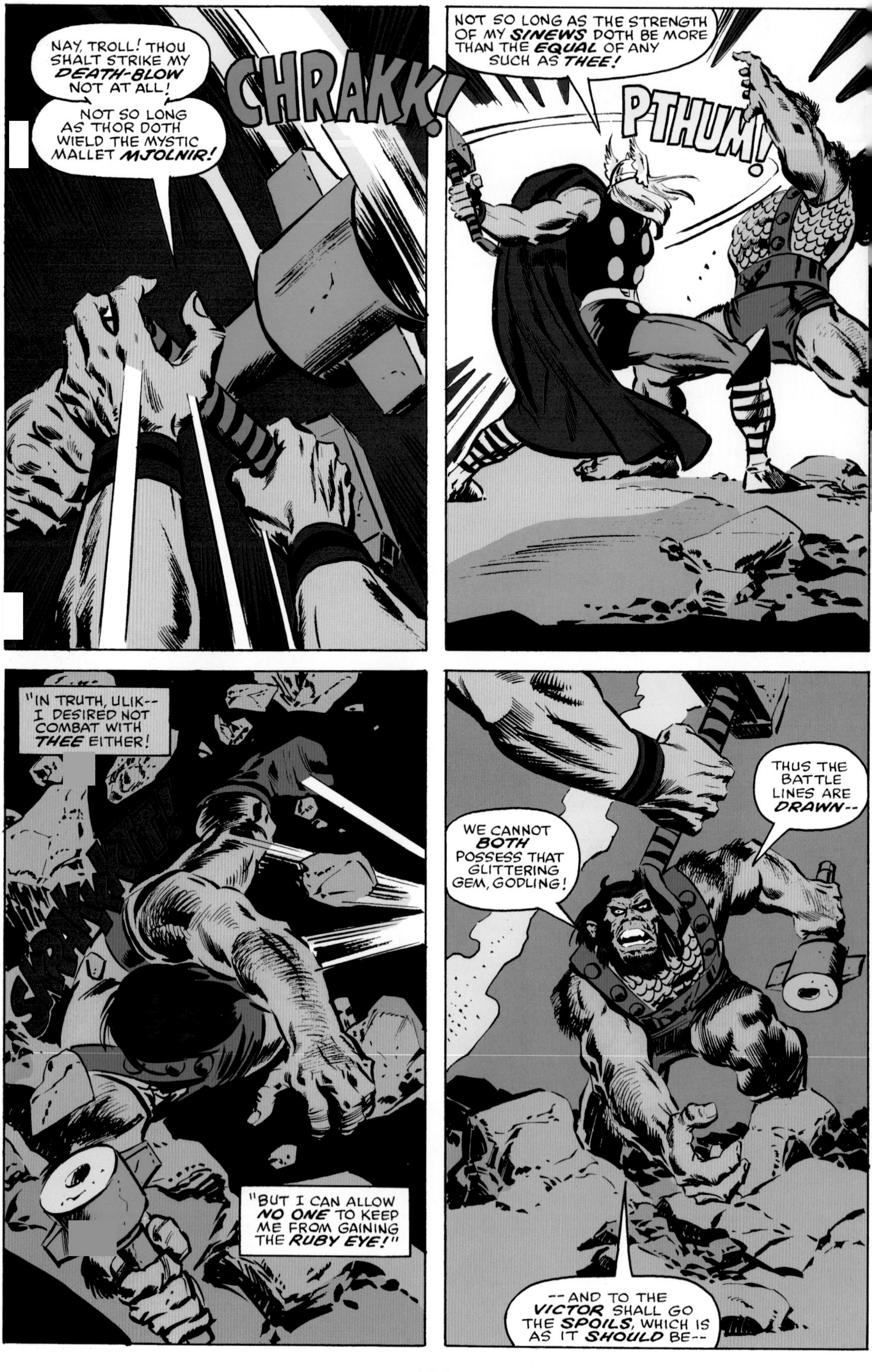
NAY, TROLL! THOU SHALT STRIKE MY DEATH-BLOW NOT AT ALL!
NOT SO LONG AS THOR DOTH WIELD THE MYSTIC MALLET MJOLNIR!
CHRAKK!
NOT SO LONG AS THE STRENGTH OF MY SINEWS DOTH BE MORE THAN THE EQUAL OF ANY SUCH AS THEE!
PTHUM!
"IN TRUTH, ULIK-- I DESIRED NOT COMBAT WITH THEE EITHER!
"BUT I CAN ALLOW NO ONE TO KEEP ME FROM GAINING THE RUBY EYE!"
WE CANNOT BOTH POSSESS THAT GLITTERING GEM, GODLING!
THUS THE BATTLE LINES ARE DRAWN--
--AND TO THE VICTOR SHALL GO THE SPOILS, WHICH IS AS IT SHOULD BE--

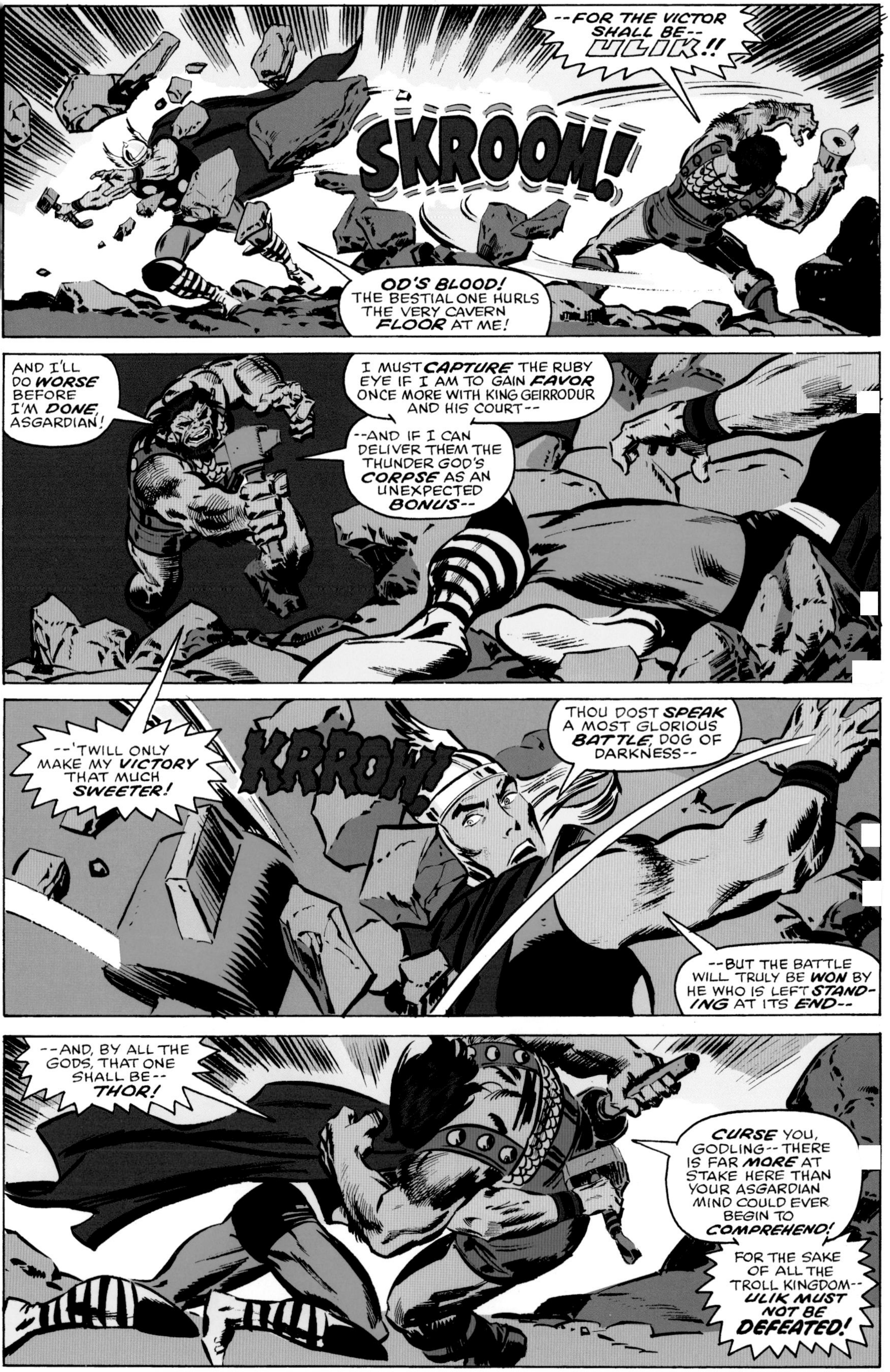
--FOR THE VICTOR SHALL BE-- ULIK!!
SKROOM!
OD'S BLOOD! THE BESTIAL ONE HURLS THE VERY CAVERN FLOOR AT ME!
AND I'LL DO WORSE BEFORE I'M DONE, ASGARDIAN!
I MUST CAPTURE THE RUBY EYE IF I AM TO GAIN FAVOR ONCE MORE WITH KING GEIRRODUR AND HIS COURT--
--AND IF I CAN DELIVER THEM THE THUNDER GOD'S CORPSE AS AN UNEXPECTED BONUS--
--'TWILL ONLY MAKE MY VICTORY THAT MUCH SWEETER!
KRROW!
THOU DOST SPEAK A MOST GLORIOUS BATTLE, DOG OF DARKNESS--
--BUT THE BATTLE WILL TRULY BE WON BY HE WHO IS LEFT STANDING AT ITS END--
--AND, BY ALL THE GODS, THAT ONE SHALL BE-- THOR!
CURSE YOU, GODLING--THERE IS FAR MORE AT STAKE HERE THAN YOUR ASGARDIAN MIND COULD EVER BEGIN TO COMPREHEND!
FOR THE SAKE OF ALL THE TROLL KINGDOM-- ULIK MUST NOT BE DEFEATED!

BY ODIN! WE HAVE TUMBLED BACK UPON THE CRUMBLING **BRIDGE** THAT STRETCHES OVER THE FLAMING **SEA!**

A SINGLE **MIS-STEP** COULD SPELL BLAZING **DOOM** FOR EITHER OF US!

YET STILL THE TROLL RISES ALMOST **BLINDLY** TO HIS FEET, HEEDLESS OF THE **DANGER!** NEVER HAVE I SEEN ULIK MORE **RESOLUTE,** MORE **DETERMINED** IN HIS PURPOSE!

COULD THERE TRULY BE **SUBSTANCE** TO THE BESTIAL ONE'S CLAIMS?

IS THE KINGDOM OF THE TROLLS REALLY IN **MORTAL PERIL?**

UNFORTUNATELY, IT DOTH NOT **MATTER.** I CANNOT SACRIFICE THE FUTURE OF **ASGARD** FOR THE SAKE OF ITS MOST BITTER **ENEMIES!**

I MUST STRUGGLE ON, EVEN AS DOTH **ULIK** -- UNTIL THE VICTORY BE **WON!**

OF ALL THOSE WHO HAVE **CHALLENGED** ULIK'S POWER, THUNDER GOD -- YOU ARE THE MOST **VALIANT** FOE OF ALL!

BUT STILL THAT SHALL NOT **STOP** ME FROM HURLING YOU BODILY INTO THE HUNGRY **FLAMES** THAT LICK AROUND US!

SPOW!

CEASE YOUR FUTILE **STRUGGLING,** ASGARDIAN!

LET ME **STRIKE** THE BLOW THAT WILL SEND YOU TO YOUR FINAL **REST!**

NAY, TROLL --!

IF ANY **BLOW** IS TO BE STRUCK HERE --

--'TWILL BE **MINE!!**

BTROK!

NEXT ISSUE: MORE MIND-BENDING *ACTION* THAN YOU'VE EVER THOUGHT POSSIBLE, AS *ULIK* GOES BERSERK! BE HERE FOR... "**CHAOS IN THE KINGDOM OF THE TROLLS!**"

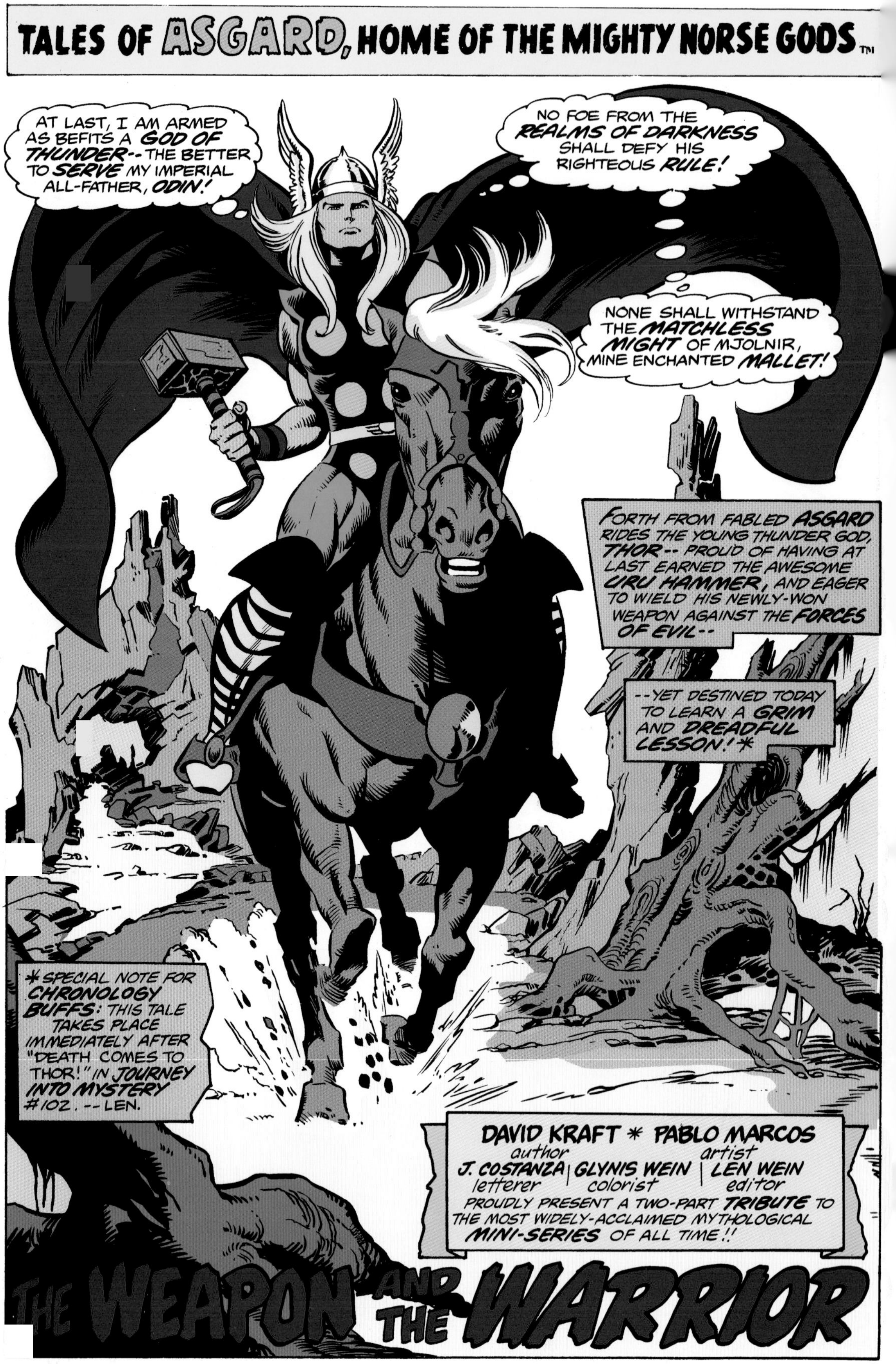
TALES OF ASGARD, HOME OF THE MIGHTY NORSE GODS™
AT LAST, I AM ARMED AS BEFITS A GOD OF THUNDER-- THE BETTER TO SERVE MY IMPERIAL ALL-FATHER, ODIN!
NO FOE FROM THE REALMS OF DARKNESS SHALL DEFY HIS RIGHTEOUS RULE!
NONE SHALL WITHSTAND THE MATCHLESS MIGHT OF MJOLNIR, MINE ENCHANTED MALLET!
FORTH FROM FABLED ASGARD RIDES THE YOUNG THUNDER GOD, THOR-- PROUD OF HAVING AT LAST EARNED THE AWESOME URU HAMMER, AND EAGER TO WIELD HIS NEWLY-WON WEAPON AGAINST THE FORCES OF EVIL--
--YET DESTINED TODAY TO LEARN A GRIM AND DREADFUL LESSON!*
*SPECIAL NOTE FOR CHRONOLOGY BUFFS: THIS TALE TAKES PLACE IMMEDIATELY AFTER "DEATH COMES TO THOR!" IN JOURNEY INTO MYSTERY #102. --LEN.
DAVID KRAFT * PABLO MARCOS
author artist
J. COSTANZA | GLYNIS WEIN | LEN WEIN
letterer colorist editor
PROUDLY PRESENT A TWO-PART TRIBUTE TO THE MOST WIDELY-ACCLAIMED MYTHOLOGICAL MINI-SERIES OF ALL TIME!!
THE WEAPON AND THE WARRIOR

OFT HAVE I **DREAMED** OF THIS DAY, WHEN I SHOULD ENTER INTO THE **FULL POWERS** OF MY BIRTHRIGHT AS A **GOD!**

LONG AND HARD HAVE I **STRUGGLED** TO **DESERVE** THE POWER-LADEN **WEAPON** WHICH NOW I CARRY!

MANY ARE THE **FIERCE FOES** I FACED AND VANQUISHED WITH **NAUGHT** SAVE SWORD AND SHIELD AND CUNNING, ERE I ACHIEVED THE STRENGTH TO WEILD THIS **MIGHTY HAMMER!**

AND WITH A THRILL OF PRIDE, THE YOUTHFUL THUNDER GOD RECALLS THE **ORDEALS** WHICH CHALLENGED AND TESTED EVERY ASPECT OF HIS HEAVEN-BORN **RIGHT** TO GODHOOD!

NEVER SHALL I FORGET THOSE **FIRST BATTLES** I FOUGHT AS A BEARD-LESS BOY!

MY LORD ODIN, THE ALL-WISE, WISHED ME TO **PROVE** MY RIGHT TO CALL MYSELF **HIS SON!**

"AND PROVE THAT RIGHT I **DID**...BEGINNING WITH THE DAY I DARED ENTER THE DREAD CASTLE OF THE **STORM GIANTS** TO RE-TRIEVE THE **GOLDEN APPLES** OF IDUNA!

PUNY GODLING... THINKEST THOU CAN CREEP UNSEEN INTO **JOTUNHEIM** AND **ESCAPE** WITH THY WORTHLESS LIFE?!!

SAVE THY **FOUL BREATH,** GIANT! 'TIS THINE OWN LIFE WHICH IS IN **DANGER**--

--FOR I AM **THOR,** SON OF **ODIN**-- AND IT IS TO THE **CHAMPIONS** OF ASGARD THOU SHALT **ANSWER** NOW FOR THE **THEFT** OF THE GOLDEN APPLES!

"AND WELL, TOO, DO I RECALL THAT DAY I STOOD **ALONE** AGAINST THE **HORDES OF EVIL** WHEN THEY LAUNCHED THEIR **FEARSOME ATTACK** ON ASGARD!

ONLY THIS **FECKLESS YOUTH** STANDS 'TWIXT US AND **VICTORY!**

SCORCH HIM WITH THY **FUR-IOUS FUMES,** O'DRAGON!

SOON THE REALM OF THE GODS SHALL BE **OURS!**

NAY! NEVER SHALL EVIL BLIGHT FAIR ASGARD WHILST I HAVE WIT AND WILL TO **STAY** YE!

"YET, EVEN THEN, I *LACKED* THE STRENGTH TO LIFT THE MIGHTY MJOLNIR!

UHNH... OH, FATHER! WILL I NEVER BE *STRONG* ENOUGH TO HURL THY ENCHANTED HAMMER!?!

PATIENCE, MY SON! IT IS THE *WARRIOR,* NOT THE WEAPON, THAT WINS BATTLES!

WHEN THOU ART FINALLY *READY,* THOU SHALT NOT EVEN FEEL THE HAMMER'S *WEIGHT!*

"TRULY DID ODIN *SPEAK* THAT DAY... FOR WHEN MY COURAGE ROSE TO FACE THE *GREATEST CHALLENGE* OF ALL, I SWUNG THE ENCHANTED HAMMER AS *LIGHTLY* AS IF IT WERE MY BOYISH SWORD!"

LET THE *STORM GIANTS* BEWARE!

NOT ONE SHALL ESCAPE THE WRATH OF THOR IF ANY *HARM* BEFALLS LOVELY *SIF,* SISTER OF MY FRIEND BALDER!

OUT OF MY *WAY,* HULKING FIENDS-- LEST YE FIND YOURSELVES *BURIED* BENEATH THE RUBBLE OF YON CASTLE!

HAVE A CARE, BROTHER! I SENSE IN THIS SMALL ONE A *WILINESS* AND *SPIRIT* THAT BODES ILL FOR ANY WHO *OPPOSE* HIM!

BOLD WORDS, PUNY GODLING! NOW PREPARE TO *EAT* THEM!

BOTH MONSTERS I *DISPOSED OF* WITHOUT EVEN PAUSING TO DO *BATTLE!*

LO! WHAT *FIGURE* DOTH STAND ON YONDER PEAK??!

HO THERE, CREATURE! WHY STAND THEE THERE WITH SUCH AN AIR OF *INSOLENCE?* THOU DOST OBSTRUCT THE WAY OF *THOR,* SON OF ODIN!

HELA HERSELF-- GODDESS OF *DEATH*-- YIELDED HER PREY TO ME WHEN SHE SAW THAT NOT EVEN HER *AWE-SOME POWER* COULD SWAY ME FROM MY WARRIOR'S VOW!

WITH BUT *WIT* AND *WILL* ALONE, SCARCE THINK-ING OF MY *MIGHTY MALLET,* I SAVED THE LOVELY SIF!

IF THOU DOST WISH TO *PASS,* FOOL-- TRY THEN TO *MOVE* ME!

BY THE BEARD OF ODIN-- THIS IS A *CHALLENGE* WHICH CANNOT BE *IGNORED!*

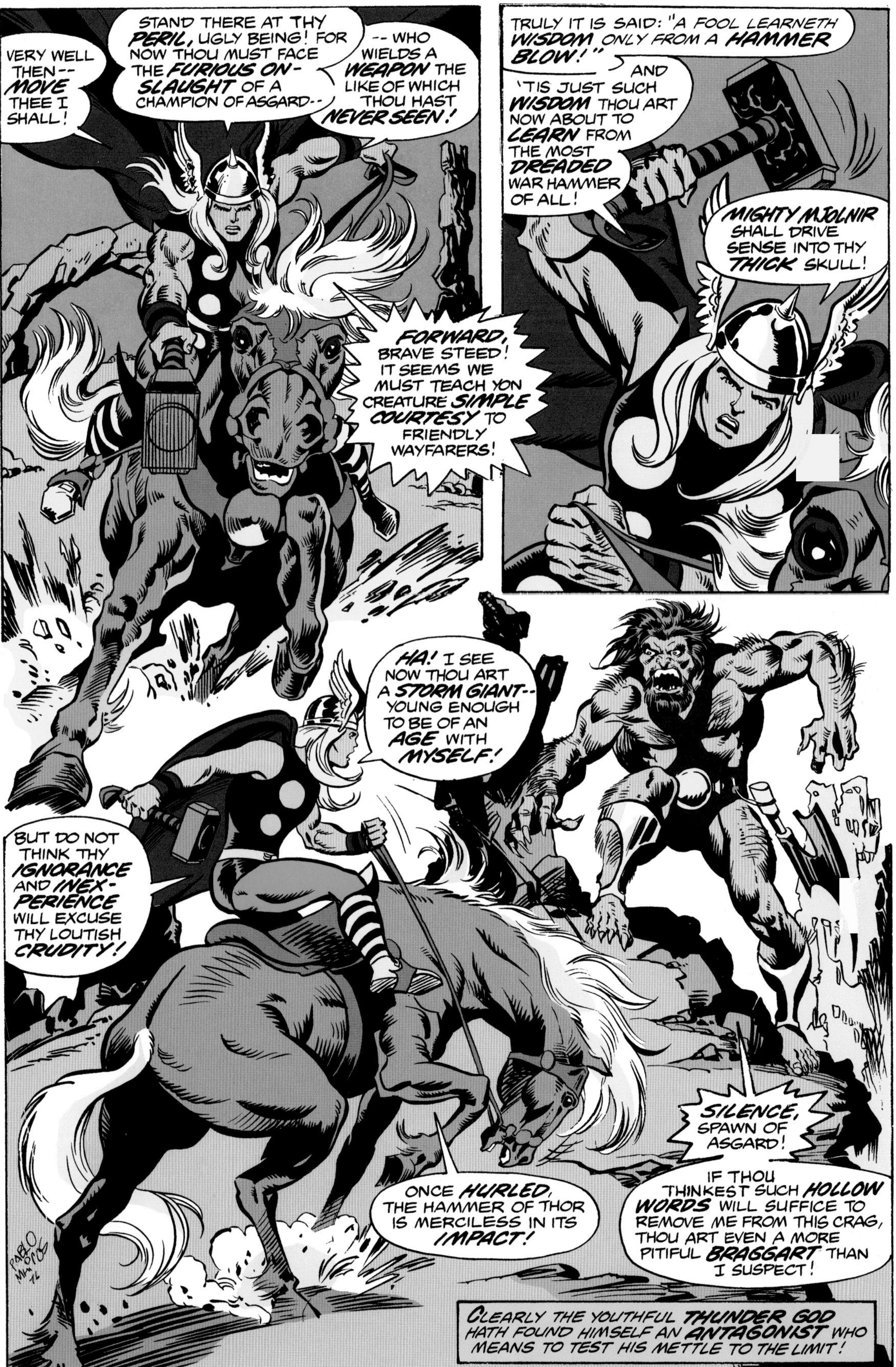
VERY WELL THEN-- MOVE THEE I SHALL!
STAND THERE AT THY PERIL, UGLY BEING! FOR NOW THOU MUST FACE THE FURIOUS ON-SLAUGHT OF A CHAMPION OF ASGARD--
--WHO WIELDS A WEAPON THE LIKE OF WHICH THOU HAST NEVER SEEN!
FORWARD, BRAVE STEED! IT SEEMS WE MUST TEACH YON CREATURE SIMPLE COURTESY TO FRIENDLY WAYFARERS!
TRULY IT IS SAID: "A FOOL LEARNETH WISDOM ONLY FROM A HAMMER BLOW!"
AND 'TIS JUST SUCH WISDOM THOU ART NOW ABOUT TO LEARN FROM THE MOST DREADED WAR HAMMER OF ALL!
MIGHTY MJOLNIR SHALL DRIVE SENSE INTO THY THICK SKULL!
HA! I SEE NOW THOU ART A STORM GIANT-- YOUNG ENOUGH TO BE OF AN AGE WITH MYSELF!
BUT DO NOT THINK THY IGNORANCE AND INEX-PERIENCE WILL EXCUSE THY LOUTISH CRUDITY!
ONCE HURLED, THE HAMMER OF THOR IS MERCILESS IN ITS IMPACT!
SILENCE, SPAWN OF ASGARD!
IF THOU THINKEST SUCH HOLLOW WORDS WILL SUFFICE TO REMOVE ME FROM THIS CRAG, THOU ART EVEN A MORE PITIFUL BRAGGART THAN I SUSPECT!
CLEARLY THE YOUTHFUL THUNDER GOD HATH FOUND HIMSELF AN ANTAGONIST WHO MEANS TO TEST HIS METTLE TO THE LIMIT!
PABLO

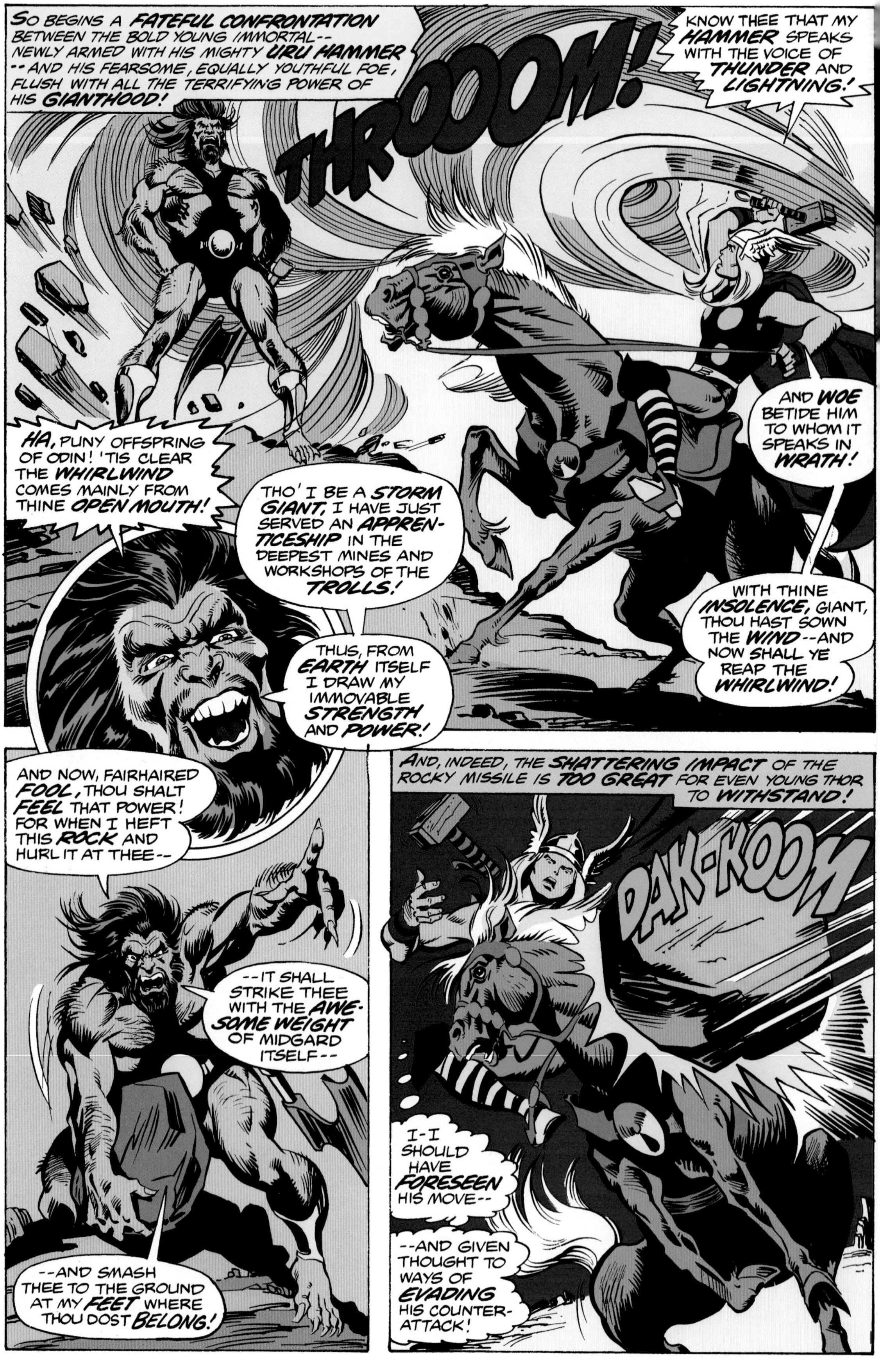

SO BEGINS A FATEFUL CONFRONTATION BETWEEN THE BOLD YOUNG IMMORTAL-- NEWLY ARMED WITH HIS MIGHTY URU HAMMER -- AND HIS FEARSOME, EQUALLY YOUTHFUL FOE, FLUSH WITH ALL THE TERRIFYING POWER OF HIS GIANTHOOD!
THROOOOM!
KNOW THEE THAT MY HAMMER SPEAKS WITH THE VOICE OF THUNDER AND LIGHTNING!
AND WOE BETIDE HIM TO WHOM IT SPEAKS IN WRATH!
HA, PUNY OFFSPRING OF ODIN! 'TIS CLEAR THE WHIRLWIND COMES MAINLY FROM THINE OPEN MOUTH!
THO' I BE A STORM GIANT, I HAVE JUST SERVED AN APPRENTICESHIP IN THE DEEPEST MINES AND WORKSHOPS OF THE TROLLS!
THUS, FROM EARTH ITSELF I DRAW MY IMMOVABLE STRENGTH AND POWER!
WITH THINE INSOLENCE, GIANT, THOU HAST SOWN THE WIND--AND NOW SHALL YE REAP THE WHIRLWIND!
AND NOW, FAIRHAIRED FOOL, THOU SHALT FEEL THAT POWER! FOR WHEN I HEFT THIS ROCK AND HURL IT AT THEE--
--IT SHALL STRIKE THEE WITH THE AWESOME WEIGHT OF MIDGARD ITSELF--
--AND SMASH THEE TO THE GROUND AT MY FEET WHERE THOU DOST BELONG!
AND, INDEED, THE SHATTERING IMPACT OF THE ROCKY MISSILE IS TOO GREAT FOR EVEN YOUNG THOR TO WITHSTAND!
DAK-KOOM
I-I SHOULD HAVE FORESEEN HIS MOVE--
--AND GIVEN THOUGHT TO WAYS OF EVADING HIS COUNTER-ATTACK!

WHAT SAY THEE *NOW*, BRASH GODLING?! DOST THOU STILL MEAN TO *REMOVE* ME FROM THY PATH?!

IF SO, WHY DOST THOU *LIE* THERE SUPINE AT MY *FEET?!*

OR HAST THY VAUNTED COURAGE *FAILED* THEE--

--NOW THAT THOU HAST FELT THE *PAINFUL EFFECTS* OF MY TERRIBLE STRENGTH?

NEVER BEFORE HAS THOR FELT SUCH INTENSE SHAME AND HUMILIATION AS HE FEELS NOW! THE PHYSICAL PAIN OF THE GIANT'S BLOW IS AS NOTHING COMPARED TO ITS PAINFUL EFFECT ON HIS HEART AND SPIRIT!

MY *HONOR* IS AT STAKE!

I MUST NOT GIVE HIM THE *SATISFACTION* OF BETRAYING EVEN THE SLIGHTEST *WEAKNESS!*

RATHER, I MUST SHOW HIM HOW A *GOD OF ASGARD* REACTS AT SUCH A MOMENT!

BUT AS THOR REACHES OUT TO RETRIEVE HIS HAMMER AND RENEW THE FIGHT--

HOLD, PUNY ONE! WHAT NEED HATH A *WORM* LIKE THEE FOR SUCH A WEAPON?!

WAR HAMMERS ARE FOR *WARRIORS*-- NOT FOR MISERABLE, *CRAWLING* THINGS SUCH AS THEE!

THINE EMPTY BOASTING IS ALREADY *EXPOSED* FOR WHAT IT IS-- NAUGHT BUT THE SHRILL *YOWLING* OF AN UN-BLOODED *WHELP!*

THE BATTLE IS NOT YET *OVER,* OGRE!

'TIS THOU WHO DOST *BOAST* NOW-- LIKE THE HOLLOW BOOMING OF AN *EMPTY TUB!*

BUT HEAR ME WELL! THY CALLOW YOUTHFULNESS WILL NOT STAY ME FROM WHAT IS TO *FOLLOW!*

FOR WHEN I *RISE* TO MY FEET, THEN TRULY WILL I BEGIN TO *FIGHT!*

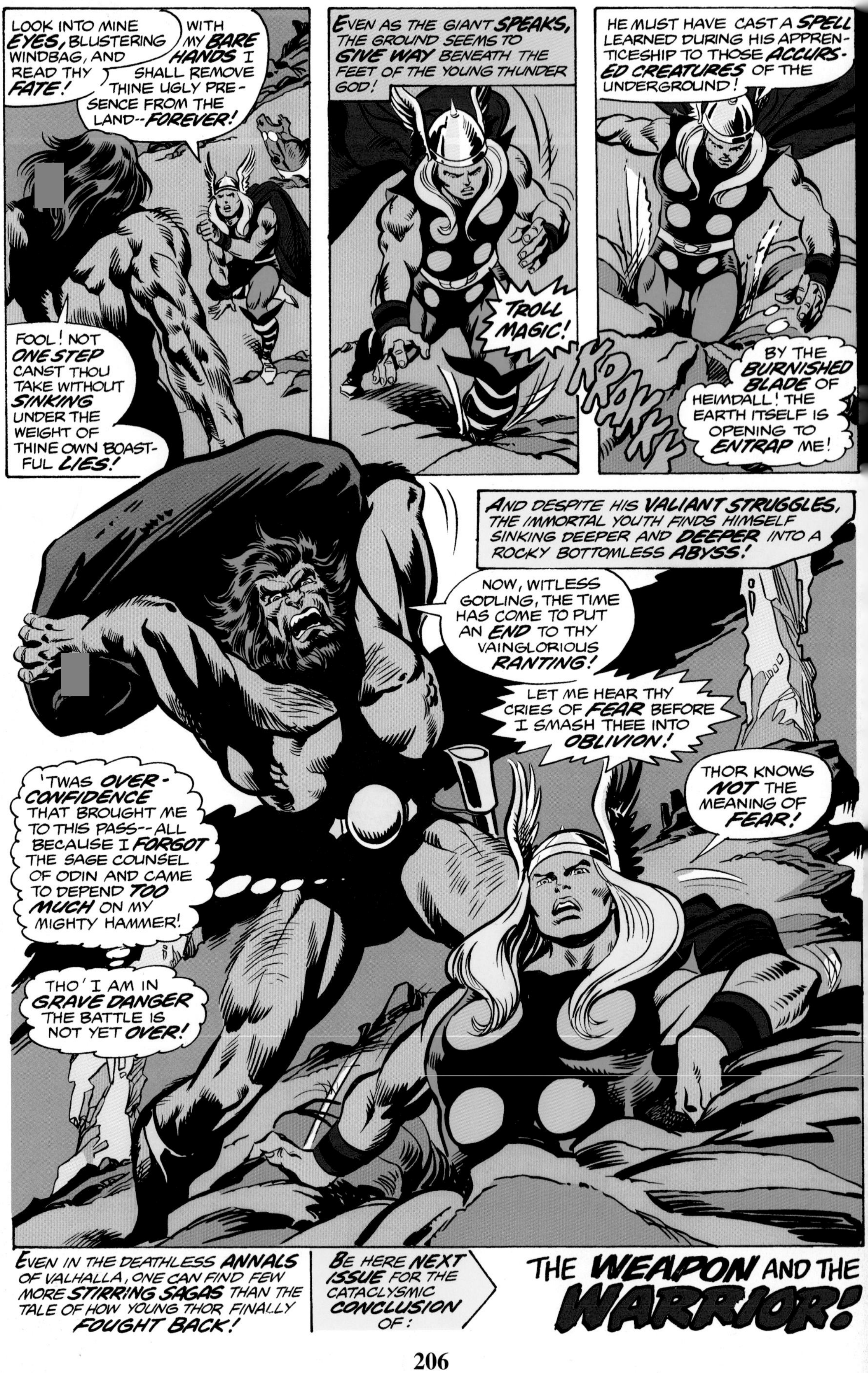
LOOK INTO MINE EYES, BLUSTERING WINDBAG, AND READ THY FATE!
WITH MY BARE HANDS I SHALL REMOVE THINE UGLY PRESENCE FROM THE LAND--FOREVER!
FOOL! NOT ONE STEP CANST THOU TAKE WITHOUT SINKING UNDER THE WEIGHT OF THINE OWN BOASTFUL LIES!
EVEN AS THE GIANT SPEAKS, THE GROUND SEEMS TO GIVE WAY BENEATH THE FEET OF THE YOUNG THUNDER GOD!
TROLL MAGIC!
HE MUST HAVE CAST A SPELL LEARNED DURING HIS APPRENTICESHIP TO THOSE ACCURSED CREATURES OF THE UNDERGROUND!
KRAKK
BY THE BURNISHED BLADE OF HEIMDALL! THE EARTH ITSELF IS OPENING TO ENTRAP ME!
AND DESPITE HIS VALIANT STRUGGLES, THE IMMORTAL YOUTH FINDS HIMSELF SINKING DEEPER AND DEEPER INTO A ROCKY BOTTOMLESS ABYSS!
NOW, WITLESS GODLING, THE TIME HAS COME TO PUT AN END TO THY VAINGLORIOUS RANTING!
LET ME HEAR THY CRIES OF FEAR BEFORE I SMASH THEE INTO OBLIVION!
THOR KNOWS NOT THE MEANING OF FEAR!
'TWAS OVER-CONFIDENCE THAT BROUGHT ME TO THIS PASS--ALL BECAUSE I FORGOT THE SAGE COUNSEL OF ODIN AND CAME TO DEPEND TOO MUCH ON MY MIGHTY HAMMER!
THO' I AM IN GRAVE DANGER THE BATTLE IS NOT YET OVER!
EVEN IN THE DEATHLESS ANNALS OF VALHALLA, ONE CAN FIND FEW MORE STIRRING SAGAS THAN THE TALE OF HOW YOUNG THOR FINALLY FOUGHT BACK!
BE HERE NEXT ISSUE FOR THE CATACLYSMIC CONCLUSION OF:
THE WEAPON AND THE WARRIOR!

THOR

MARVEL COMICS GROUP™

APPROVED BY THE COMICS CODE AUTHORITY

30¢ CC

253 NOV 02450

THE MIGHTY THOR®

SIDE-BY-SIDE WITH ULIK!

THUNDER GOD and TROLL-- TOGETHER AGAINST THE MOST AWESOME MONSTER OF ALL!

When lame Dr. DONALD BLAKE strikes his wooden walking stick upon the ground, it becomes the mystic mallet MJOLNIR—and Blake is transformed into the Norse God of Thunder, Master of the Storm and the Lightning, Heir to the Throne of Immortal Asgard...

Stan Lee PRESENTS: THE MIGHTY THOR!™

CHAOS IN THE KINGDOM OF THE TROLLS

THE BATTLE AT LAST IS OVER, ASGARDIAN-- AND 'TIS ULIK WHO CLAIMS THE FINAL VICTORY!

A MOMENT AGO, HE WAS LOCKED IN MORTAL COMBAT WITH THE DREAD ULIK, MOST TERRIBLE OF ALL THE SAVAGE TROLLS WHO DWELL BENEATH THE EARTH!

NOW THE GOD OF THUNDER PLUNGES HEADLONG FROM THE ROCK-HEWN BRIDGE THAT SPANS AN ALL-CONSUMING OCEAN OF FLAME--

--AND, SO DOING, IT SEEMS HE HAS SEALED THE FATE OF IMMORTAL ASGARD!

EXPERIENCE BOUNDLESS WONDERMENT AT THE SIDE OF THESE STALWARTS!

LEN WEIN
WRITER / EDITOR

JOHN BUSCEMA / TONY DeZUNIGA
ILLUSTRATORS

M. SEVERIN • COLORIST
CONDOY • LETTERER

WE PROMISE YOU WON'T BE DISAPPOINTED!

YOU FOUGHT *WELL*, THUNDER GOD-- BUT YOUR *GUILELESS GALLANTRY* WAS YOUR *DOWNFALL!*

BY SHOWING ME *MERCY* WHEN YOU THOUGHT ME *DEFEATED*, YOU LEFT YOURSELF *OPEN* FOR MY MOST TREACHEROUS *BLOW!*

I WARNED YOU IN *BATTLE*, ASGARDIAN, THAT ONLY *ONE* OF US COULD LIVE TO CLAIM THE *RUBY EYE* OF YON *DRAGON*--

--HE WHO *GUARDS* THE GOLDEN GATES TO THE *REALM BELOW*--

--AND THAT ONE SHALL BE-- *ULIK!*

A SAVAGE CRY OF *BATTLE* ON HIS SLAVERING LIPS, THE MONSTROUS *TROLL* THUNDERS FORTH TO MEET THE GREAT BELLOWING *GUARDIAN*...

...AND SPEAKING OF *THUNDER*...!

VERILY, IF THOR DOTH NOW *PERISH*, 'TWILL MEAN THE *END* OF THE REALM ETERNAL!

FOR I HAVE SWORN TO *PRESENT* THE RUBY EYE TO THE ALL-KNOWING *MIMIR*, THAT HE MIGHT TELL ME THE *WHEREABOUTS* OF THE LONG-MISSING *ODIN*--

--AND NOT ALL THE FLAMES OF THE *FIERY PIT* NOR ALL THE *MIGHT* OF THE VILE TROLL EMPIRE SHALL STAY ME FROM MY *QUEST!*

NOT SO LONG AS THE *MYSTIC MALLET MJOLNIR* IS STILL MINE TO *COMMAND!*

NOT SO LONG AS THOR IS STILL *GOD OF THUNDER!!*

'TIS AS I *SUSPECTED!* THINKING ME *DEAD*, ULIK HATH RETURNED TO HIS *PRIMARY* TASK--

--AND VERILY, 'TIS A MOST *DISTASTEFUL* TASK INDEED!

THUS, IT IS A TASK THAT ULIK *REVELS* IN PERFORMING, HIS BLUDGEONING *BATTLE-MACE* SLASHING SAVAGELY THRU THE SWELTERING AIR, DRIVING THE LEGENDARY GUARDIAN *BACK*--

--BACK--

--UNTIL, AT LAST, THE BLOODY-HANDED CAVE-BRUTE PROVES THAT EVEN A LEGEND CAN *DIE!*

THUS PERISH *ALL* WHO STAND IN ULIK'S *WAY!*

SKROOM!

AND, HIS GRISLY TASK *COMPLETED*, ULIK CLAIMS HIS *PRIZE!*

THERE! THIS GLITTERING GEM IS FINALLY *MINE!*

IN MY HAND, I HOLD THE *FUTURE* OF ALL THE MIGHTY *TROLL EMPIRE!*

BUT THOU MUST PASS BY *ME* TO RETURN TO THY KINGDOM, BESTIAL ONE--

--AND THOU HAST NOT *POWER* ENOW TO *ACCOMPLISH* THAT TASK!

SO, ASGARDIAN, YOU STILL *LIVE*--

--BUT THAT IS AN *OVERSIGHT* THAT CAN QUICKLY BE *CORRECTED!*

THOU ATTACKEST *BOLDLY*, TROLL!

AARRGGHH!!

BROK!

CAN IT BE THOU HAST SO SOON FORGOTTEN THE *POWER* OF MINE ENCHANTED *HAMMER?*

OR THE AWESOME *STRENGTH* OF MINE OWN IMMORTAL *SINEWS?*

CHUDD!

I SAY THEE, ULIK -- *RELEASE* THE RUBY EYE!

IN ODIN'S NAME -- *IT MUST BE MINE!*

ALL THAT WILL BE *YOURS* HERE, THUNDER GOD, IS A SWIFT AND FLAMING *DEATH!*

THEIR BATTLE IS THE STUFF OF *MYTH* AND *MAJESTY*, AND THE VERY CAVERNS *TREMBLE* BEFORE THEIR *RAGE* --

-- UNTIL THE CRUMBLING *BRIDGE* UPON WHICH THEY STRUGGLE CAN BEAR THE STRAIN *NO LONGER* --

-- AND, GROANING, IT *COLLAPSES!*

ODIN'S EYES! WE ARE *UNDONE!*

THE CURSED BRIDGE *FALLS AWAY* BENEATH US!

UNLESS MY GRIP IS *SURE*, MY DOOM IS *SEALED!*

BUT IT SEEMS ULIK'S GRIP UPON THE JAGGED ROCK IS FAR MORE *CERTAIN* THAN HIS GRIP UPON ONE SOLITARY *GEM*...

SURTUR'S FLAMES! I'VE DROPPED THE *RUBY EYE!*

211

NAY! IF THE JEWEL DOTH PLUNGE INTO YON HUNGRY *FLAMES,* 'TIS LOST TO US *BOTH!*

ONLY MINE ENCHANTED *MALLET* CAN HOPE TO RETRIEVE IT *NOW!*

THUS, FOR THE SAKE OF THE *REALM ETERNAL,* LET MINE ARM BE *STRONG--*

--LET MINE AIM BE *TRUE--*

--AND LET THE MYSTIC *MJOLNIR* DELIVER UNTO ME MY LONG-SOUGHT *PRIZE!*

IT'S A PRIZE YOU'LL *NOT* LIVE TO *DEPART* WITH, ASGARDIAN!

THE FATE OF THE ENTIRE *TROLL EMPIRE* HANGS ON MY *RETURNING* THERE WITH THE *RUBY EYE--*

--AND I WILL *SLAY* YOU, THUNDER GOD, OR BE SLAIN *MYSELF* BEFORE I WILL *GIVE IT UP!*

THY WORDS ARE HOLLOW *ECHOES* IN A BLACK AND BITTER *WIND,* BESTIAL ONE!

WHAT NEED HAVE TROLLS FOR A *GEM* SUCH AS THIS, WHEN THOU HAST SUCH AWESOME *WEAPONRY* ALREADY AT THY COMMAND?

BUT 'TIS EXACTLY SUCH *WEAPONRY* THAT HAS BROUGHT THIS SHADOW OF DOOM *UPON* US, BLONDHAIR!

FOR CENTURIES UNTOLD, WE TROLLS HAVE TOILED *CEASELESSLY* BENEATH THE EARTH--

--OUR UNMATCHED MACHINERY *DIGGING,* FOREVER *DIGGING--*

"--TO HELP US ACHIEVE OUR INEVITABLE *DOMINATION* OVER EVERYTHING THAT LIVES!

212

"WE WERE USING OUR *NEWEST*, MOST *POWER-FUL* DRILLERNAUT WHEN WE BROKE THRU THE TUNNEL *WALL*--

"--INTO AN *UNKNOWN* CAVERN BEYOND, OR PERHAPS INTO ANOTHER *DIMENSION*--

"--WHEREIN LURKED THE CURSED CREATURE CALLED--*TROGG*!!"

"*TROLLS* BEYOND NUMBER *PERISHED*, ATTEMPTING TO SEAL THE *PORTAL* BETWEEN TROGG'S WORLD AND OURS--

"--BUT, AT LAST, WE CONSTRUCT-ED A PROTECTIVE *BARRICADE* ACROSS THE PORTAL--

"--A BARRICADE THAT EVEN NOW THREATENS TO *GIVE WAY!*"

ONLY THE *RUBY EYE* CAN SEAL THE PORTAL *PERMANENTLY*, THUNDER GOD-- --AND I MEAN TO *POSSESS* IT--OR *DIE!*

ODIN'S TRUTH! I *BELIEVE* THEE, TROLL!

BUT MAYHAP THERE IS A WAY THAT *NEITHER* OF US NEEDS PERISH OVER THAT GLITTER-ING *JEWEL*.

WHAT IF THOR WERE TO *RETURN* WITH THEE TO THY KINGDOM, ULIK--AND HELP THEE *DEFEAT* THIS TROGG *WITH-OUT* SACRIFICING THE RUBY EYE?

THEN WE WOULD *BOTH* HAVE THAT WHICH WE SO *DESIRE!*

WHAT?!?

ALLY MYSELF WITH *YOU*--MY MOST BITTER *ENEMY*? I WOULD SOONER...

NO.

PERHAPS YOU ARE *RIGHT*, ASGARDIAN. PERHAPS THERE *IS* NO OTHER WAY.

THUS, THOUGH MY VERY SOUL *CURDLES* AT THE THOUGHT, ASGARDIAN--

--YOU MAY ACCOMPANY ME... *HOME!*

DOWN TWISTING *CORRIDORS*, THRU TUNNELS THICK WITH ANCIENT *DUST*, THE RELUCTANT COMPANIONS TRAVEL.

UNTIL, AT LENGTH...

HAIL, KING GEIRRODUR--WISEST OF ALL THE *TROLLS!*

HAIL, ULIK! HAVE YOU...?

FAFNIR'S BREATH! WHAT MANNER OF *MADNESS* IS THIS?

ARE YOU *INSANE*, ULIK, BRINGING *THOR*-- THE VERY *PRINCE* OF ACCURSED ASGARD, WITH WHOM WE HAVE *WARRED* FOR CENTURIES BEYOND RECKONING-- RIGHT INTO OUR *MIDST*?

BUT THE THUNDER GOD DOES *NOT* COME AS A *FOE*, GEIRRODUR.

HE HAS COME TO BATTLE *TROGG*!

VERILY, GEIRRODUR-- ULIK SPEAKS *TRUE*! I MEAN TO *HARM* TO THEE AND THINE.

ON THAT, THOU HAST THE MOST SOLEMN WORD OF *THOR*!

AND THE *HONOR* OF THE FOOLISH ASGARDIAN IS *LEGENDARY*, ISN'T IT?

VERY WELL, ULIK-- TAKE THE GODLING AND DO WHATEVER YOU *MUST*!

THE EVIL SOUND OF THE TROLL KING'S MALEVOLENT *CHUCKLING* FADES INTO THE DISTANCE AS THOR AND HIS BRUTISH *ALLY* MOVE BOLDLY THRU THE UNDER-DWELLERS' DESOLATE *KINGDOM*...

THEN, SLOWLY, A *NEW* SOUND INTRUDES UPON THE SCENE, A SOUND NOT UNLIKE THE AWESOME RUMBLE OF *THUNDER*--

--OR THE GRIM POUNDING OF A *FUNERAL DRUM*!

POOM!

POOM!

POOM!

DO YOU *SEE* ASGARDIAN? EVEN AS WE SPEAK, *TROGG* SEEKS TO *SHATTER* THE BARRICADE THAT CONTAINS HIM!

THEN WE MUST NEEDS *PLAN* OUR FIRST MOVE MOST *CAREFULLY*, ULIK--!

214

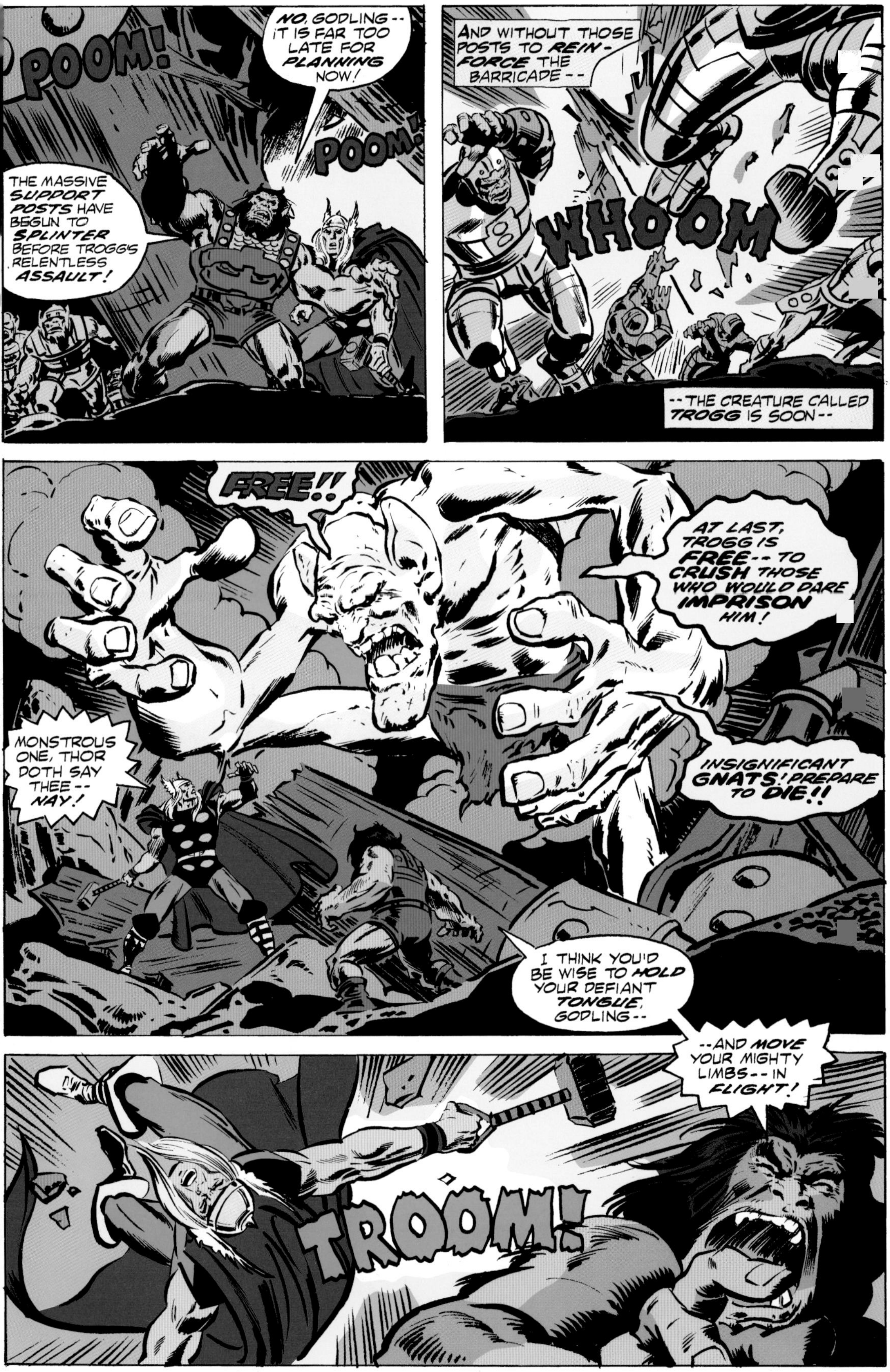

POOM!
NO, GODLING -- IT IS FAR TOO LATE FOR PLANNING NOW!
POOM!
THE MASSIVE SUPPORT POSTS HAVE BEGUN TO SPLINTER BEFORE TROGG'S RELENTLESS ASSAULT!
AND WITHOUT THOSE POSTS TO REIN-FORCE THE BARRICADE --
WHOOM
-- THE CREATURE CALLED TROGG IS SOON --
FREE!!
AT LAST, TROGG IS FREE -- TO CRUSH THOSE WHO WOULD DARE IMPRISON HIM!
MONSTROUS ONE, THOR DOTH SAY THEE -- NAY!
INSIGNIFICANT GNATS! PREPARE TO DIE!!
I THINK YOU'D BE WISE TO HOLD YOUR DEFIANT TONGUE, GODLING --
-- AND MOVE YOUR MIGHTY LIMBS -- IN FLIGHT!
TROOM!

YOU ARE MORE *AGILE* THAN I IMAGINED, LITTLE *GNATS!* YOU *AVOIDED* THE BRUNT OF MY *FIRST BLOW!*

BUT NOTHING THAT LIVES CAN ELUDE THE INFERNAL *POWER* THAT IS *TROGG'S* ALONE!

BEWARE, THUNDER GOD-- PROTECT YOUR *FLANK!*

THE SON OF ODIN NEED NO *LESSONS* IN THE ART OF *BATTLE*, TROLL !

THOR IS A *WARRIOR BORN!*

SHOOM!

STAND STILL, LITTLE *GNATS!* CURSE YOU-- STAND STILL!!

I WARN YOU-- THE VENGEANCE OF TROGG IS ALL-CONSUMING!

SWIFTLY, ULIK, WHILST I DRAW THE GIANT'S *FIRE*--

--ATTACK!!

MY ASSAULT IS ALREADY *BEGUN*, ASGARDIAN!

THE BATTLE IS *JOINED*--

--AND THE *VICTOR* SHALL BE-- *ULIK !*

BROK!

BUT IT APPEARS THAT SUBJECT IS STILL OPEN TO *DISPUTE*.

FOR, WITH HARDLY A *SHRUG*, THE THING CALLED TROGG TOSSES ULIK *ASIDE*--

SKRAKK!

--AND THUS LEAVES HIMSELF UNGUARDED FOR THE THUNDER GOD'S *ATTACK!*

I KNOW NOT WHAT MANNER OF *CREATURE* THOU ART, TROGG--

--BUT, IN TRUTH, IT MATTERS *LITTLE!*

BTOW!

I KNOW ONLY THAT THOU MUST BE *DEFEATED* IF I AM TO CLAIM THE *RUBY EYE* WITH IMPUNITY--

PTROK!

--AND THUS, IN ODIN'S NAME-- I *STRIKE!*

YOUR HAMMER HAS DONE ITS JOB *WELL*, ASGARDIAN!

NOW LEAVE THE REST TO *ULIK!*

NAY, TROLL! TOGETHER WE *BEGAN* THIS BATTLE--

--AND *TOGETHER* WILL WE *RETURN* THIS MONSTROUS ONE TO HIS MYSTERIOUS DOMAIN!

SINCE BEFORE THE DAWN OF TIME HAS TROGG DWELT IN *DARK-NESS!*

BUT NO MORE, LITTLE GNATS-- *NO MORE!*

NO!!

THAMM!

THE CHOICE IS NOT THINE TO *MAKE,* MONS-TROUS ONE!

THOU CANST NOT BE ALLOWED TO *RUN RAMPANT* THRU THE KINGDOM OF THE *TROLLS*--

--AND THEN, MAYHAP, THRU FABLED *ASGARD* ITSELF!

CURSE YOU, THUNDER GOD-- *HOLD YOUR GROUND!*

THE TOWERING TROGG MUST BE *KEPT AT BAY* A MOMENT LONGER--

AARRGHH!!!

--UNTIL ULIK IS IN POSITION TO DO-- *THIS!*

TRUNCHEON IN HAND, I FORCE THE GIANT *BACK*--BACK INTO HIS OWN UNKNOWN *WORLD!*

NEVER, LITTLE GNAT! TROGG WILL SOON *SPLINTER* YOUR CRUDE WEAPON--

--AND THEN TROGG WILL SPLINTER *YOU!*

AYE, TROGG WILL TURN YOUR WORLD TO SMOKING *RUINS*-- BEFORE HE WILL *SURRENDER!!*

ZOUNDS!

THOU HAST DRIVEN THE UNGAINLY BEHE-MOTH BACK TO THE VERY *BRINK* OF HIS INK-DARK *REALM!*

QUICKLY, ULIK--THRUST HIM *BACK* THRU THE YAWNING *PORTAL!*

DON'T YOU THINK I'M *TRYING* TO, ASGARDIAN?

THE GIANT'S STRENGTH IS *OVERWHELMING!*

EVEN *I* CANNOT HOLD THE GIANT BACK MUCH *LONGER*, ASGARDIAN!

YOU'LL HAVE TO USE THE *RUBY EYE* TO SEAL THE PORTAL-- AND USE IT *SWIFTLY!*

NAY, TROLL! TO *SACRIFICE* THE RUBY EYE NOW WOULD BE TO *CONDEMN* THE REALM ETERNAL!

IN THE NAME OF *MERCY,* ULIK-- I CANNOT *BETRAY* MY PEOPLE'S *TRUST* IN ME!

YES, YOUR PEOPLE *PRIDE* THEMSELVES ON THEIR MERCY-- *DON'T* THEY, THOR? THEY CLAIM IT IS THE SINGLE QUALITY THAT *SEPERATES* THEM FROM THE *TROLLS!*

USE THE CURSED *GEM,* THUNDER GOD-- OR, IN TRUTH, YOU ARE NO BETTER THAN *ME!*

I SAY THEE, TROLL -- *ENOUGH!*

I'LL HEAR *NO MORE!*

THOUGH THEE AND THINE STAND FOR ALL THAT IS *BASE* AND *EVIL* IN THIS UNIVERSE...

THOUGH THOU HAST OFTEN SOUGHT MY *DEATH* AND MOCKED ME TO MY *FACE...*

...STILL WILL I USE THE RUBY EYE TO *SAVE* THY KINGDOM, ULIK...

...AND MAY *ODIN* HAVE MERCY ON MY *SOUL!*

A MOMENT MORE-- AND TROGG WILL BE *FREE* ONCE AGAIN!

A MOMENT MORE-- AND *NOTHING* WILL STOP ME FROM *DESTROY-ING* YOUR *CURSED...*

THE EXPLOSION IS INCREDIBLY *BRIEF*--

KWHOOM!

--BUT UNARGUABLY *FINAL!*

AND WHEN THE ACRID *SMOKE* AND SWIRLING *DUST* AT LAST HAVE *CLEARED*...

GONE!

THE CREATURE CALLED TROGG HAS *VANISHED*--ALONG WITH THE GAPING PORTAL THAT GAVE HIM *ENTRY* TO THIS WORLD!

AYE, ULIK--AND WITH HIM WENT THE *RUBY EYE OF THE DRAGON*--

--AND MY FINAL HOPE OF *FINDING* THE LONG-MISSING *ODIN!*

IT IS NO MORE THAN YOU *DESERVE*, GODLING! ONLY AN UTTER *FOOL* SACRIFICES HIS OWN ENDS FOR THE SAKE OF HIS MOST BITTER *ENEMY!*

THOU DOST DARE SPEAK THUS TO THE *GOD OF THUNDER*, TROLL?

ASGARD HELP ME, ULIK... BUT THOU SPEAKEST *A'RIGHT.*

VERILY, WE SHALL MEET *AGAIN*, BESTIAL ONE...

...AND I SHALL *REMEMBER* THE LESSON I LEARNED HERE TODAY!

THEN, HEAD BOWED, SHOULDERS SLUMPED IN RESIGNATION, THE PRINCE OF ASGARD TURNS AND *DEPARTS* THE UNDERGROUND KINGDOM--

--WHILE THE TAUNTING *LAUGHTER* OF THE ASSEMBLED TROLLS CUTS *THRU* HIM LIKE A WORN AND RUSTED *SWORD!*

NEXT ISSUE: WOULD'JA BELIEVE... THE **STONE MEN** FROM **SATURN!**

FLUSHED WITH YOUTHFUL **PRIDE** IN HIS NEWLY-WON WEAPON--THE MIGHTY URU HAMMER, **MJOLNIR**-- THOR HAS RUSHED RECKLESSLY INTO BATTLE WITH A YOUNG **STORM GIANT**--

--ONLY TO SUFFER A HUMILIATING MAGICAL **ENTRAPMENT** THAT HAS PLUNGED HIM TO THE VERY BRINK OF **DOOM!**

LOOK THY **LAST**, PUNY GODLY, UPON THE GLORIOUS LIGHT OF DAY--

--BEFORE THE CRUSHING **WEIGHT** OF THIS BOULDER **SMASHES** THEE DEEP INTO THE BOWELS OF THE **EARTH!**

NAY, OGRE! OUR FIGHT IS **FAR** FROM FINISHED!

THOUGH MY PLIGHT BE TRULY **DESPERATE**--BY THE BEARD OF **ODIN**, I SHALL **BEST** THEE YET!

THIS **IS IT!** THE CATACLYSMIC CONCLUDING CHAPTER!

THE WEAPON AND THE WARRIOR!

DAVID KRAFT,
WRITER
PABLO MARCOS
ARTIST
I. WATANABE,
LETTERER
GLYNIS WEIN,
COLORIST
LEN WEIN, EDITOR

'TWAS BRASH **OVERCONFIDENCE** AND UNTHINKING **DEPENDENCE** UPON MY MIGHTY MALLET THAT DELIVERED ME TO THIS **IGNOBLE** PLIGHT.

BUT NOW I SHALL PROVE THAT THERE IS FAR **MORE** TO MY POWER THAN ANY MERE **WEAPON!**

WITNESS THE **MIGHT** AND THE **MAJESTY** OF THOR!

KRAAAKR!

OD'S BLOOD!!

NOW, TO **ME,** MJOLNIR--FOR YOU GIBBERING **GIANT** SHALL SOON LEARN--

--THAT THOR, TOO, CAN BE AN **EARTH-SHAKER!**

KLONK!

THE MATCHLESS **MIGHT** OF MJOLNIR BREAKS THRU THE CRUST OF THE MOUNTAINSIDE--

--FREEING THE YOUNG **GOD OF THUNDER**--

--AND PLUNGING BOTH COMBATANTS INTO A HIDDEN **SUBTERRANEAN CHASM!**

222

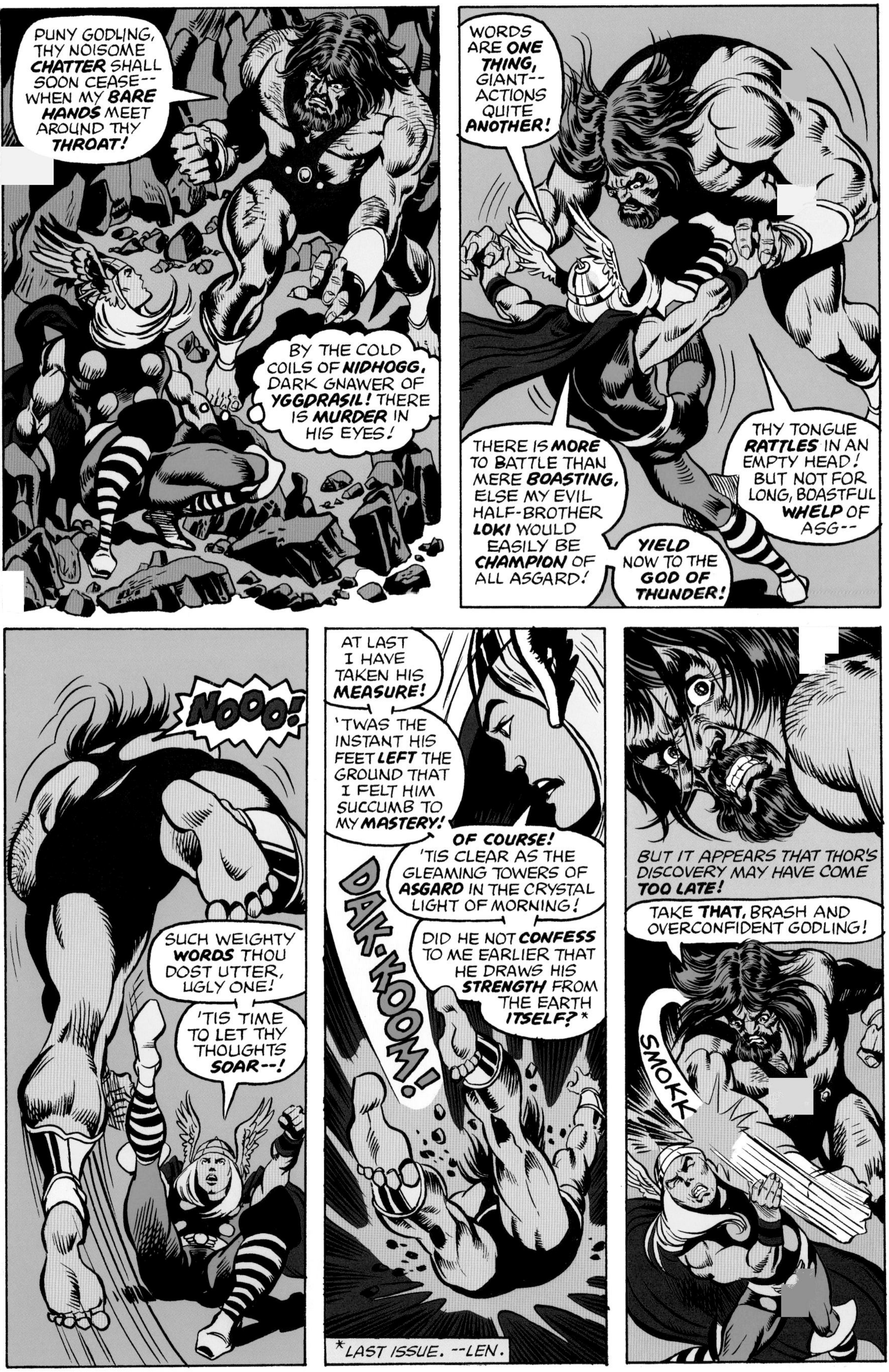
PUNY GODLING, THY NOISOME CHATTER SHALL SOON CEASE-- WHEN MY BARE HANDS MEET AROUND THY THROAT!
BY THE COLD COILS OF NIDHOGG, DARK GNAWER OF YGGDRASIL! THERE IS MURDER IN HIS EYES!
WORDS ARE ONE THING, GIANT-- ACTIONS QUITE ANOTHER!
THERE IS MORE TO BATTLE THAN MERE BOASTING, ELSE MY EVIL HALF-BROTHER LOKI WOULD EASILY BE CHAMPION OF ALL ASGARD!
THY TONGUE RATTLES IN AN EMPTY HEAD! BUT NOT FOR LONG, BOASTFUL WHELP OF ASG--
YIELD NOW TO THE GOD OF THUNDER!
NOOO!
SUCH WEIGHTY WORDS THOU DOST UTTER, UGLY ONE!
'TIS TIME TO LET THY THOUGHTS SOAR--!
AT LAST I HAVE TAKEN HIS MEASURE!
'TWAS THE INSTANT HIS FEET LEFT THE GROUND THAT I FELT HIM SUCCUMB TO MY MASTERY!
OF COURSE! 'TIS CLEAR AS THE GLEAMING TOWERS OF ASGARD IN THE CRYSTAL LIGHT OF MORNING!
DID HE NOT CONFESS TO ME EARLIER THAT HE DRAWS HIS STRENGTH FROM THE EARTH ITSELF? *
DAK-KOOM!
*LAST ISSUE. --LEN.
BUT IT APPEARS THAT THOR'S DISCOVERY MAY HAVE COME TOO LATE!
TAKE THAT, BRASH AND OVERCONFIDENT GODLING!
SMOKK

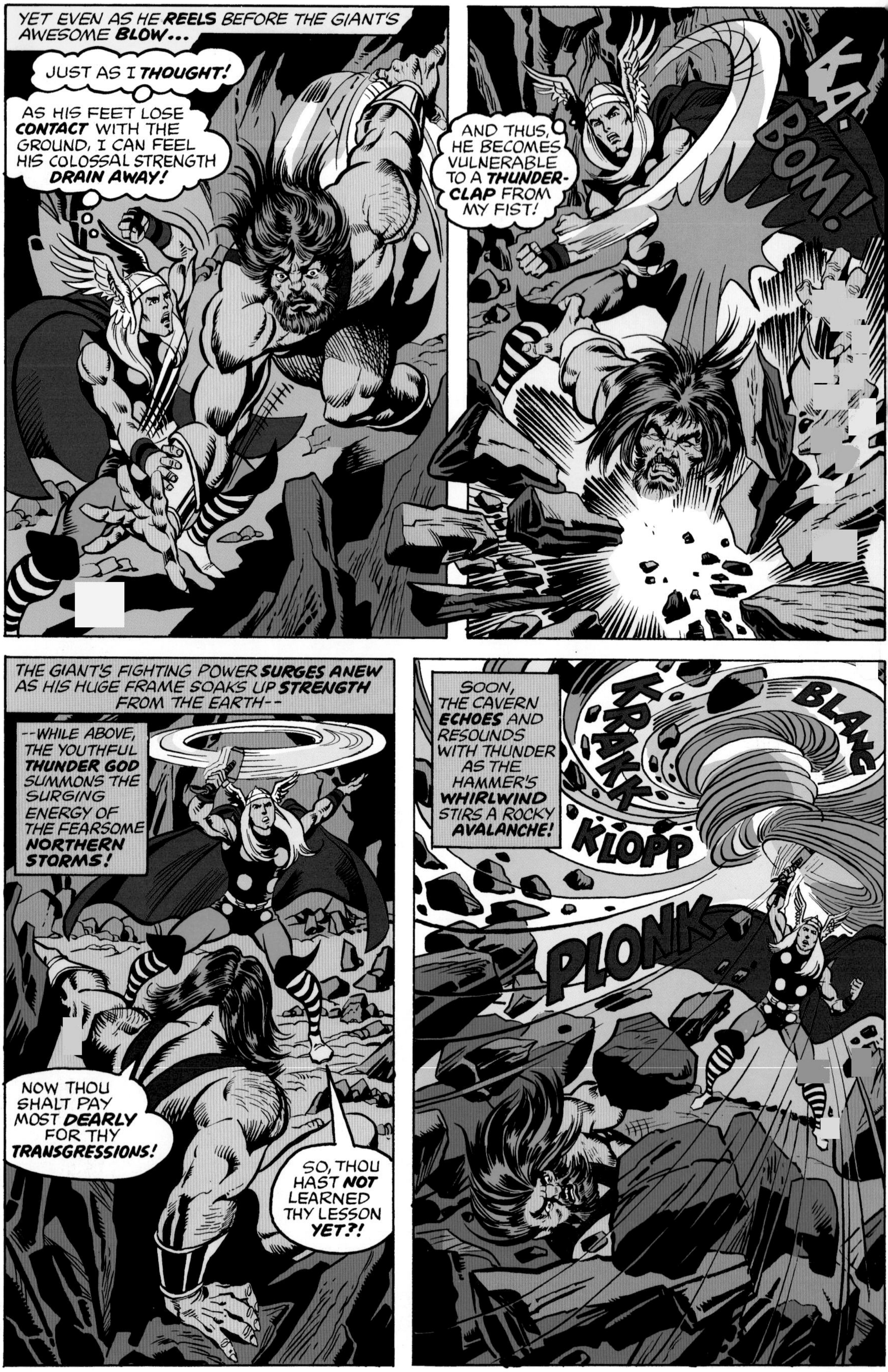
YET EVEN AS HE REELS BEFORE THE GIANT'S AWESOME BLOW...
JUST AS I THOUGHT!
AS HIS FEET LOSE CONTACT WITH THE GROUND, I CAN FEEL HIS COLOSSAL STRENGTH DRAIN AWAY!
AND THUS, HE BECOMES VULNERABLE TO A THUNDER-CLAP FROM MY FIST!
KA-BOM!
THE GIANT'S FIGHTING POWER SURGES ANEW AS HIS HUGE FRAME SOAKS UP STRENGTH FROM THE EARTH--
--WHILE ABOVE, THE YOUTHFUL THUNDER GOD SUMMONS THE SURGING ENERGY OF THE FEARSOME NORTHERN STORMS!
NOW THOU SHALT PAY MOST DEARLY FOR THY TRANSGRESSIONS!
SO, THOU HAST NOT LEARNED THY LESSON YET?!
SOON, THE CAVERN ECHOES AND RESOUNDS WITH THUNDER AS THE HAMMER'S WHIRLWIND STIRS A ROCKY AVALANCHE!
KRAKK
BLANG
KLOPP
PLONK

STILL THE FIERCE YOUNG GIANT **REFUSES** TO ADMIT DEFEAT... NOR HAS THOR LOST HIS BERSERKER'S THIRST FOR **BATTLE**--

--THOUGH **BOTH** HAVE SUFFERED **SORELY** FROM THE FRAY!

FOR A LONG MOMENT, THE TWO **GLARE** AT EACH OTHER IN TENSE **SILENCE**...

...AND THEN, WITHOUT WARNING, THE GIANT SUDDENLY BURSTS INTO BELLOWING **LAUGHTER**!

THOR LIKEWISE FINDS HIMSELF **INFECTED** BY THE **RIDICULOUSNESS** OF THE SITUATION ...AND HE, TOO, ERUPTS IN SAVAGE **MIRTH**!

ZOUNDS, GODLING-- WE ARE FAIRLY **MATCHED**! WE COULD GO ON **FIGHTING** POINTLESSLY FOR **DAYS**!

AYE! BUT WHY IN THE NAME OF **HELA** ARE WE TRULY BATTLING?!

HA-HA·HA·H̅! HA·HA·H̅

AND THUS RELIEVED OF THE ONEROUS DUTIES OF **COMBAT**...

FARE THEE **WELL**, GODLING! THOU HAST FOUGHT A **GOOD** FIGHT!

BUT NEXT TIME WE MEET-- **BEWARE**!

THOU TOO **BEWARE**, UGLY ONE! WHEN NEXT I **TOSS** THEE, IT MAY BE DOWN A **BOTTOMLESS WELL**!

FOR MANY A LONG YEAR, THE YOUNG GOD OF THUNDER WILL **REMEMBER** THE LESSON HE HAS LEARNED THIS DAY...

MJOLNIR, MY FRIEND, A WEAPON OF THY MATCHLESS MIGHT IS A **TREASURE** BEYOND PRICE!

YET NEVER AGAIN WILL I RELY SOLELY ON **THEE** TO DO MY FIGHTING --WITHOUT LOOKING FIRST TO MY OWN **BRAINS** AND **BRAWN**!

FOR WELL AND TRULY HATH THE ALL-FATHER **ODIN** SAID:

"IT IS THE **WARRIOR,** NOT THE WEAPON THAT **WINS** BATTLES!"

The END

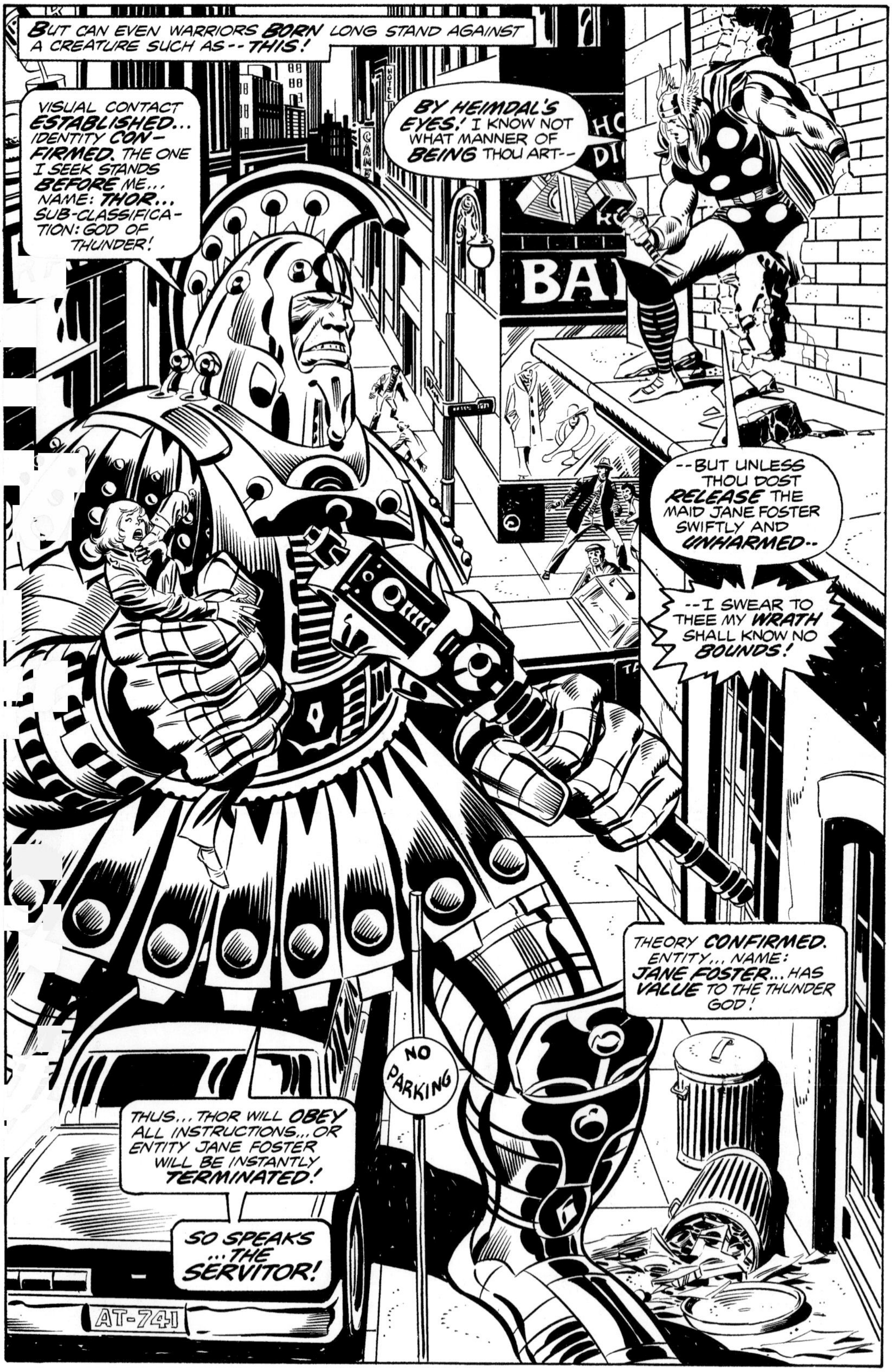
BUT CAN EVEN WARRIORS BORN LONG STAND AGAINST A CREATURE SUCH AS--THIS!
VISUAL CONTACT ESTABLISHED... IDENTITY CONFIRMED. THE ONE I SEEK STANDS BEFORE ME... NAME: THOR... SUB-CLASSIFICATION: GOD OF THUNDER!
BY HEIMDAL'S EYES! I KNOW NOT WHAT MANNER OF BEING THOU ART--
--BUT UNLESS THOU DOST RELEASE THE MAID JANE FOSTER SWIFTLY AND UNHARMED--
--I SWEAR TO THEE MY WRATH SHALL KNOW NO BOUNDS!
THEORY CONFIRMED. ENTITY... NAME: JANE FOSTER...HAS VALUE TO THE THUNDER GOD!
NO PARKING
THUS... THOR WILL OBEY ALL INSTRUCTIONS... OR ENTITY JANE FOSTER WILL BE INSTANTLY TERMINATED!
SO SPEAKS ...THE SERVITOR!
AT-741

INKED ART FOR THOR #242 PAGE 8 BY JOHN BUSCEMA & JOE SINNOTT

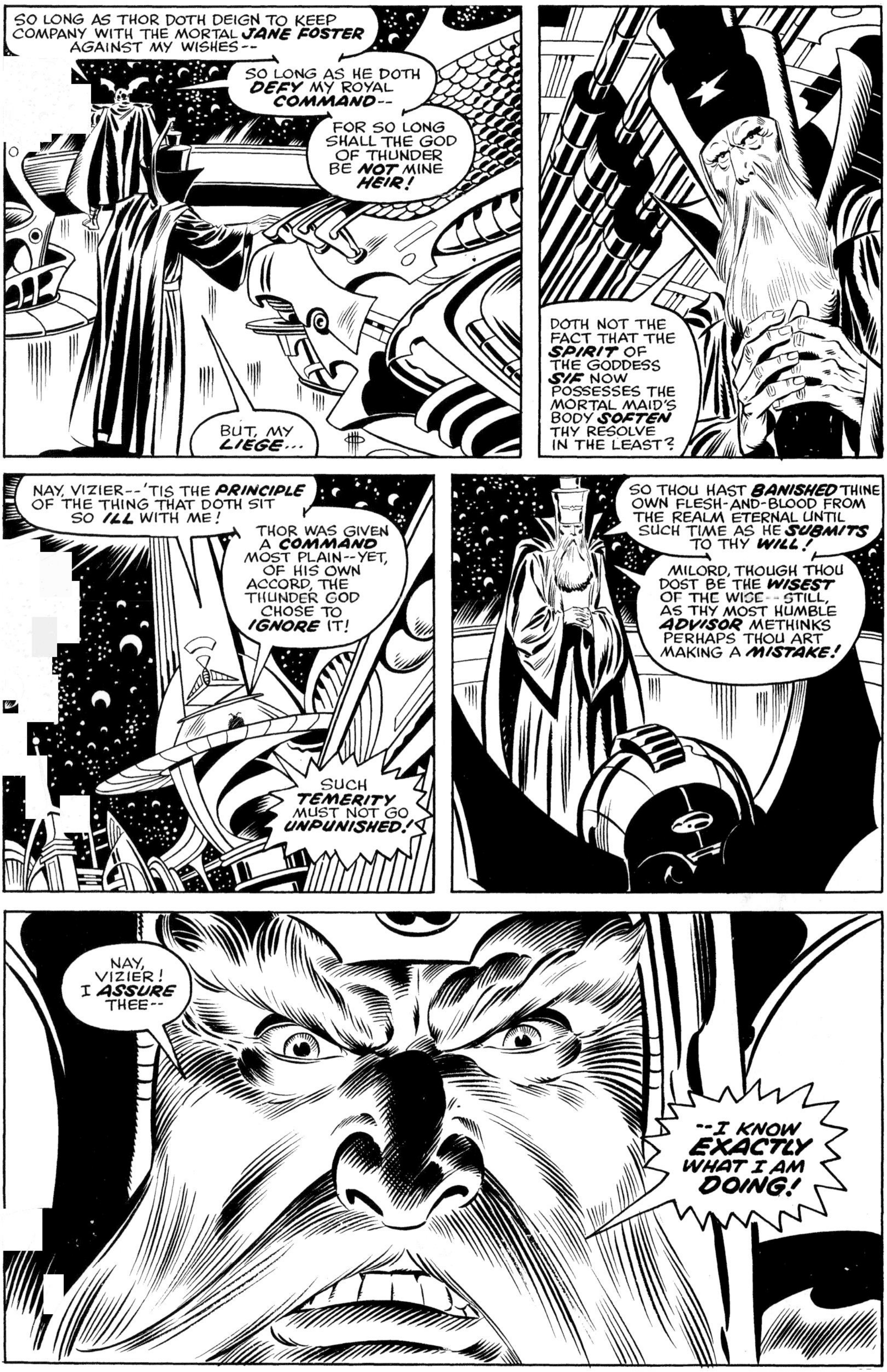

SO LONG AS THOR DOTH DEIGN TO KEEP COMPANY WITH THE MORTAL JANE FOSTER AGAINST MY WISHES--
SO LONG AS HE DOTH DEFY MY ROYAL COMMAND--
FOR SO LONG SHALL THE GOD OF THUNDER BE NOT MINE HEIR!
BUT, MY LIEGE...
DOTH NOT THE FACT THAT THE SPIRIT OF THE GODDESS SIF NOW POSSESSES THE MORTAL MAID'S BODY SOFTEN THY RESOLVE IN THE LEAST?
NAY, VIZIER--'TIS THE PRINCIPLE OF THE THING THAT DOTH SIT SO ILL WITH ME!
THOR WAS GIVEN A COMMAND MOST PLAIN--YET, OF HIS OWN ACCORD, THE THUNDER GOD CHOSE TO IGNORE IT!
SUCH TEMERITY MUST NOT GO UNPUNISHED!
SO THOU HAST BANISHED THINE OWN FLESH-AND-BLOOD FROM THE REALM ETERNAL UNTIL SUCH TIME AS HE SUBMITS TO THY WILL!
MILORD, THOUGH THOU DOST BE THE WISEST OF THE WISE--STILL, AS THY MOST HUMBLE ADVISOR METHINKS PERHAPS THOU ART MAKING A MISTAKE!
NAY, VIZIER! I ASSURE THEE--
--I KNOW EXACTLY WHAT I AM DOING!

Inked art for THOR #243 page 7 by John Buscema & Joe Sinnott

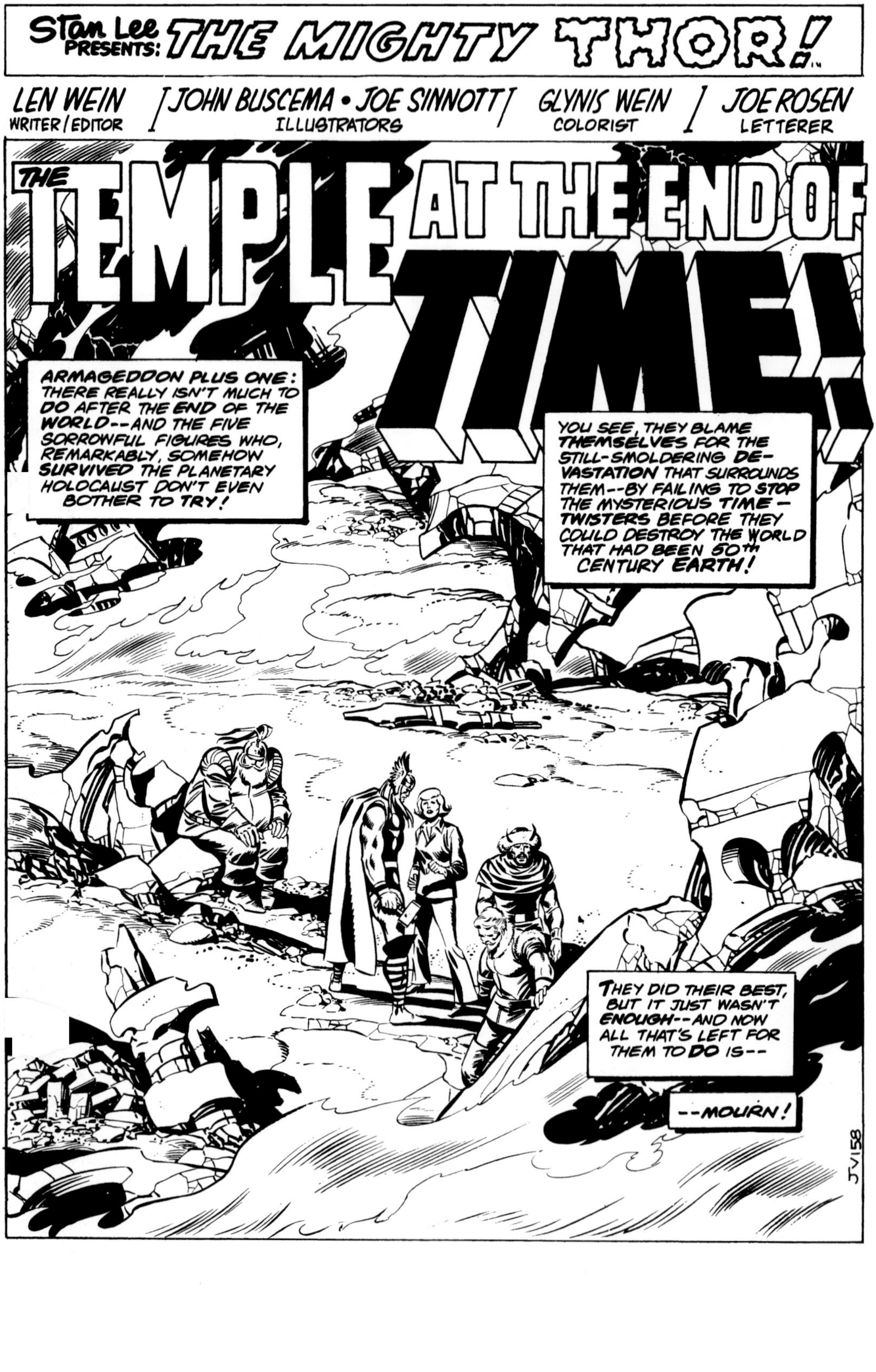
Stan Lee PRESENTS: THE MIGHTY THOR!
LEN WEIN WRITER/EDITOR
JOHN BUSCEMA • JOE SINNOTT ILLUSTRATORS
GLYNIS WEIN COLORIST
JOE ROSEN LETTERER
THE TEMPLE AT THE END OF TIME!
ARMAGEDDON PLUS ONE: THERE REALLY ISN'T MUCH TO DO AFTER THE END OF THE WORLD--AND THE FIVE SORROWFUL FIGURES WHO, REMARKABLY, SOMEHOW SURVIVED THE PLANETARY HOLOCAUST DON'T EVEN BOTHER TO TRY!
YOU SEE, THEY BLAME THEMSELVES FOR THE STILL-SMOLDERING DEVASTATION THAT SURROUNDS THEM--BY FAILING TO STOP THE MYSTERIOUS TIME-TWISTERS BEFORE THEY COULD DESTROY THE WORLD THAT HAD BEEN 50TH CENTURY EARTH!
THEY DID THEIR BEST, BUT IT JUST WASN'T ENOUGH--AND NOW ALL THAT'S LEFT FOR THEM TO DO IS--
--MOURN!
JV158

Inked art for THOR #245 page 1 by John Buscema & Joe Sinnott

When lame Dr. DONALD BLAKE strikes his wooden walking stick upon the ground, it becomes the mystic mallet MJOLNIR—and Blake is transformed into the Norse God of Thunder, Master of the Storm and the Lightning, Heir to the Throne of Immortal Asgard...

Stan Lee PRESENTS: THE MIGHTY THOR!

LEN WEIN	JOHN BUSCEMA & JOE SINNOTT	G. WEIN	J. ROSEN	MARV WOLFMAN
WRITER•EDITOR	ILLUSTRATORS	COLORIST	LETTERER	TOKEN GRINGO

KNOW YE THIS! THE GOD OF THUNDER HATH SEEMINGLY GONE MAD!

NOW, AT THE SIDE OF THE ALIEN CALLED FIRELORD, HE DOTH BATTLE THE DESPERATE ARMY OF THE REVOLUTION-TORN REPUBLIC CALLED COSTE VERDE--

--AND IT DOTH SEEM THERE BE NOTHING 'PON ALL THE EARTH THAT MAY STOP HIM!

WE'LL FILL IN THE DETAILS AS WE GO ALONG, FAITHFUL ONE--'CAUSE FROM HERE ON, IT'S ACTION-TIME!

THE FLAME AND THE HAMMER!

BUT ALMOST BEFORE THE ECHOES OF MIMIR'S BONE-CHILLING LAUGH HAVE *FADED*, THE GOD OF THUNDER AND HIS COMPANIONS STAND UPON THE VERY *THRESHHOLD* OF THE MYSTERIOUS *REALM BELOW*...

VERILY, THIS CRATER DOTH YAWN DOWN INTO A DARKNESS THAT SEEMS TO *SWALLOW* ALL LIGHT... AND ALL *HOPE*.

ART THOU CERTAIN THOU SHOULDST *RISK* THIS MAD ENDEAVOR, FRIEND THOR?

IN TRUTH, THE THUNDER GOD DOTH HAVE NO *CHOICE*, BALDER.

INDEED, NORN QUEEN, AS MY FATHER'S *SON*, I DO WHAT *MUST* BE DONE-- THOUGH MY *SOUL* SHALL KNOW NO *SATISFACTION* FROM THE DEED!

KEEP THYSELF *WELL*, MILADY SIF. I SWEAR I SHALL *RETURN* TO THEE ERE LONG.

AND SIF SHALL BE *WAITING*, MY LOVE... AS *ALWAYS*.

FEAR *NOT*, MY PRINCE. WE SHALL GUARD THE REALM ETERNAL *WELL* IN THINE ABSENCE.

AND I COULD LEAVE GOLDEN ASGARD IN NO *SAFER* HANDS THAN *THINE*, BRAVE BALDER.

SO IT HATH COME TO *THIS* THEN--

--THAT A *PRINCE OF THE REALM* SHOULD DESCEND INTO THIS SMOLDERING EMBODIMENT OF DESPAIR AS NOTHING MORE THAN A COMMON *THIEF*!

THERE BE LITTLE ENOUGH OF *VALUE* IN THIS DESOLATE DOMAIN ALREADY.

WOULD THAT I WERE NOT FORCED TO *STEAL* THE SINGLE SOURCE OF *LIGHT* THAT REMAINS HERE.

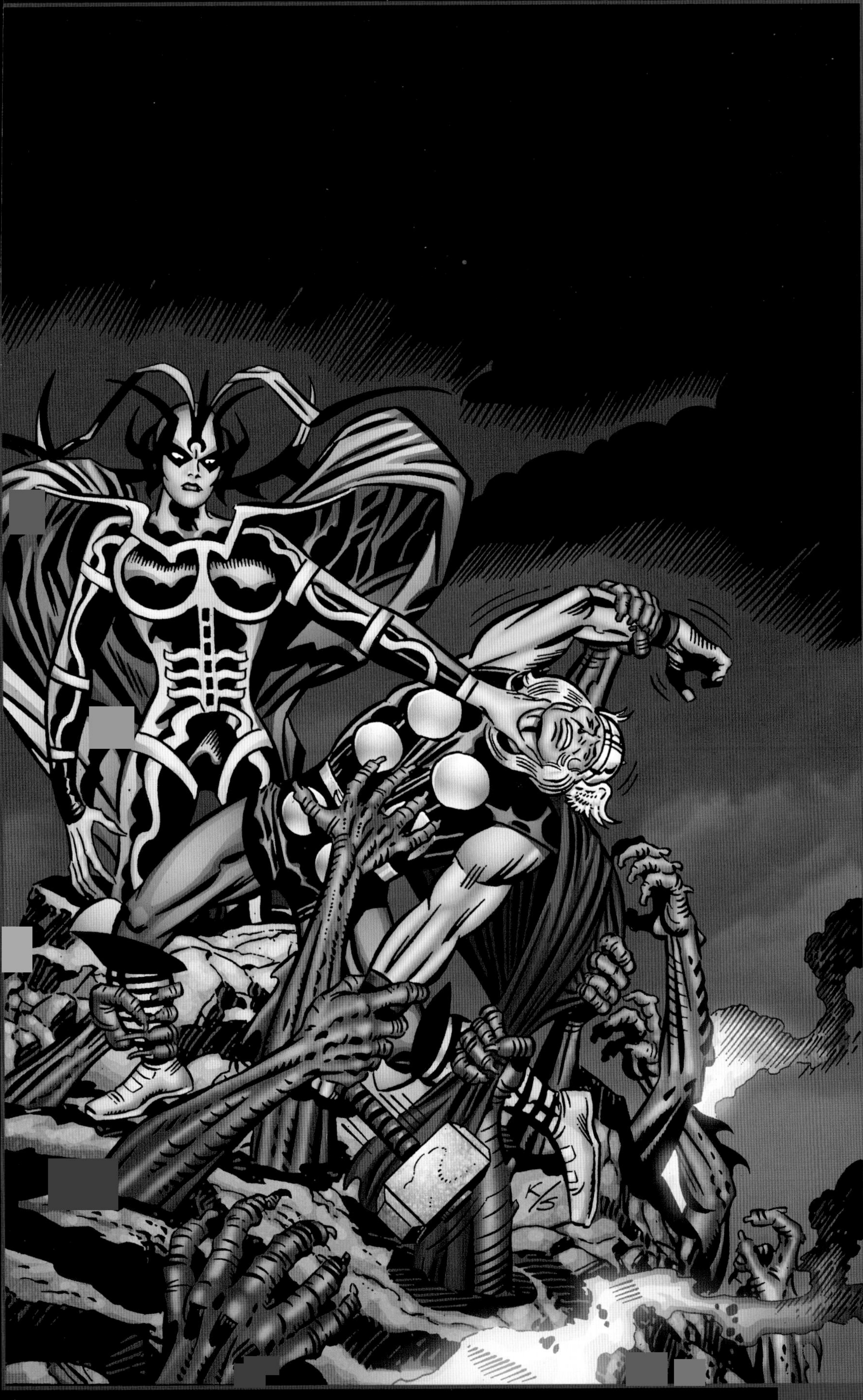

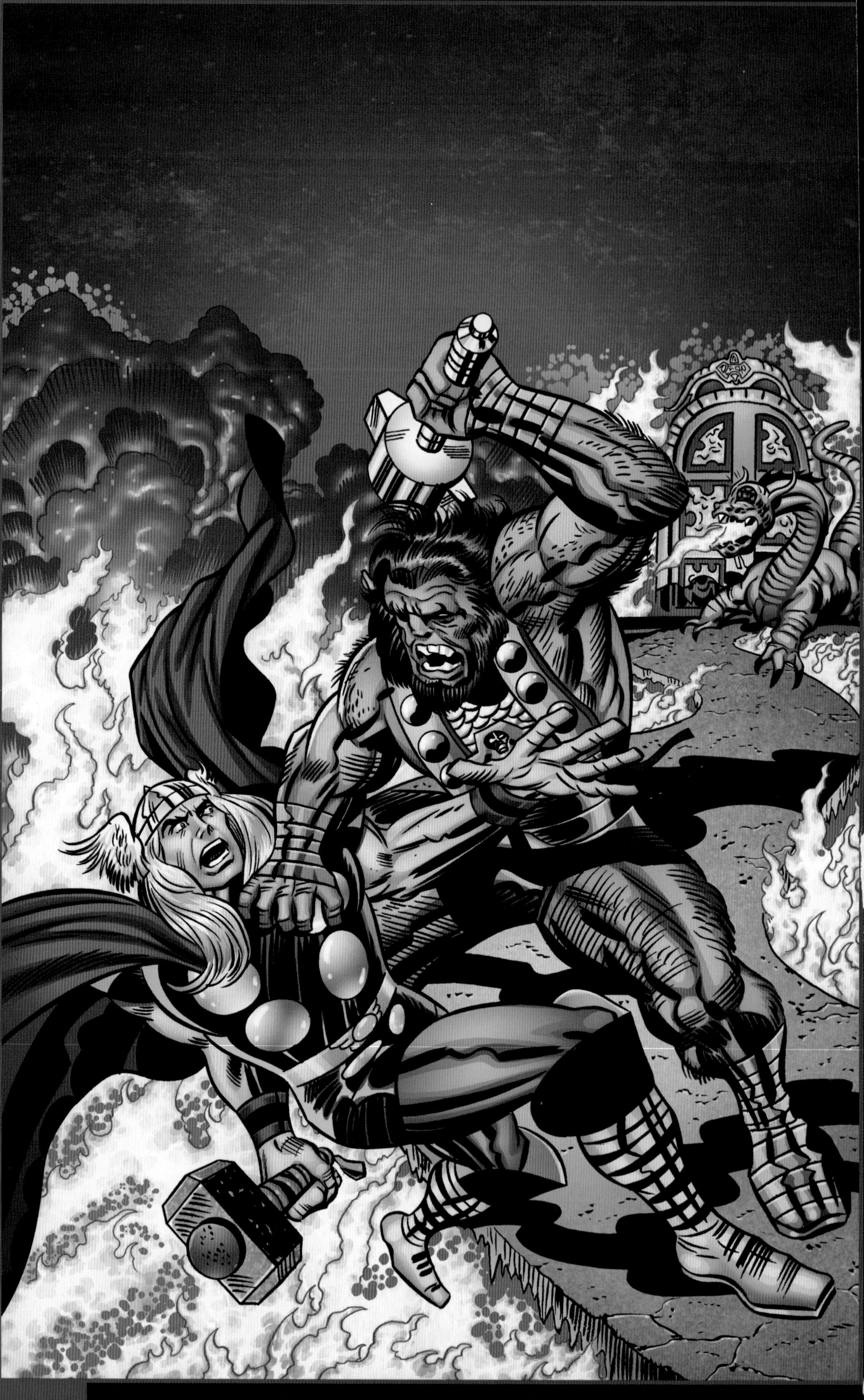